Hospital Emergency Response Teams

Hospital Emergency Response Teams
Triage for Optimal Disaster Response

Jan Glarum

Don Birou

Edward Cetaruk, MD

ELSEVIER

AMSTERDAM • BOSTON • HEIDELBERG • LONDON
NEW YORK • OXFORD • PARIS • SAN DIEGO
SAN FRANCISCO • SINGAPORE • SYDNEY • TOKYO

Butterworth-Heinemann is an imprint of Elsevier

Butterworth-Heinemann is an imprint of Elsevier
30 Corporate Drive, Suite 400, Burlington, MA 01803, USA
The Boulevard, Langford Lane, Kidlington, Oxford, OX5 1GB, UK

Library of Congress Cataloging-in-Publication Data
Application submitted

British Library Cataloguing-in-Publication Data
A catalogue record for this book is available from the British Library.

ISBN: 978-1-85617-701-6

Printed in the United States of America
09 10 11 12 13   10 9 8 7 6 5 4 3 2 1

For information on rights, translations, and bulk sales, contact Matt Pedersen, Commercial Sales Director and Rights; email: *m.pedersen@elsevier.com*

For information on all Butterworth–Heinemann publications
visit our Web site at *www.elsevierdirect.com*

Publisher: Laura Colantoni
Acquisitions Editor: Pam Chester
Development Editor: David Bevans

Project Manager: Paul Gottehrer
Designer: Joanne Blank
Typeset by: diacriTech, India

Dedicated to my beautiful and loving wife, Sue, and daughter, Jennifer.

—D. B.

To Kristi, Abby, Kate & Emerson. Thank you for all your love, support and patience.

—E. C.

I would like to thank my family for the idiosyncrasies I demonstrated as I went through the throes of contributing to this text. After several decades of being the one who responded to other people's emergencies, I am hoping this text will one day serve me well should one of my family members need the services provided by one of the readers. The eighth anniversary of the attacks of September 11, 2001, has just passed as I pen this, and this text is dedicated to reminding us all of the need to never forget what happened that day.

—J. G.

Contents

Preface

This hospital emergency response team (HERT) textbook was born out of nearly three decades of participating and observing in emergency medical response, planning, training and exercises, with both civilian and military medical entities. Day in and day out, personnel who have dedicated their lives to taking care of others perform admirably. In this author's experience, units that operate at the peak of efficiency and effectiveness share the attributes of good training, on-the-job experience, and leadership. Disasters pose a challenge to these traits observed in high-performing teams. Rarely is training adequate, few personnel have disaster response experience, and unfortunately, expending limited hospital resources on disaster preparedness does not often lengthen any Chief Executive Officer's tenure.

Having trained for response in the medical field, fire service, and tactical police operations, this author noted an interesting trend. My experience with SWAT training involved very little "pretending." We were training as we planned on fighting. Fire department training varied, but a "burn to learn" approach was treated very seriously as poor performance here could lead to fire fighter injury or death. Medical training, conversely, involved a tremendous amount of pretending: verbalizing what I would have done, and paper drills. When police and fire perform poorly, they get hurt, but when medical personnel perform poorly, their patient gets hurt.

The author was helping assess and train medical personnel on Okinawa when an event occurred that cemented his philosophy that the medical field must engage in simpler but more robust training. A hospital had scheduled a drill for their field and emergency department personnel. I went out in the field to observe the response to a traffic accident scenario, which had been set up near a sports field. The call was placed to dispatch and while waiting for the units to arrive I noticed a handful of Marines practicing hand to hand combat, as their next stop from here was the Middle East. Time after time, they repeated various moves, gaining that muscle memory that they hoped would keep them alive. I was brought back to the drill when I heard radio traffic which indicated that the medical personnel were questioning the need to respond to the drill. It took several additional phone calls to get any medical personnel to show up and train. Throughout the ordeal of getting the medical personnel to report for training, this handful of Marines continued going through their evolutions, apparently oblivious to the lack of interest in training by the very medical personnel they would be counting on to save their lives should things go badly.

This book is about training hospital personnel in the same manner you want them to fight. Choosing your battlefield always gives you an advantage; however, disasters present us with an environment that is very unfamiliar to us, so we must also train outside the comfort of our facility walls. Disasters also tend to be non-discriminatory, they affect all of us the same, and therefore we need to realize that when disaster strikes, the entire community has a problem that is best solved by everyone working together to mitigate the event. Life safety should always be your first priority and by developing your HERT as outlined within this text, adopting a rigorous and regular training program, you will not just be giving lip service to disaster preparedness, you will be building a real capacity to change patient outcomes in the worst event of your career.

—Jan Glarum

1 ::::

Command and Control

- Review NIMS Implementation Activities for Hospitals and Health Care Systems
- Understand the mission of HICS IV
- Describe implementation issues, requirements, and timelines in establishing an internal HICS IV program

Introduction

Any type of crisis or disaster, occurring anytime, can impact the operation of healthcare facilities if the facility has not taken the opportunity to prepare before-hand. An all hazards approach helps healthcare facilities prepare for any type of event. The Hospital Emergency Response Team (HERT) is not like the Trauma Team, Cardiac Team or Stroke Team, which are designed to address routine "emergencies." The HERT is designed for disaster or crisis response for incidents that may impact hospital operations brief in duration (e.g., explosion, fire, multiple gunshot victims) or may be prolonged over a period of days or weeks (e.g., floods, severe weather, pandemics). For our purposes we will define a crisis as a rapidly occurring event for which there are not established policies, procedures or protocols.

It is also important to recognize the healthcare sector's financial climate balanced against the challenges facing hospitals as they attempt to improve crisis or disaster response capabilities:

- Medical economics in the global economic crisis
- Just-in-time inventory
- Remuneration
- Lack of preparedness assistance
- Distraction of attention by administrators, clinicians and nursing

Despite these challenges, hospital administrators must maintain a sense of obligation to be prepared to respond to the community they serve, not just on a daily basis, but for the possibility of a once-in-a-lifetime event that will have

1

lasting impact on the facility's reputation in its capture area. In essence, any capability for a hospital to respond on its own, during at least the initial phase of a mass casualty event, is dependent upon secure leadership, not just having the staff complete a series of Incident Command System (ICS) classes. It is not enough to delegate creation of a HERT program to the director of plant engineering, security, emergency management, or the emergency department without continuous engagement and support from the administration.

Healthcare institutions have systems that allow them to integrate disparate hospital functions into a single system to achieve a common goal during every 24-hour, 7 day a week operating cycle. A hospital's system will take into consideration typical emergency operations, but oft times the structure breaks down when it comes to organizational response for most of the low-frequency, but quite predictable, hazards that may result in mass casualty incidents. This chapter will address those components this author believes can provide healthcare facilities with a means to establish a scalable incident management process that can be adapted to any event.

In the experience of this author, the components that contribute to an incident being mitigated in the most efficient and effective manner (taking into consideration the available skill sets of employees and the totality of incident circumstances and operating conditions) are command, control, coordination, communication and collaboration. If your incident management system accounts for each of these components, you will have given your staff, patients, and supporting agencies the best possible opportunity to deal with the majority of events your facility may face.

We will explore each of these components to ensure there is clarity of the meaning of each, within the context of this book. This book was not designed to test your knowledge of incident management systems or the incident command system specifically; this guide, along with adoption of a training and education program, is designed to help your HERT become operationally proficient. There are numerous ICS courses available either online or in a traditional classroom setting if one needs to pass a test as part of their job or accreditation requirement.

Command Passing an ICS course with a perfect score does not make you the best candidate for the command position, nor does it make those around you safe during a crisis. While seeking education is important, having the proper temperament, experience, command presence and ability to transfer classroom information into practice is key. It is also important to realize that the person filling the command position should not necessarily be the Chief Executive Officer, the head of security, or shift supervisor. This is not to say that any one of these individuals is not competent to serve in the position of command, but they typically have unique positions within the upper levels of management of the hospital itself. It is much more beneficial to both command and the facility if these individuals are free from command responsibilities in order to carry out the tasks only they have the authority to address.

Control The best way to gain and maintain control is to slow the event down for your team by establishing simple, clear and attainable goals. Gaining control may require taking on numerous actions that encompass a host of issues. However, control elements can be broken down into several groupings, making them easier to manage.

Physical Fixed Property The facility structure, parking lots, access corridors, adjacent building complexes and utility infrastructure are all considered fixed property. The goal is to ensure the structure and all support services remain functional, as well as compensate for the higher demand and increased load that will be placed on the system when a major incident occurs. Under the "support services remain functional" category you will also have to ensure that security access and control procedures are adequate, as failure to properly control the hospital's footprint as a whole can, and usually does, result in an uncontrolled and chaotic incident.

FIGURE 1.1 A fixed property that could be considered when selecting areas of security and control.

FIGURE 1.2 Parking facilities can also be used for support services in an emergency.

Equipment HERT equipment control and accountability issues are closely related to the current equipment system utilized by your hospital; the exception here is the specialized equipment needed to fulfill the HERT mission. Such equipment may only be used during the incident and may or may not be returned to service afterward. Control measures may include ensuring the equipment is current, functional, operational, and accessible. A related control measure is accountability during routine checks.

Personnel A well-trained and practiced HERT provides the best command and control element when it comes to organizing and deploying individuals. Control is conveyed by the ability to communicate clear and concise directives, which will result in effective operational goals being achieved with little-to-no confusion or conflict.

Coordination Any incident that is beyond the normal scope of hospital activities creates disruption and taxes the system. An incident that requires deployment of the HERT will obviously enhance that level of disruption and prove a challenge. Coordination should be thought of on a multi-level, systemic approach; the scope of what needs to be coordinated without affecting normal hospital operational needs will involve coordination at a high, "big-picture" level. Delegation of duties and span of control remain the keystones to effectively coordinating large incidents.

Communication Communications for a disaster incident should not get lost or confused with routine communication that occurs amongst hospital staff. The hospital setting already utilizes a specific and clear line of communicating to ensure that proper and accurate information is communicated at all levels of patient and staff operations. This strict yet effective communication protocol works well under normal operations and is still useful during a HERT incident, but that is where the similarities end. During an incident, not only do you need to communicate general information on a person-to-person basis, but you will most likely have to communicate to other operational groups or teams, which will likely involve a portable radio or other communication device. Add to this the use of personal protective equipment, which will hinder direct verbal communication capabilities, and high noise environments, and you have the makings of a communications nightmare. Communications at this level require well-thought-out communications equipment that is easy to use, easy to replace, and functions through fortress-type walls. When using portable devices, you may want to consider securing multiple channels if numerous operational teams are active simultaneously; for instance, security on one channel, HERT another, support on yet another. It may be difficult, in the midst of an incident, to keep track of numerous channels simultaneously, so a radio liaison may be of assistance here; someone to scan the channels and relay priority information.

Communications should also encompass sharing pertinent or priority information with all teams and hospital staff affected by the incident. In disaster incident situations, the adage "no news is good news" does not apply; no communications or no information does not always equate to nothing being wrong. Communicate the essentials and resist the urge to elaborate; provide clear, concise directives and remain focused.

Collaboration Collaborative effort does not just happen; however, collaboration can best be achieved through joint practical exercises that allow all team members to understand the needs of all involved. Collaboration among the internal hospital staff might be assumed, but bear in mind that the HERT may indeed be comprised of many individuals from the hospital who rarely have the opportunity to work together, and thus are unfamiliar with one another.

A second consideration for collaboration is among external entities such as ambulance crews, fire departments, police/law enforcement, other mutual aid hospital staff, emergency management support groups or agencies, and news media. Collaboration at this level requires joint practical planning, exercises and training, and refinement of communications practices.

It will be helpful to review recommendations on the development of an incident command system by the National Incident Management System (NIMS) and the Hospital Incident Command System (HICS).

History of Incident Command Systems Development

Creation of Incident Command Systems (ICS) resulted from the obvious need for a new approach to the management of rapidly moving wildfires in the early 1970s. At that time, emergency managers faced a number of problems:

- Too many people reporting to one supervisor.
- Different emergency response organizational structures.
- Lack of reliable incident information.
- Inadequate and incompatible communications.
- Lack of a structure for coordinated planning between agencies.
- Unclear lines of authority.
- Terminology differences between agencies.
- Unclear or unspecified incident objectives.

Designing a standardized emergency management system to remedy the problems listed above took several years and extensive field testing. The Incident Command System was developed by an interagency taskforce working in a cooperative local, state, and federal interagency effort called FIRESCOPE (Firefighting Resources of California Organized for Potential Emergencies). Early in the development process, four essential requirements became clear:

1. The system must be organizationally flexible to meet the needs of incidents of any kind and size.
2. Agencies must be able to use the system on a day-to-day basis for routine situations as well as for major emergencies.
3. The system must be sufficiently standard to allow personnel from a variety of agencies and diverse geographic locations to rapidly meld into a common management structure.
4. The system must be cost-effective.

Initial ICS applications were designed for responding to disastrous wildland fires. It is interesting to note that the characteristics of these wildland fire incidents are similar to those seen in many law enforcement, hazardous materials, and other disaster situations:

- They can occur with no advance notice.
- They develop rapidly.

- Unchecked, they may grow in size or complexity.
- Personal risk for response personnel can be high.
- There are often several agencies with some on-scene responsibility.
- They can very easily become multi-jurisdictional.
- They often have high public and media visibility.
- Risk of life and property loss can be high.
- Cost of response is always a major consideration.

ICS is now widely used throughout the United States by fire-fighting agencies and is increasingly used for law enforcement, other public safety applications, and for emergency and event management.

First responders have used ICS for a number of years to manage incidents of all sizes. The British Columbia Emergency Response Management System (BCERMS) defines a process for organizing and managing a response to emergencies and disasters based on a framework of five components: operations and control, qualifications, technology, training, and publications. The BCERMS is modular with four levels of operation, including site, site support, provincial regional coordination, and provincial central coordination. These four levels allow elements to be activated or deactivated as the needs of the incident/emergency change over time. The system also provides for expansion as additional resources are required.

Many have asked the question, "Can ICS be effectively used in a healthcare environment?" To answer this question, the Joint Commission (a healthcare accreditation organization, formerly the Joint Commission on the Accreditation of Healthcare Organizations (JCAHO)) has studied a variety of disasters that have impacted healthcare organizations. The Commission's study involved debriefings with the organizations impacted by these disasters, discussions with emergency management experts, service on national emergency management panels, and review of the contemporary emergency management literature. The disasters include floods, widespread extended electrical utility outages, wildfires, the terrorist attacks of September 11, the four back-to-back Florida hurricanes in 2004, and Hurricanes Katrina and Rita on the Gulf Coast in 2005. Based on the information gathered, the Joint Commission has made the following determinations:

During a community-wide emergency, a single event can escalate into multiple events. For example, Hurricane Katrina escalated to flooding because of failed levees, and the flooding further escalated into civil unrest in some communities. Therefore, it is not sufficient that healthcare organizations plan for a single event; rather, they must develop the capacity to respond to combinations of escalating events.

FIGURE 1.3 Hurricane Katrina and Hurricane Ike devastated the Gulf Coast and compromised numerous healthcare organizations.

Regardless of the cause of the disaster, key elements of the organization must be effectively managed. These include communications; patient safety; organization's resources/assets, including staff; clinical care; and the integrity of building utilities. Planning with attention to these elements is integral to an "all-hazards" approach to emergency preparedness.

It is important that healthcare organizations consider, in their plans, the potential for disasters of long duration, such as those that occurred during and after the Florida and Gulf Coast hurricanes.

During these events, the healthcare infrastructure became compromised because healthcare organizations could not rely on their usual suppliers and response partners in the weeks that followed the immediate disaster.

Many of the same incident characteristics facing first responders challenge our healthcare system during major events.

History of Hospital Emergency Incident Command System

In 1987, the Hospital Council of Northern California completed work on the adaptation of the ICS to hospital emergency response functions in a publication entitled, Earthquake Preparedness Guidelines for Hospitals. That document served as a corner stone in the development of the original Hospital Emergency Incident Command System (HEICS), written by Orange County Emergency Medical Services in 1991 with a grant from the State of California Emergency Medical Services Authority. In 1992, Orange County EMS began work on the second edition of HEICS with funding provided by the State EMS Authority. This major rewriting of the HEICS was done with the intention of making the original document easier to use and implement within the hospital environment. The second edition attempted to retain those same characteristics that made the original ICS-based plan so appealing. The third edition of HEICS was produced by the County of San Mateo Emergency Medical Services Agency with a grant from the State EMS Authority. The Project began in the fall of 1996 with the intention of gathering data regarding the usage of HEICS. From this input, a revised edition of HEICS was created. The 1998 version, HEICS III, rapidly became the standard for hospital emergency management across the nation.

However, the world seemed to change on September 11, 2001. Some of the response issues that emerged on those days included:

- Lack of a systematic planning process, with no predictable chain of command
- Lack of accountability
- Lack of common terminology
- Poor communication
- Incident commanders unable to keep up with the developing situation
- No method to integrate multiple disciplines and response agencies
- Resultant health and safety issues, unnecessary damage, ineffective resource management and economic losses

As a result of the terrorist attacks and the issues associated with the response, a number of significant presidential directives were issued and the Department of Homeland Security was formed.

As a result of Homeland Security Presidential Directive 5 (HSPD-5), NIMS (the National Incident Management System) was created in March of 2004. We now have a truly consistent, standardized, nationwide approach for federal, state, tribal, and local governments to work together to prepare for, respond to, and recover from domestic incidents regardless of their cause, size, or complexity.

From the very beginning, local, state and federal agencies were expected to comply with published guidelines. NIMS was envisioned to:

- Provide a consistent template for government, private sector, and non-government organizations to work together during an incident

- Promote interoperability and coordination
- Provide a flexible framework
- Address all phases of an incident, regardless of size, complexity and location

The NIMS Organizational Design comprises three levels:

- Incident Command System
  - Defines operating characteristics, management components, and incident management structure for an incident
- Multi-agency Coordination System
  - Defines how support entities will be integrated and provide assistance
- Public Information System
  - Processes and procedures for communicating timely and accurate information to the public during an emergency

NIMS provides a core set of concepts, principles, terminology, and technologies that, when taken together, provide all responders with the tools needed to effectively and efficiently manage a variety of incidents. NIMS consists of six major components:

- Command and management
- Preparedness
- Resource management
- Communications and information management
- Supporting technologies
- Ongoing management and maintenance

Hospital Incident Command System IV (HICS IV)

In October 2004, the Emergency Medical Services Authority (EMSA) launched a project to review and revise the current version of HEICS. The HEICS IV project was sponsored by the California EMS Authority, with contract support from the Washington Hospital Center Institute for Public Health and Emergency Readiness (WHC IPHER) and Kaiser Permanente. HEICS IV was created by a multi-disciplinary 27-member national work group with representatives from the American Hospital Association (AHA), the American Society of Chemical Engineers (ASCHE), the Joint Commission, the Department of Health and Human Services (DHHS), and the National Integration Center (NIC).

The HEICS III, published in 1998, served as a foundation for the revision. There was additional material review and input from a multi-disciplinary, approximately 80-member secondary review group that included vendors. They were tasked with reviewing draft materials and providing comments. The entire group had to:

- Collaborate through face-to-face meetings and teleconferences
- Build a consensus document
- Update and incorporate current emergency management practices into the system
- Enhance the system by integrating chemical, biological, radiological, nuclear and explosive (CBRNE) events into the management structure
- Address and develop a standardized configuration of HEICS to address rural and small hospital needs
- Develop a standardized HEICS IV curriculum and teaching aids (CD or video)
- Develop an instructor credentialing and certification process to ensure standardization in all hospitals across the nation
- Clarify the components of HEICS and its relationship to the National Incident Management System (NIMS)

The HEICS IV project strove to ensure the applicability of HEICS in hospitals across the nation. In order to accomplish that goal, the HEICS (HICS) IV project committee membership included healthcare professionals from across the nation. The project continues to be funded by the State of California Hospital Bioterrorism Preparedness Program with monies allocated to the State from the Health Resources and Services Administration (HRSA) Bioterrorism Hospital Preparedness Program. As part of this project, HEICS was officially renamed simply HICS for Hospital Incident Command System.

Why Was It Called HICS?

The incident command principles embodied in HICS are applicable to emergent and non-emergent incidents. Thus, the letter "E" was dropped from the original acronym to reinforce this practical point of importance. "HEICS IV" is the name of the project that led to the new HICS. The HEICS IV project, funded by California EMS Authority using a HRSA grant, resulted in the creation of HICS.

HEICS vs. HICS

HICS is a revision of HEICS III and is:

- "All hazards" in design
- Intended for non-emergency events, not just emergency incidents
- Better designed to be used by any size hospital
- More compact, with a scalable Incident Management Team (IMT) design

- Contains modified Job Action Sheets (JAS)
- Composed of a variety of other planning and response tools, such as:
  - Incident Planning Guides (IPGs)
  - Incident Response Guides (IRGs)
  - Forms

The HICS IV project team embraced the principles of NIMS in the new document. Prior to the release of HICS IV, in a memorandum dated May 26, 2006, from Albert H. Fluman, Acting Director, NIMS Integration Center, DHS/FEMA, and CDR Melissa Sanders, Branch Chief, Bioterrorism Hospital Preparedness, HRSA, HHS, hospitals were informed that NIMS compliance was mandatory for HRSA participation.

On the one hand, an effective emergency management system must permit a team effort from those used to responding to emergencies. On the other hand, it must also integrate the jurisdictional needs of the municipality's elected officials. The system must factor in the involvement of these elected officials, who most likely have little experience with emergency response, but who must ultimately shoulder the responsibility for whatever response occurs.

Within Canada, there are three basic systems to manage disasters. Within these systems there are variations reflecting provincial standards, organizational culture, and to a lesser degree, the preference of those who employ these systems. These systems include the Incident Command System (ICS), the British Columbia Emergency Response Management System (BCERMS) and the Emergency Site Management System (ESM). These systems have some common elements and some unique features.

The Incident Command System (ICS) has been addressed earlier in this chapter and will not be covered here. The British Columbia Emergency Response Management System, developed by the B.C. government through its Interagency Emergency Preparedness Council (IEPC) is designed as a comprehensive "all hazards" provincial emergency operations system. This BCERMS identifies "the standardized approach to emergency response management to be utilized and practiced by provincial government ministries, agencies and crown corporations." BCERMS is based upon the Incident Command System as developed and practiced throughout the United States. Since the fall of 1992, the B.C. provincial government endorsed this emergency management response system and mandated its application for all its ministries.

Site Level
At the site level, resources are utilized to manage problems presented by an emergency incident.

   The BC Incident Command System (ICS) is used to manage the response, using responders from all levels of government and the private sector. A single command or unified command from an on-site incident command post structure is utilized.

Site Support Level
When the site level response requires off-site support, an Emergency Operations Center (EOC) may be activated as a second level of response. The EOC supports the site by providing communication with the site level, establishing policy guidance, managing the local multiple agency support to the site, as well as acquiring and deploying additional resources at the incident site, as required.

Provincial Regional Coordination Level
This third level of activation provides further support to the site level or EOC, if required by an escalation in the magnitude of emergency. The provincial regional coordination level manages the assignment of multiple ministry and agency support to individual site support locations or multiple site support level locations. It acquires and deploys requests from the site support level and provides emergency

FIGURE 1.4 Communications are an integral part of any emergency response.

response services where incidents cross local authority boundaries or where local authorities are not organized to fulfill their role. This regional level does not normally communicate directly with the site level, but rather communicates through the EOC or site support level.

Provincial Center Coordination Level

The fourth level exists to expand support into an overall provincial government response. Persons within this level would have the responsibility for the provision of support for the regional levels. It is within this level of activation that authority of the minister for a declaration of a provincial emergency is obtained, direction of senior elected officials is sought, and provincial policy and priority guidance is provided. This group is responsible for managing the provincial emergency public information activities as well as the acquisition and deployment of provincial, federal, inter-provincial and international resources. If required, this group would provide coordination and other support services to provincial Ministry Operation Centers (MOCs) and Crown Corporation's centers as well as Federal emergency response agencies. The system is used not only in emergency situations, but in private sector emergency response and management programs, as well as for planned events such as celebrations, parades, and concerts. It thus allows more practice and familiarity with the system should it be needed in an emergency. The "all hazards" approach in British Columbia includes fires, HAZMAT, multi-casualty incidents, search and rescue missions, oil spill response and recovery incidents, and air, rain water or ground transportation accidents. It is also an integral part of British Columbia's earthquake preparedness and response plans.

Canadian emergency services tend to receive training manuals and reading material from the United States, where the pool of resources is significantly larger. Therefore, most services are aware of and practice, some form of the ICS system. Although not as widely used or known as the ICS system, another approach called Emergency Site Management (ESM) has been documented for Canadian communities as a guide during community-wide disasters or emergencies.

Emergency Preparedness Canada (EPC) initially formulated the Emergency Site Management (ESM) system in the early 1980's. The ESM system started out being a replica of the ICS approach. However, over time it developed its own structure, mandate, roles and responsibilities, to the point that it is now an independent and unique approach to the management of disasters, both at the scene and away from the site at the local Emergency Operations Center (EOC).

The ESM unique approach is based on the Canadian system of emergency management. More often than not that approach places the focus of emergency planning and disaster response squarely on the shoulders of municipal elected officials who are ultimately responsible for the effectiveness of their municipal plans and response effort. The ESM approach considers and addresses two areas of operation: the site and the municipal EOC. The EOC is designed to contain all key decision makers whose input may be of significance to the operation as a whole. Their role is to support the operational effort at the scene, as well as to carry on the day-to-day business of the rest of the community. While removed from the scene (or site), the members of the EOC are nevertheless of great value because they are the formal link between the site and the rest of the world.

Disaster situations involve many organizations from diverse jurisdictions. By the time a community realizes it is confronting a disaster, rather than a day-to-day emergency that is manageable by emergency services alone, a number of things have happened. Various agencies have begun their individual response to the incident. Those at the site have tried to work together. Someone assumed the role of a Site Manager coordinating efforts at the scene and a call may have gone out to activate the EOC. Once activated, the EOC personnel formally appoint a Site Manager and advise all responding agencies of his/her identity (this person is typically recruited or appointed from the ranks of the local fire, police or EMS services, depending on the nature of the disaster). From that point on, all key functions at the site are typically coordinated through the Site Manager. This appointment allows incoming resource agencies to have a contact person.

The Site Manager has a challenging role. He or she must accept that every key agency at the site will maintain its own chain of command, mandate, and roles. But at the same time, the Site Manager must create the operational structure at the scene that will provide an effective process to manage information, delegate responsibilities or resources, and coordinate action among the diverse agencies on site. Additionally, the Site Manager must maintain a link between the scene and the municipal EOC. This allows communication to flow from those involved in tasks at the scene to their lead officer, from that lead officer to the overall site manager, and from the site manager to the municipal EOC. The flow of communication also works in reverse when being initiated from the EOC to the site.

In essence, everything within the perimeter boundary of the site is the responsibility of the Site Manager and the site team. This 'team' includes the senior representatives of the key agencies as well as the Incident Commander, who commands the Fire Services resources at the scene. This group, under the guidance and coordination of the Site Manager, manages the response to the disaster event at the site.

The EOC team is responsible for everything outside the outer boundary of the site, such as coordinating with hospitals. The EOC team must also be available to support the operation within that site boundary, if and when requested. Roles

and responsibilities for the EOC team include media contacts, resource allocation, integration and communication with other communities and government,
and public information access. Such responsibilities are not far from the daily
responsibilities of these elected officials and allow for a smooth transition from
daily operational to disaster mode.

The ESM system allows each organization to employ the process that best fits
its needs, while still maintaining operational coordination and communication
both at the site as well as between the site and the EOC. For example, fire personnel could continue to use the Incident Command System without detracting from
the ESM process. Similarly, municipal officials are encouraged to employ their
own operational system and to make strategic decisions away from the chaos of
the site. Hospitals may use whatever incident management structure suits their
particular needs, such as HICS, ICS or others, but must be aware of and practice
coordination with, the other agencies to ensure each fully understands how best
to work together. There are essentially three systems to manage disasters at community or municipal level currently utilized within Canada. The ICS system is
well known by most first responders in Canada, particularly those from the fire
services. Responders at site level who wish to manage emergencies and follow an
existing chain of command frequently use the ICS system. Because of their prior
knowledge of this system and its application, ICS often becomes the preferred or
default system for large scale emergencies. Unfortunately, many municipal officials may not have experience with the ICS system or be aware of the terminology
and intricate command structure or reporting procedures.

Their lack of understanding combined with their overall responsibility for an
effective disaster management could lead to confusion, awkward shifts of command and control, and ultimately an uncoordinated response.

The ESM model was designed to address this concern and clearly indicates
the roles and responsibilities of municipal officials. The problem with this system however, is the lack of regular exposure to the process. Many communities
and their diverse agencies do not regularly plan or train for disasters. Their three
key response agencies (i.e., fire, EMS, and police) plan and regularly train their
personnel. They also have regular exposure to emergencies and typically use the
structure (i.e., ICS) that suits their respective professional needs during 'normal'
emergencies. When these emergencies expand to require more agencies to work
together, the three response agencies may be reluctant to switch to the ESM
model. This reluctance may occur because the ESM system has not been properly
practiced or due to an initial commitment at the site to the ICS approach. Without
regular training and practice, hospitals will also be hard pressed to function properly. In times of stress, and most disasters are stressful, people revert to what they

know or are comfortable with rather than try new methods. Consequently, the ESM system, which otherwise would assist in coordination and communication, is left untried. This may be particularly confusing and frustrating for municipal officials who are not familiar with any of the existing roles and responsibilities.

British Columbia may have developed a solution to the problem by customizing the ICS system to incorporate municipal leaders and government officials with the intention of providing harmony. Although the system should provide effective emergency management practices within the province in which it was designed, it may cause significant conflicts in cross-border disaster situations when other provinces or states respond by using other systems. The BC system also requires fairly extensive training by all those who would perform a role in the various levels of activation.

In the final analysis, any system will work if there is an agreed-upon plan among all responding agencies and officials to use it. Before a disaster occurs, if everyone agrees on which process will be used, and is trained in its application, the system is very likely to work. Conversely, no system, no matter how well-designed, will work during a disaster if those who are responsible for overall management are unaware or unwilling to use the system.

Education and practice involving all those who would respond to disaster is essential. Effective models exist but are not useful if they are not practiced and understood by responders and government leaders. Training in disaster response at the community level is essential to ensure smooth transition from 'normal' emergencies to disaster response with its multi-agency effort.

2

Assessment of Likely Mass Casualty Events and Potential Hospital Impact

CHAPTER OBJECTIVES

- To familiarize HERT members with the hospital response to mass casualty events (MCEs)
- Introduce the concept of surge capacity and how a hospital and HERT can increase a hospital's surge capacity
- Introduce the "all hazards" approach to HERT preparation for MCEs
- Introduce the use of toxidromes for the management of chemical MCEs
- Provide a basis of knowledge to management likely types of MCEs, including chemical, biological, radiological, and explosive (CBRNE)

A mass casualty event (MCE), by definition, is a public health emergency involving multiple patients that overwhelms local resources. A mass casualty event may simply be the result of a multiple victim motor vehicle accident (MVA) where the number of patients received at a medical facility exceeds that facility's ability to routinely care for them or it could be a terrorist chemical agent attack. An MCE may compromise and/or overwhelm, at least in the short term, the ability of a local or regional health system to deliver their normal level and number of services. This often necessitates a transition from what is called the "standard of care" to a "sufficiency of care" where typical practices may be altered to manage large numbers of patients.

Historically, most MCEs are the result of either natural disasters or large scale accidental events which are obviously not planned, but they also are not unpredictable. These events do not typically occur when the healthcare and emergency response communities are at the ready. Therefore, it is essential that these communities prepare ahead of time so as to be as ready as possible.

The exceptions to the concept that disasters are not planned are those disasters that result from terrorist acts. These events are typically the result of extensive preparation and planning on the part of the terrorists. History has shown us that terrorists plan their attacks to cause the largest number of casualties as possible and to occur when our communities are least prepared (e.g. during rush hour on a crowded commuter train). They may occur amidst a large gathering of people, such as a sporting event or convention. They may also occur where and when the emergency response system is least prepared to deal with them.

MCEs typically result in a sufficient number of casualties to overwhelm existing medical resources. A terrorist MCE may occur in such a fashion as to specifically overload a medical response community with inordinately large numbers of victims, target the responders, or exploit our lack of preparedness to create additional chaos.

A mass casualty event may be an obvious event such as a bomb blast. Instantaneous events such as explosive or chemical attacks are very recognizable and typically swift in producing large numbers of casualties. The closest hospital to this event may get very short notification from the local 911 system, field responders or may receive no notification at all. Without a well-trained and effective HERT in place, they very quickly may be overwhelmed with patients.

In contrast, an MCE such as a biological event, whether it is naturally-occurring, accidental, or terrorist-invoked, may not have a sentinel event to forewarn the medical community that it has occurred. Examples of this include a pandemic flu that results in mass casualties increasing in number over time or the release of a biological agent that produces casualties only after an incubation period of several days and the victims have dispersed and/or traveled away from the attack site. Later in this chapter we describe the mnemonic D.O.C.T.O.R. as a simple tool to help personnel determine when to adopt the appropriate protective posture.

Natural disasters are by far the most common cause of mass casualty events. In North America, hurricanes, tornadoes and earthquakes are the most likely causes of MCEs, while elsewhere in the world they may also be due to floods and tsunamis.

MCEs may include hazardous materials events such as train derailments. In North America an enormous quantity of hazardous materials is transported by rail on a daily basis. There have been multiple events in recent years that resulted in large releases of chemical agents into populated areas. MCEs may result from the release of chemicals from fixed facilities as well. Such an event occurred in Bopal, India in 1984, resulting in thousands of deaths. Additionally, the Texas City harbor explosion in 1947 resulted in hundreds of deaths and thousands of victims. These types of events should be sources of study for "lessons learned" for those involved in planning emergency response.

Other MCEs include building collapses and multiple victim MVAs, such as multiple car pileups on highways and/or bus accidents. Pandemic influenza may represent a global MCE incident. The infrequency of MCEs can create a false

THE TEXAS CITY DISASTER

On April 16, 1947, a ship called the "Grandcamp," a freighter that was loaded with ammonium nitrate, docked at Texas City, Texas, caught fire and exploded. The resultant course of events from this massive explosion illustrates the suddenness and large impact that a mass casualty event may have on a community. The resources of the local community were quickly overwhelmed. Although many of the neighboring Texas communities responded by sending assistance, this was during an era with no advanced systems for disaster management and response. The explosion of the S.S. Grandcamp set off a chain of related explosions and fires, causing hundreds of deaths and thousands injured (United States Coast Guard, 1947).

Once the Grandcamp caught fire, the fire department arrived on the scene and a crowd of people gathered to watch. The standard plan for towing a dangerously burning ship from the harbor was not implemented until it was too late, and the tugboat didn't arrive in time to pull the ship to safety. At a little after 9:00 a.m. the Grandcamp exploded. A great column of smoke shot up an estimated two thousand feet, followed ten seconds later by another, even more violent, shockwave. Within moments of the second blast, the Monsanto Chemical Plant was in flames resulting from broken lines and shattered containers. As entire buildings collapsed, trapping people inside, fires quickly spread to the refineries that made up the Texas City indusial complex.

Adding to the catastrophe was a miniature tidal wave that was created when water from the bay, which had been driven out by the explosion, rushed in over the docks and continued as far as 150 feet inland, sweeping everything in its path with it. All day long the work of caring for the injured and fighting the fires continued. By nightfall, the town was filled with rescue workers and ambulances had made repeated trips to area hospitals. Rescue efforts continued through the night, even as fear mounted because another freighter, also loaded with ammonium nitrate as well as sulfur, had also been burning all day. Tugs had tried in vain to tow her out of the ruined harbor. At 1:10 a.m. on April 17, the S.S. High Flyer exploded in the most violent of all the blasts, taking with her another ship, the Wilson B. Keene. It also destroyed a concrete warehouse and a grain elevator and triggered even more fires. Almost the entire fire department had been lost in the first explosion, along with plant workers, dockworkers, school children, and other bystanders.

The losses from the disaster were unprecedented: nearly 600 deaths, over 2,000 injuries, and property loss of over $67 million. Dreadful as the disaster was, it brought the people of Texas City together as nothing else had ever done. Those that remained were determined to rebuild and all of the industries that were damaged, stayed and rebuilt. It must be remembered that the disaster was not caused by an indusial accident, but by a ship in port that exploded. No one could have predicted this unprecedented disaster.

sense of security in delaying preparedness initiatives until after another event occurs. It is likely we will see more terrorist attacks that create MCEs, and if we choose to not develop a robust HERT capability at our healthcare facilities the results may be fatal. This chapter will look at potential MCE causative agents and how healthcare facilities can prepare for them.

As noted above, terrorist attacks are by design intended to cause as many casualties as possible. They target the unprepared as well as structures and places that may have additional symbolic and/or strategic value. The Oklahoma City bombing in 1995 targeted the Alfred P. Murrah Federal Building, a U.S. government office complex in downtown Oklahoma City, Oklahoma. The attack, which involved an ammonium nitrate truck bomb, claimed 168 lives, including 19 children, and left over 800 injured. Around the same time, the Aum Shinrikyo committed two terrorist attacks using a sarin nerve agent, in Matsumoto and Tokyo, Japan, in 1994 and 1995, respectively. These attacks resulted in 19 deaths and thousands injured, with several hundred requiring hospitalization.

Mass shootings have often resulted in many victims. The West Virginia Tech shootings in 2007, were comprised of two separate attacks about two hours apart on the Virginia Tech campus in Blacksburg, Virginia. Seung-Hui Cho killed 32 people and wounded 25 before committing suicide, making it the deadliest shooting in modern U.S. history. The Columbine high school shooting occurred on April 20, 1999, at Columbine High School in Littleton, Colorado. Two students, Eric Harris and Dylan Klebold, carried out a shooting rampage, killing 12 students and a teacher, as well as wounding 24 others, before committing suicide.

The terrorist attacks of September 11, 2001, resulted in 3,000 deaths and hundreds more injured. The response to this event by local hospitals is also a source of study on the hospital response to a large MCE.

Planning Practicality

Hospitals exist to treat the medical conditions and injuries of their communities. This mission does not change during a disaster or MCE. The goal remains to minimize the suffering of those injured and/or ill as well as to save lives. In an MCE this goal is tempered by the need to triage a hospital's resources to best serve many patients at one time.

Additionally, hospital disaster planning must provide for the continued care of those patients already in the hospital, as well as those in the community with medical conditions requiring care, not as a result of the disaster and MCE. Ultimately, the hospital may be overwhelmed by the additional patient load resulting from the MCE but will nonetheless need to maintain services for those patients already in hospital. Healthcare facilities must make plans to insure that they can maintain operations during and after an MCE. Hospital disaster planning should include these general goals as a basis for their planning.

Hospitals have a responsibility both to their staff and to their community to be prepared for disasters, and need to include MCE planning in their disaster preparedness plans. Proper planning and development of their HERT will enhance a hospital's ability to respond to MCEs such as a chemical terrorist attack or a natural disaster (e.g., earthquake) and also ensure the safety of its staff during the event.

At a basic level, even small hospitals must develop at least a minimal level of preparedness to receive and treat contaminated victims. This would include the development of procedures to be able to accept, decontaminate, and treat at least one non-ambulatory chemically-contaminated patient. Once a hospital has developed the ability to decontaminate and treat one patient, planning and training to decontaminate many more patients is achievable.

Hospital disaster preparedness should also include plans to manage the potential influx of mass casualties. The hospital will be the location where MCE patients will be transported for care. If hospitals are not prepared to receive and effectively treat these patients, little will be accomplished other than relocating the disaster from the scene to the hospital. Ideally, hospital disaster plans should integrate with the local, regional, and state disaster plans and resources to better improve the community's response to a disaster.

One of the initial steps to disaster preparedness for a hospital is to determine the potential hazards it may face in its local community. A hazard and vulnerability analysis (HVA) is a tool to screen for potential hazards. It involves a systematic approach to identify both internal and external hazards the hospital may face (see Chapter 3). More importantly, it studies the potential vulnerabilities the hospital may have to these hazards. Ultimately, this type of hazard analysis is best done with a multi-disciplinary team that includes hospital administrators, subject matter experts (e.g., toxicologists, radiation safety officers), and other emergency responders such as hazardous materials specialists, infection control specialists, industrial hygienists, emergency managers and planners, and public health personnel. The goal of the hazard and vulnerability analysis is to enable the hospital to better respond to disasters and MCEs while continuing to provide care to other patients in the community and protect their staff from potential hazards and threats. Although not a new concept in the field of emergency response, the hazard and vulnerability analysis became a Joint Commission (formerly JCAHO) requirement for hospitals in 2001.

"Plans must be simple and flexible. They should be made by the people who are going to execute them." This quote from General George S. Patton typifies the approach that should be employed for hospital MCE planning. The committee(s) or group(s) doing the MCE planning for a hospital should include representation from all departments or services that would be involved in an MCE response. For example, administrative and executive officers of the hospital, physicians and nursing staff, the emergency department, pharmacy, security and all other stakeholders would be needed to respond to an MCE. If all stakeholders have had input into the plan, it will likely be more achievable and effective.

A basic component of any hospital-based MCE response plan is that it should always be operational in terms of personnel (adequately trained staff) and equipment (available, functional with staff trained in its use). Hospital MCE plans should be able to integrate with existing incident command systems both within the hospital (hospital incident command) as well as external incident command systems, such as those used by EMS and fire departments. Also, as a result of federal legislation, all hospitals in the United States must have plans compliant with the National Incident Management System (NIMS).

As disasters and resultant MCEs typically occur without warning, hospital MCE plans should be able to use existing personnel in the hospital for initial HERT response and include means to quickly augment their personnel. The plan should include provisions to protect employees from potential injuries and/or illness. This includes training in the proper use of PPE as well as policies and procedures and infrastructure modifications to minimize staff exposure to chemical or infectious agents. It should also include stockpiling appropriate antibiotics for prophylaxis against infectious agents as well as antidotes for chemical exposure.

Overall, hospital mass casualty event planning is a complicated but critically important task. Ultimately, a HERT must be able to balance the treatment of many patients against limited resources. Therefore, the goals and plans set forth in a hospital MCE plan should be achievable and cost effective, but also adequate. If the operations are to be successful in their implementation they must also be efficient in their use of human resources. As much as other resources may be limited, hospital personnel to respond to the MCE are also likely to be limited. Therefore, the MCE plan should include a system to train sufficient numbers of staff to allow for rotation of HERT personnel during a MCE.

Additionally, a hospital should include the use of other community response assets, if available, to augment the hospital's ability to respond to the MCE. Prior planning, such as establishing mutual aid agreements and training with other local emergency response agencies and/or hospitals, is essential if this is to be a reliable component of the plan. Often the hospital that is most overwhelmed in an MCE is the one that is geographically closest to the event and not necessarily the one that is best equipped to respond. Therefore, other hospitals may be available to share and/or provide focused resources such as a HERT, specific medications, or other equipment. Local EMS, police and fire systems, state office of emergency management, and local public health departments should be aware of the capabilities and limitations of a hospital plan, such that they can integrate their own response with that of the hospital. This integration is important for effective communication and coordination during the course of the MCE. Participation in Local Emergency Planning Committees (LEPCs) is highly recommended. Community-wide coordination is best accomplished through planning as well as regular and realistic training *before an event occurs.* A well-coordinated response plan will prevent waste and inefficiency and ultimately improve the ability for the hospital to save lives.

The simplicity of any response plan is often critical to its success. As a plan becomes increasingly complex the likelihood that it will break down and not be functional at the time it is needed increases. This is apparent in the roles of personnel involved in the response. Ultimately, staffing a HERT requires personnel to expand their duties during the course of an MCE response. Generally, personnel function best in familiar roles. But by expending the effort to build up an effective HERT, personnel will be assigned duties that are similar to their normal hospital duties, and will have had specialized training that allows them to operate with increased safety during an MCE. Economically speaking, as well as functionally speaking, your HERT will likely work better if key components are already established, tested and well-known. Utilizing existing systems within the hospital as much as possible during an MCE will also help keep the plans simple.

Flexibility is a critical component for any all-hazards-all-threats response plan. Maintaining significant flexibility in the hospital MCE plan allows the hospital to effectively adjust its response (e.g., small vs. large event, chemical vs. traumatic injuries). For example, a flexible plan may include phased responses, such that a "lower" level of a disaster plan implementation is initially used. This type of plan would include procedures to bring in additional HERT resources as needed, or as the condition permits, to stand down the HERT response in an organized and incremental fashion. Additionally, flexibility within the plan also allows for the response to be adjusted as a disaster evolves (e.g., initial victims of a terrorist attack have traumatic injuries due to a bomb, but subsequent victims have chemical weapon poisoning due to a chemical secondary device and need decontamination). Flexibility allows for additional outside response assets to be incorporated into existing HERT operations as the event changes or increases in scale.

Coordination of a hospital disaster/MCE response reflects the ability of the HERT to work in an organized and efficient fashion. In other words, personnel are able to coordinate their efforts such that the response is efficient and maximizes the hospital's ability to respond to the MCE. This may include simply knowing who is in charge and knowing what your role is at the time of the MCE response. Having a basic understanding of what everybody else's jobs in the HERT are, and how to work together, will also increase the efficiency of the team's response.

Leadership is the key component of any plan. In the hospital setting, the Hospital Incident Commander (HIC) has the authority and responsibility of coordinating the hospital's overall MCE response. The HERT Commander is responsible for the team's actions. The individuals in leadership roles must be familiar with all aspects of the hospital's MCE plan before an event occurs. This is essential as the HIC is best able to coordinate the response only if he or she has an adequate understanding of the assets available, as well as the capabilities and limitations of the HERT. The HIC is a critical position in a hospital MCE plan, but the HERT Commander is often pivotal in determining the success, or failure, of the emergency response.

Overall, the HIC best serves this role by remaining calm and effectively directing the response of the entire hospital. This may involve dealing with many personnel and/or agencies both within and outside the hospital. The HIC should be able to clearly and concisely direct personnel regarding coordination of the hospital MCE response, continually re-evaluate the situation as an event evolves, and reorder priorities depending upon changing needs during the course of the response. The HIC must effectively delegate certain operational functions and tasks to best coordinate the hospital's response to the MCE; allowing the HERT to function as designed and trained will be critical.

Communication is often the most critical function in any response to a large disaster or event. It is also considered the most vulnerable to failure in any disaster response. During disasters the communication systems within a small community can be quickly overloaded. Additionally, the communication infrastructure also may become involved in the disaster and be compromised, further making communication difficult. Communication plans for the hospital should be redundant and be integrated with surrounding agencies. They need to be evaluated on a periodic basis to make sure they are both operational as well as interoperational with outside agencies. The best guarantee of success for the HERT in the event of predictable communication failures is achieved through repetitive training, which leads to quiet confidence in staff being able to perform their tasks without communication adjuncts.

In summary, hospital MCE planning should be based on learning the principles of disaster planning and management in a way that the hospital develops a plan that can be applied to any situation. A basic, robust and flexible HERT capability that is focused on a generic mass casualty response can be augmented to respond to specific types of MCEs such as chemical, biological, or nuclear attacks, as well as natural disasters.

Hospital surgical capacity is an important component of a hospital's ability to respond to a MCE and can be measured in multiple ways. The hospital's human resources and/or personnel are part of the surgical capacity; this includes medical care providers such as doctors and nurses and the many specific job types and skills that are essential and/or critical to the efficient and effective response to a MCE. A hospital MCE response plan should identify specific jobs and critical positions within the hospital that will be essential for an MCE response and ensure these positions are filled when a MCE occurs.

Equipment, both durable and disposable, may very well become a rate-limiting factor in a hospital's ability to respond to an MCE (e.g., mechanical ventilators). Other disposable supplies such as endotracheal tubes, intravenous supplies, bandages, and other burn or trauma supplies are also essential aspects of surge capacity. Furthermore, surgical capacity can be determined by the infrastructure of the hospital (e.g., the number of operating or isolation rooms). Pharmaceutical supplies are certainly a critical aspect of a hospital's ability to respond. This may include specific medications such as antidotes for nerve agent or cyanide poisoning, and antibiotics. The surge capacity of a hospital's pharmacy can be augmented both through stockpiling of specific medications and/or implementation of procedures to bring external supplies of pharmaceuticals or pharmacists into the hospital in the event of an MCE.

Ultimately a hospital will reach a finite bed capacity to treat patients. This aspect of surge capacity can best be addressed by the establishment of agreements with alternate care facilities that the hospital may be able to divert and/or transfer patients to for care. A properly trained HERT triage team working at the initial reception point will be decisive in the hospital's ability to maintain throughput of patients over time. Not unlike the National Disaster Medical System (NDMS), a hospital's surge capacity would be augmented if there were plans and procedures in place to route or transfer patients to other facilities as appropriate, allowing the hospital to continue to receive and treat new patients. This would be important in protracted MCEs, such as a biological weapons attack, that continue to generate new patients over a longer period of time.

Stockpiling of PPE for surge response staff requires careful consideration and should be included in any hospital MCE response plan. Additionally, some respirators and PPE require fit testing and training to be used safely and effectively, which will have to be accomplished before an MCE occurs. Sufficient PPE must be on hand to allow for hands-on training in the PPE, and operational efficiency, confidence, and safety for all personnel anticipated being a part of the HERT.

Chemical, Biological, Radiological and Explosive Threats

The following information is included in this text, as HERT members are in the best position to become subject matter experts in recognizing and dealing with unconventional threats. Allowing a patient into the facility without appropriate recognition of the threat can lead to delays in detection and containment, and possibly result in unnecessary exposure of other hospital personnel.

Chemical Threats

The possibility of an MCE resulting from the release of a toxic chemical compound is relatively high given the history of such events. There have been numerous instances in which the release of toxic chemical compounds has sent patients to the hospital. More often than not, these releases result in only a few victims. However, a large chemical release involving a vapor or a gas may result in an MCE. The characteristics of the vapor or gas are important. Specifically, heavier-than-air gases will remain close to the ground, in the breathing zone of potential victims. The release of chemicals may be an insidious event, such as the failure of a tank fitting, or it may be an explosive release, such as an uncontrolled chemical reaction resulting in the failure of a pressurized vessel. The explosive event might be from sabotage designed to release the compound, or an event preceding the intentional release of the chemical. Such tactics have been used recently in Iraq, where car bombs have also contained chlorine tanks.

Additionally, mass casualty events involving a chemical release may involve the hospital itself. If the release is of significant magnitude, the chemical plume may envelope the hospital and may comprise that hospital's ability to respond. For instance, in January 2002, Trinity hospital in Minot, ND was enveloped by a cloud of anhydrous ammonia that blanketed the entire city after a nearby train derailment. The hospital itself might be targeted by a terrorist either as a primary or a secondary target, in which case a strong HERT security capability to control access to the healthcare facility is important.

A chemical release causing an MCE is likely to be quickly recognized. Very often patients will self-evacuate from the scene and may arrive at the hospital prior to the hospital even being notified of the event. Typically, the nearest hospital to the event is overwhelmed by people escaping the exposure and seeking the nearest source of medical care. This was the case during the sarin nerve agent release in Tokyo in 1995 when Saint Luke's hospital received hundreds of patients within an hour of the release.

Victims of a large chemical release may vary widely in their severity of poisoning, from the critically ill to the "worried well." Paradoxically, the more severely affected victims will reach the hospital later than less affected victims. This is because mildly or moderately affected victims will typically self-evacuate and be en route to the hospital prior to EMS arrival at the scene. Statistically, as many as 70–85% of victims will arrive at the hospital without the assistance of EMS.

In the Tokyo sarin attacks, large numbers of victims arrived at area hospitals from the scene without clinically significant poisoning and/or even evidence of exposure. These victims are often referred to as "psychological casualties." They may not require medical treatment, but will certainly impact hospital response as they will still need to be medically screened and dispositioned, which will slow the delivery of care to those victims in need of treatment. Therefore, the HERT reception area should consider large numbers of psychological casualties in their plans. Procedures should be made for these patients to be evaluated quickly and moved through the system as expeditiously as possible, so that the hospital can provide care for other more significantly affected victims.

Often, plans for responding to MCEs resulting from large chemical releases involve developing lists of chemicals. However, it is very important for the basic HERT MCE plan not to be driven by such lists. Response protocols should be based on responding to an unknown, undifferentiated, and undiagnosed chemical exposure. The plan can then have different branches that can be employed as information becomes available. There are, however, a certain number of chemicals that are of higher toxicity and/or require specific treatment that need to be specifically considered in the hospital MCE response plans. In general, chemical MCE response plans should include specific provisions to respond to chemicals that are known to be weaponized as chemical warfare agents (such nerve agents that require antidotes) or toxic chemicals known to be stored within the community.

There are also numerous toxic industrial chemicals (TICs) and toxic industrial materials (TIMs) that represent a significant threat due to their availability and potential to be used as chemical weapons of opportunity. In short, chemicals that are of concern would include those that are available in large quantities, available locally and have high toxicity. The risk of these chemicals causing an MCE should be assessed with a hazard and vulnerability analysis (HVA) done by the hospital in conjunction with the surrounding community. Any chemical with sufficient toxicity, availability and quantity can cause an MCE.

In as much as the HERT response protocols for a chemical MCE should be flexible and general enough to respond to any potential chemical release, there are certain chemicals that would require early identification to optimize medical management and survival of the victims. These would be chemicals that require a specific antidote and/or specific treatments, such as nerve agents, organophosphate pesticides, or cyanide. Should a hazard vulnerability analysis of a hospital and its community reveal chemicals that may cause a large MCE at that hospital and require specific antidotal therapy, then that hospital should plan to Stock the required treatment and/or antidote.

Chemical agents that could be encountered in a terrorist attack or in an accidental chemical release share some degree of overlap. Chemical warfare agents typically include nerve agents and/or vesicant agents. In the past they have also included agents such as chlorine, phosgene and cyanide. These agents have been abandoned as viable chemical warfare agents since WWI. However, they are still found in large quantities in industry and in our communities and may be used as chemical agents of opportunity for a terrorist attack or could be accidentally released. For instance, there are numerous releases of anhydrous ammonia, chlorine and other chemicals in our industries annually. Although very few of these resulted in any large number of exposed victims, it does demonstrate the fact that highly toxic chemicals are still available and somewhat ubiquitous. The importance of this is the fact that there are numerous chemical weapons of opportunity in our communities that may result in chemical MCEs and your HERT must be prepared to be effective and safe.

Many chemical MCEs are the result of a chemical that is not readily identifiable at the time of the victims' presentation to the hospital. Indeed, the sarin nerve agent released in the Tokyo subway in 1995 was initially mistakenly identified as a cyanide compound. Therefore, it is important for the HERT to develop and practice a chemical MCE response plan based on the likelihood that the chemical will not be identified at the time event. Moreover, most chemical exposures can be treated with supportive care without specific identification of the chemical. Medical management includes airway and respiratory management per advanced life support protocols. Further management can be tailored as the patient's condition changes and/or specific information about the chemical becomes available.

Basic chemical MCE HERT response protocols may be augmented by specific protocols or procedures for chemicals that are known to be in that hospital's community. Emergency planners can utilize the Emergency Planning and Community Right to Know Act (SARA Title III) to obtain information about the industries in the hospital's area to identify specific chemicals that may cause a chemical MCE. Additional plans may include the stockpiling of related antidotes. It may be helpful to develop specific procedures and protocols to integrate the HERT response with the local industry that may be using those chemicals.

In summary, it is important for the HERT MCE response plan not to be based on a list of chemicals, but to be based on a basic, robust and flexible chemical MCE response plan. Additional specific responses based on what chemicals might be found locally, or other chemicals that require specific treatment or antidotes, can be annexed to this base plan.

Toxidromes

An essential clinical tool for the diagnosis and management of chemical exposures is the use of toxidromes. By definition, a toxidrome is a constellation of clinical signs and/or symptoms specific to a particular chemical or a class of chemicals or drugs. They are useful to help diagnose the responsible chemical or drug in an intoxicated patient. Common toxidromes include opioid (also called the opiate), sympathomimetic, sedative-hypnotic, cholinergic and anticholinergic. Therefore, the HERT chemical MCE response should include training of personnel on the team in the use of toxidromes to rapidly diagnose and treat undifferentiated poisoned patients. A working knowledge of the use of toxidromes will help a hospital-based provider to diagnose and treat based on the clinical presentation of the patient, or patients, without identification of the causative drug and/or chemical (which could be delayed).

Toxidromes, as mentioned above, are a clinical collection of signs and symptoms that can be assessed by an examiner. The clinical evaluation to determine a toxidrome includes: a qualitative assessment of vital signs, assessment of pupils (dilated or constricted); respiratory status (hyperventilating, hypoventilating or some degree of respiratory distress); neurological status (depressed neurological system such as coma or unresponsiveness or a stimulated neurological system such as seizures or agitation); skin (dry or diaphoretic) as well as other specific clinical signs and symptoms. It is important to note that a specific patient may not have every feature of a toxidrome. In a MCE, many patients may present with similar clinical findings that may not be completely consistent with a specific toxidrome. However, when all the patients' presentations are considered in aggregate they may lead to a clinical diagnosis and potentially the identification of the chemical responsible as well.

The opioid toxidrome is what we would expect to see from someone intoxicated on narcotics or opiates. It typically is exemplified by decreased mental status which may range from coma to lethargy, constricted pupils, and depressed, shallow, or apneic respirations. The patient may also have bradycardia, decreased bowel sounds or hypothermia. The essential symptoms of decreased mental status, decreased respiratory status and constricted pupils are the most consistent presentation of this toxidrome. Opioids are not often considered to be a likely cause of an MCE. However, on October 23, 2002, more than 800 people attending a play in Moscow were taken hostage by about 50 Chechen rebels. After several days of a hostage standoff and fears that the terrorists would soon detonate their explosives, the Russian military introduced an incapacitating chemical agent into the theatre, which caused coma and respiratory arrest in the rebels as well as a large number of the hostages. The end result was that out of the 800 hostages, 127 actually died of exposure to this agent, which was later identified as a fentanyl derivative. This is an example of a mass casualty event resulting from the use of an opioid compound.

The cholinergic toxidrome is the presenting toxidrome of a nerve agent or organophosphate pesticide poisoned patient. It is a direct result of excess acetylcholine binding to acetylcholine receptors in the central nervous system, the autonomic nervous system, and at the neuromuscular junction. Muscarinic manifestations of nerve agent poisoning include excess exocrine gland secretions and smooth muscle contraction. These effects are often summarized in the mnemonics SLUDGE or DUMBELS which include: salivation, lacrimation, urination, gastrointestinal distress, defecation or diarrhea, emesis, bronchoconstriction and bronchorrhea, and miosis. Paralysis of the skeletal muscles of respiration and the diaphragm worsens muscarinic-mediated respiratory bronchorrhea and bronchoconstriction and can rapidly lead to respiratory arrest. The interested reader is encouraged to further study the concept of toxidromes such that HERT team members may be familiar with toxidromes and may use them in the event of an MCE.

In managing a chemical MCE it is important for the HERT to keep focused on an all threats, all hazards approach. By HERT members maintaining a wide differential diagnosis when presented with a victim of chemical agent exposure, the patient is more likely to receive life-saving intervention in a timely fashion. Treatment should be based on the clinical presentation of the patient. Regardless of the actual chemical agent involved, treatment priorities remain the ABCs (airway, breathing, circulation). If a toxidrome that requires an antidote is identified, then the antidote can be administered as well. Although ultimately important, identification of the actual chemical released may not impact the emergent treatment on the patient's initial presentation.

Care in the HERT treatment area should be tailored appropriately as additional information becomes known and/or certain determinations as to the patient's condition are made. For example, should information become available that the patient was exposed to cyanide then the appropriate cyanide antidote should be immediately administered. Additionally, as diagnoses are made in the hospital they should be communicated to the other responding agencies such that the information can be shared with other hospitals and/or utilized in the pre-hospital setting as well. The value of toxidromes and the sharing of information is illustrated by the fact that in the 1995 Tokyo subway attacks a physician who had treated victims of the 1994 Matsumoto sarin nerve agent attack (and was watching live television coverage of victims arriving at hospitals) recognized the cholinergic toxidrome and called the hospitals to notify them that it was nerve agent that they were dealing with.

Up to this point, the emphasis has been the all-hazards, all-threats approach to mass casualty event response. This has been the case with the chemical MCE response as well. However, there are a number of chemical agents that deserve specific attention. These agents have high toxicity, may be more readily available, or may be available in larger quantities and therefore more likely to be encountered as the cause of a chemical MCE. Some of these are known to have been weaponized, such as nerve agents, and some require specific antidotes, such as nerve agents or cyanide. Therefore, the following sections should serve as a primer for HERT teams to develop a knowledge base about potential agents that could cause MCEs. A large number of toxic industrial chemicals are classified as irritant gases or pulmonary agents. These include chlorine, anhydrous ammonia, phosgene and others. The pathophysiology of the lung injury caused by these gases is determined by the physical characteristics and chemistry of the gas. Those gases with high water solubility, such as chlorine, will irritate the mucous membranes of the upper respiratory tract, providing a noxious warning property to these gases. Other gases with poorer water solubility often will not interact quickly with the moisture found in the upper airways and instead penetrate deep into the respiratory tract, causing a significant amount of injury in the distal or lower airways, such as the alveoli.

Often these gases generate an acid or an alkaline that will react with and injure tissue. This could lead to upper airway edema and airway compromise leading to asphyxiation. In the lower airways they can cause tissue injury at the level of the alveoli, resulting in a non-cardiogenic pulmonary edema (often delayed), possibly leading to asphyxiation. Pulmonary agents can also be very irritating to the smooth muscle that lines the respiratory tract and may cause a significant amount of bronchospasm as well.

Chlorine

Chlorine has good warning characteristics, such as a green-yellowish cloud and a very pungent and well-recognized odor. It becomes a gas at an ambient temperature of 34°C and will likely be in a gaseous state when released. Its vapor density is 2.5 compared to that of air (1.0). Therefore, it will travel downhill and remain close to the ground, settling in geographical depressions. It is heavily transported and typically shipped as a liquefied pressurized gas. It is highly reactive with many compounds and can react explosively. These characteristics make it a good candidate for use as a chemical weapon of opportunity. This was the case in Iraq from 2006 to 2007 when numerous car and truck bombs were detonated with chlorine tanks in the vehicles.

Chlorine is a ubiquitous chemical found in many places around our communities. It can be found at fixed facilities such as water treatment plants and other facilities that utilize chlorine in large quantities. Importantly, it can be found in transit, either on the highways or in rail cars. An important aspect of a local HVA is to determine where fixed facilities might exist in the community as well as local transportation routes. Identify possible or most likely sites for chlorine release, due to either a rail car derailment and/or a terrorist attack on rail tank cars carrying chlorine.

When chlorine interacts with water found in the mucous membranes it will form hydrochloric acid. This hydrochloric acid subsequently interacts with the tissues, causing mucous membrane irritation at low levels and tissue necrosis at high levels. This interaction is also responsible for the characteristic effects of chlorine including irritation of the eyes, nose, and throat, causing coughing, laryngospasm and bronchospasm. At higher concentrations chlorine will reach the peripheral airways of the respiratory tract. In the peripheral airways a second chemical reaction occurs that generates oxygen free radicals. These free radicals attack the alveolar-capillary membrane, producing non-cardiogenic pulmonary edema.

After initial assessment and decontamination, treatment priorities include airway and pulmonary management. Aggressive airway management is important given the possibility of progressive upper airway edema leading to airway obstruction. Management of lower airway injury includes the administration of oxygen, bronchodilators to treat bronchospasm, and supportive ICU care with or without mechanical ventilation. Less severely injured patients may be observed and put at bedrest pending resolution of their symptoms. It should be noted that victims of chemical agent inhalation injury should be observed for latent symptoms such as non-cardiogenic pulmonary edema.

Phosgene

Phosgene was a World War I chemical weapon and is widely used in the chemical industry as an intermediate for chemical syntheses such as the production of diisocyanates for polyurethane production. Phosgene is a highly toxic gas with an OSHA immediately dangerous to life and health (IDLH) limit of 2 ppm. It is a colorless and highly toxic gas with a relatively innocuous odor. During WWI, when it was introduced as a chemical weapon, soldiers were often cautioned to be alert for the unexplained odor of mown hay or grass. This smell, although characteristic, is not terribly offensive, lacking the warning properties noted with chlorine. This is primarily due to its poor water solubility compared to chlorine. It has a vapor density of 3.4, and when released it will remain close to the ground, travelling downhill and into geographical depressions.

Phosgene, as mentioned above, is a common chemical intermediate. A vast majority of this is used for the production of isocyanates, which subsequently are used for the production of polyurethane as well as pesticides. Although it may be shipped as a liquefied, pressurized gas, 99% of phosgene is utilized onsite where it was produced. Therefore, it is less likely to be a hazard in transit. Nonetheless, a community threat assessment should determine whether any fixed chemical facilities within the area indeed manufacture and/or stockpile phosgene.

Although poorly water soluble, in high enough concentration phosgene will interact with water in the mucous membranes to liberate hydrochloric acid, similar to the chemical interaction in which chlorine produces hydrochloric acid. Due to its poor water solubility, most inhaled phosgene reaches the distal airways. In the distal airway the carbonyl group of phosgene (a highly reactive free radical) damages alveolar-capillary membranes, producing non-cardiogenic pulmonary edema. It is very important to note this process can occur in a delayed fashion, resulting in delayed onset of a severe and potentially life-threatening lung injury even after an initial presentation without significant symptoms.

Exposure to low concentrations of phosgene may produce mild cough, a sense of chest discomfort, and dyspnea. High concentrations may trigger a rapidly developing pulmonary edema with attendant severe cough, dyspnea, laryngospasm, and frothy sputum. Onset of pulmonary edema within 2 to 6 hours is predictive of severe injury.

Depending on the intensity of exposure, chest tightness with moderate dyspnea at rest and prominent exertional dyspnea becomes evident within the first 12 hours after exposure. These symptoms often precede the development of pulmonary edema, which may be delayed many hours.

Pulmonary edema is the most serious clinical aspect of phosgene exposure and begins with few, if any, clinical signs. Consequently, early diagnosis of pulmonary edema requires that careful attention by the HERT treatment area staff be paid to any symptoms of dyspnea or chest tightness. If present, these symptoms require further evaluation of the victim's respiratory status, chest x-rays and/or arterial blood gases as needed, and observation.

Anhydrous Ammonia

Ammonia is a highly water-soluble alkaline colorless gas with a pungent odor. It is often transported as a pressurized liquid. It is used widely in refrigeration and cold storage facilities, agriculture and industry.

Ammonia is a severe respiratory hazard and eye irritant with an IDLH value of 300 ppm. The odor threshold of ammonia is approximately 3–5 ppm, and it has a characteristic pungent odor. High concentrations of ammonia vapor are visible as a white fog. Ammonia vapors are generally lighter than air and in open environments they will readily dissipate to the atmosphere, but ammonia can also react with water in the atmosphere to form an ammonium hydroxide vapor that is heavier than air.

Upon contact with moist mucosal membranes such as the eyes and respiratory tract, ammonia reacts with water to form a strong alkali (ammonia hydroxide). This is a strong alkaline caustic agent that produces burns to the cornea, skin, and respiratory tract. Inhalation can cause severe caustic injury to both the upper and lower airways, including upper airway obstruction from edema and sloughing of the airway lining, as well as pulmonary edema.

At approximately 1:37 a.m. on January 18, 2002, a freight train derailed 31 of its 112 cars about ½ mile west of the city limits of Minot, North Dakota. Five tank cars carrying anhydrous ammonia as a liquefied compressed gas catastrophically ruptured and a vapor plume covered the derailment site and surrounding area. About 11,600 people lived in the area affected by the vapor plume. As a result of the accident, one person died, 11 people sustained serious injuries, and 322 people, including the 2 train crewmembers, sustained minor injuries.

Trinity Hospital activated its disaster plan, "Code Green," at 2:25 a.m., 35 minutes after the emergency room was notified of the derailment. Approximately 200 medical personnel came to the hospital in response to the Code Green. The additional personnel supplemented the 41 staff members already at the hospital. Staff secured the hospital against the hazardous vapors by shutting down air handlers, setting up a portable air-handling unit in the emergency room, and establishing an alternate emergency room entrance away from the vapor cloud. The emergency room staff consulted a material safety data sheet to find out how to effectively treat persons exposed to ammonia. Additionally, Trinity Hospital sent a representative to the emergency operations center. By 4:15 a.m., the ammonia cloud had drifted to and encompassed the hospital. Throughout the emergency, Trinity Hospital treated approximately 300 people.

Methyl Isocyanate (MIC)

Methyl isocyanate is used in the production of synthetic rubber, adhesives, pesticides and herbicide intermediates. It is extremely toxic by inhalation, ingestion and skin absorption. Inhalation of MIC causes cough, dizziness, shortness of breath, sore throat and unconsciousness. It is corrosive to the skin and eyes. Short-term exposures also lead to death or adverse effects like pulmonary edema (respiratory inflammation), bronchitis, bronchial pneumonia and reproductive effects.

On the night of December 2, 1984, a large quantity of water entered a storage tank containing MIC at the Union Carbide pesticide plant in Bhopal, India in December 1984. The plant used MIC as a chemical intermediate to produce the pesticide Carbaryl. This triggered a runaway reaction resulting in a tremendous increase of temperature and pressure in the tank and the release of approximately 40 tons of MIC, hydrogen cyanide and other reaction products into the night air of Bhopal. Thousands were killed in the hours after the release and thousands later developed chronic lung disease and other complications of the exposure. MIC is used in the United States as well, making a similar, although smaller scale event possible. The Bhopal disaster is a chemical MCE worth additional study.

Cyanide

Each year, the United States produces approximately three quarters of a million tons of cyanide. Cyanide is easily obtainable by virtue of its widespread use in industry and research laboratories. Modest quantities are easily obtained via the internet. It is transported by truck and rail, both of which are susceptible to theft, hijacking attempts, and other terrorist acts that could culminate in use of cyanide as a weapon.

Unlike other biological or chemical weapons that require specific technological or scientific proficiency for effective use, cyanide incidents can be planned and successfully executed by individuals without specific expertise or training. Cyanide is capable of causing mass casualties if released in sufficient quantities in enclosed spaces (e.g., concert hall, sports arena). Due to its high toxicity and rapid onset of potentially lethal effects, victims of cyanide poisoning require prompt treatment with cyanide antidote—a challenging task if faced with several hundred critically ill victims. Therefore, HERTs should be familiar with the diagnosis and treatment of cyanide poisoning, including the administration of cyanide antidotes.

The attractiveness of cyanide to the terrorist is underlined by several recent incidents in which cyanide was planned for use as a weapon of terror:

- Court transcripts regarding the 1993 World Trade Center bombing indicate cyanide was used in the attack (Sauer, 2001).
- At the time of the 1995 Tokyo subway attack, precursors of cyanide, which terrorists allegedly planned to use in addition to sarin, were found in the subway bathrooms (Sauer, 2001).

- UK officials foiled an attempt by al-Qaeda members to use cyanide gas to kill commuters on the London Underground in 2002 (Anonymous, Sunday Herald, 2002).
- In February 2002, four Moroccans with links to al-Qaeda were arrested for plotting to use cyanide to poison water supplies around the U.S. embassy in Rome (Anonymous, 2004).
- In December 2002, a cyanide store linked to three suspected al-Qaeda operatives was recovered in a raid in Paris (Cloud, 2004).
- In May 2003, a cyanide bomb was discovered on the premises of storage units rented by white supremacists in Texas (Anonymous, Jan. 2004).

Cyanide is a chemical asphyxiant that poisons cells by preventing them from utilizing oxygen in the production of ATP. Clinical manifestations of cyanide poisoning primarily reflect the effects of oxygen deprivation on the heart and brain. The time between initial exposure to cyanide and symptom onset can vary from seconds to hours, depending primarily on the intensity and route of cyanide exposure. Death can occur within minutes after exposure. Exposure to moderate-to-high concentrations of cyanide can cause loss of consciousness in seconds, and respiratory depression and cardiac arrest can follow within minutes. Early symptoms of acute cyanide poisoning include neurologic manifestations such as giddiness, confusion, headache, and dizziness; nausea and vomiting; palpitations and hyperventilation or shortness of breath; and eye irritation. Later symptoms of acute cyanide poisoning reflect neurological and cardiopulmonary failure due to tissue hypoxia and include hypoventilation, hypotension, stupor, seizures and loss of consciousness.

The complexity of administration and the potential serious adverse effects of the Cyanide Antidote Kit (also known as the American Cyanide Antidote Kit, The Lilly Kit) make it ill-suited for use in MCEs involving cyanide poisoning. Hydroxocobalamin (vitamin B_{12a}) is also approved in the United States for the treatment of cyanide poisoning. Hydroxocobalamin (marketed under the name Cyanokit) neutralizes cyanide by binding with it to form vitamin B_{12}. It appears to be as effective as the Cyanide Antidote Kit in the treatment of cyanide poisoning but is not associated with the same serious adverse effects. Because the safety risks of administering hydroxocobalamin are negligible, the antidote can be quickly administered to many victims in the HERT emergency treatment area. Because of its favorable risk:benefit ratio, hydroxocobalamin need not be reserved for cases of confirmed cyanide poisoning, but can be administered in cases of suspected poisoning. Both of these attributes lead to more rapid initiation of treatment than is possible with the Cyanide Antidote Kit and thereby can improve outcomes in a cyanide disaster.

Organophosphates

Nerve agents are extremely toxic organophosphate compounds that were initially developed by the German chemist, Gerhard Schrader, who synthesized tabun in 1937 (GA) while researching new insecticides. Tabun was followed by the development of sarin (GB) in 1938, soman (GD) in 1944, and then VX in 1952. Although stockpiled in great quantities during World War II, nerve agents were not employed in warfare until the Iran-Iraq war during the 1980s. Resources are readily available that provide detailed information regarding the preparation of nerve agents, as well as other chemical weapons (Ledgard, 2003).

All nerve agents are organic ester derivatives of phosphoric acid with different chemical functional groups replacing the hydroxyl radical group of the basic phosphate structure. All G agents are volatile liquids at room temperature, colorless, tasteless, and odorless, while the V agents have relatively low volatility. Several of the G agents have been reported to have a fruity or sweet smell (Neitlich, 1965). Their vapors are all heavier than air and tend to remain close to the ground, traveling downwind, downhill, and into geographical depressions. These physical characteristics make them ideal for controlled release by terrorists, although weather conditions can unpredictably disperse chemical agent releases, resulting in exposure to the terrorists who released the agent (Tu, 1999). Volatility and vapor pressure determine the likelihood that a chemical agent will be an inhalational threat. At room temperature nerve agents exist as liquids and therefore must be aerosolized or evaporated to become inhalational threats.

To date, the most significant uses of nerve agents against civilians by a terrorist group have been by the Aum Shinrikyo cult of Japan. The Aum chemical weapons program was able to produce significant quantities of VX and sarin, and lesser amounts of other nerve agents, mustard agent, phosgene, and cyanide. Nerve agents were used in a number of assassinations of cult "enemies," as well as two large-scale attacks (Tu, 1999; Tu, 2001; Okomura, 1995; Ohbu, 1997). The first was in Matsumoto, Japan on June 27, 1994 when the cult released approximately 20 kilograms of sarin vapor from a specially equipped van in an effort to assassinate three district court judges hearing a civil suit brought against the cult. This attack killed seven people, and sent several hundred more to local hospitals, with 58 being admitted for treatment. The Aum subsequently perpetrated another, larger scale nerve agent attack in Tokyo on March 20, 1995. In this attack, approximately 159 ounces of sarin was released from eight nylon-polyethylene bags (3 additional bags were recovered intact) that were punctured by Aum cult members between 7:46 a.m. and 8:01 a.m. on five of Tokyo's main subway lines causing 12 deaths. Ultimately, Tokyo hospitals and clinics saw 5,510 patients: 17 critical, 37 severe and 984 moderately ill. Over 70% of those presenting for treatment had no objective signs of nerve agent poisoning. Because this dissemination method was relatively inefficient, it caused only 12 fatalities instead of potentially hundreds or thousands.

The hospital response to a terrorist nerve agent attack should anticipate mass casualties arriving unannounced, contaminated, and in a disorganized fashion. Saint Luke's hospital's first victim arrived on foot 30 minutes after the attack and was followed by approximately 500 more within the next 30 minutes. Among 640 victims who presented to Saint Luke's Hospital on the day of the attack, 15% arrived by emergency vehicle (only 10% by ambulance), 48% by foot or private vehicle, and 25% by taxi. Radio-dispatched taxis played a significant role in transporting victims from the scene and were also important in communicating information (Okomura; Ohbu). Typically, as they are the most able to flee the incident scene and make their way to the hospital, most of the early presenters are less severely affected than those incapacitated at the scene.

Another important characteristic of nerve agents is persistence: the ability to remain present and active in the environment after dissemination. Although nerve agents with high volatility pose a significant inhalation hazard, they soon evaporate and dissipate, limiting their persistency. Agents with low volatility and vapor pressure, such as the V agents, do not readily evaporate, and therefore do not pose an inhalational threat, but are persistent. Ambient temperature directly correlates with an agent's rate of evaporation, and inversely correlates with its persistence.

CLINICAL PRESENTATION

The characteristic clinical toxicity of nerve agents is a cholinergic toxidrome, which is a direct result of excess acetylcholine binding to acetylcholine receptors in the central and autonomic nervous systems, and at the neuromuscular junction. Muscarinic manifestations of nerve agent poisoning include excess exocrine gland secretions and smooth muscle contraction. These effects are often summarized in the mnemonics SLUDGE or DUMBELS which include: salivation, lacrimation, urination, gastrointestinal distress, defecation or diarrhea, emesis, bronchoconstriction, bronchorrhea, and miosis. The respiratory effects, should be the focus of clinical assessment, treatment, and antidote administration. Nicotinic manifestations of nerve agent poisoning are primarily the result of excess acetylcholine at the neuromuscular junction causing skeletal muscle fasciculations followed by weakness and eventually paralysis. Diaphoresis can also be seen as a result of excessive cholinergic tone at the autonomic ganglia of sweat glands.

As mentioned above, the respiratory system is the site of the most serious acute clinical manifestations of nerve agent poisoning. The direct effects of the nerve agent on the respiratory tract (bronchorrhea and bronchoconstriction), inhibition of the CNS medullary respiratory center and paralysis of the diaphragm and skeletal muscles associated with respiration (Rickett, 1986; Wright, 1954) combine to cause respiratory failure. Neurological symptoms include seizures, coma, muscular weakness and paralysis, and delayed neuropsychiatric effects including depression and anxiety. Gastrointestinal symptoms include vomiting, abdominal cramping and diarrhea. Respiratory arrest is the ultimate cause of death following nerve agent poisoning.

The severity (i.e., intensity and dose) and route of exposure are significant factors in determining the clinical presentation of nerve agent poisoning. Nerve agents are well absorbed by all routes (e.g., inhalation, ingestion, and dermal). Absorption via the inhalation route will cause onset of symptoms within seconds to minutes of exposure, while absorption via the dermal route may result in a delay in onset of symptoms due to the time required for the agent to be systemically absorbed. Victims of a vapor or aerosol nerve agent exposure may initially complain of eye pain exacerbated by accommodation, loss of dark adaptation, dim and/or blurred vision, conjunctival irritation, lacrimation, and miosis. These effects are thought to result both from direct exposure of the eye to the nerve agent vapor as well as central nervous system effects (Rengstorff, 1985; Rubin, 1957). Upper respiratory tract symptoms (e.g., rhinorrhea and nasal congestion) are followed by progressive respiratory complaints including chest tightness, dyspnea, wheezing, shortness of breath, cough, and increased bronchial secretions. If the exposure is significant and/or prolonged, other signs of respiratory toxicity will rapidly develop, including severe bronchoconstriction, wheezing, bronchorrhea, respiratory distress and arrest. Inhalational exposure to nerve agents results in the most rapid onset of symptoms due to rapid absorption of nerve agent via the large surface area of the pulmonary bed. If the concentration of the inhaled nerve agent vapor is high, patients may not develop symptoms in a typical "respiratory route pattern" but may rapidly lose consciousness, and suffer respiratory arrest and seizures due to rapid systemic absorption of the agent.

Dermally-absorbed nerve agents will initially cause localized symptoms at the site of exposure (e.g., fasciculations, diaphoresis) before generalized signs and symptoms develop. As the nerve agent is systemically absorbed, victims will develop other cholinergic symptoms, such as respiratory and gastrointestinal symptoms, muscle weakness and seizures. It is important to note that dermal exposure to nerve agents may result in latent or progressive intoxication, even after appropriate skin decontamination, due to delayed systemic absorption of nerve agent already absorbed into the skin (Blank, 1952; Craig, 1977). Therefore, victims of dermal nerve agent exposure must be observed for a minimum of

18 hours after decontamination for the delayed development of toxicity. Sidell reported a case in which a 33-year-old man was splashed in the face and mouth with approximately 1 ml of a 25% (v/v) soman solution. He immediately rinsed his face and mouth with water and was asymptomatic until collapsing approximately 10 minutes after the exposure. He was immediately treated with atropine (4 mg IV, 8 mg IM) and 2-PAM (2 gm IV over 30 minutes). Endotracheal intubation was unsuccessful due to trismus. Signs and symptoms included miosis, coma, markedly injected conjunctiva, marked oral and nasal secretions, prominent muscular fasciculations, tachycardia, cyanosis, bronchoconstriction and decreased respiratory rate and amplitude. He began to awaken after 30 minutes but continued to have fasciculations, tremor, nausea, vomiting, abdominal pain, restlessness over the next 36 hours. Red blood cell cholinesterase activity was undetectable until 10 days after the exposure (Sidell, 1973). Sidell also reported a case of a 52-year-old male with an inhalational exposure to sarin. Within minutes of noticing increased nasal and oral secretions and difficult breathing while wearing a protective gas mask (later determined to have been damaged), he developed seizures, respiratory distress, miosis, muscular fasciculations, cyanosis, wheezing, and copious secretions. His respirations were less labored and cyanosis decreased within minutes of being treated with atropine (IM and IV), 2-PAM IV, and oxygen. He received a total of 14 milligrams of atropine and 6 grams of 2-PAM were administered over 1 hour. An electrocardiogram (EKG) obtained one hour after admission showed global ST segment depression. Additional EKGs obtained 18 and 42 hours after admission showed ST segment elevations as well as T wave inversions. No cardiac enzymes were obtained and the patient's EKG normalized within 4 months (Sidell, 1973).

ASSESSMENT

The diagnosis of nerve agent poisoning may be made on the basis of a single patient's presentation (i.e., a cholinergic toxidrome) and on a situational basis, in which multiple patients present with similar or identical symptoms that, collectively, suggest a diagnosis of nerve agent poisoning (Nozaki, 1995). Regardless of how the diagnosis is arrived at, due to the extreme toxicity of nerve agents, victims must be evaluated as quickly as possible to determine their need for airway management (i.e., intubation) and the administration of antidotal therapy (e.g., atropine and oxime). Therefore, the clinical assessment of a nerve agent victim is based upon the severity of their cholinergic toxidrome. Although useful retrospectively, the measurement of cholinesterase activity is not practical in the acute assessment of a nerve agent victim due to the delay in obtaining results. Further, in the case of a mass casualty incident (MCI), the initial assessment of victims must be accomplished in a rapid and efficient manner so as to triage victims for treatment.

Victims of a vapor nerve agent exposure will likely present with ocular and upper respiratory symptoms as described above. Miosis is the earliest sign of a vapor nerve agent exposure, but may be absent or delayed in a dermal exposure. Patients with only miosis and upper respiratory tract symptoms can be observed without treatment. Patients with lower respiratory tract manifestations (e.g., wheezing, dyspnea), neurological symptoms (e.g., seizures, weakness) or multiple organ system involvement should receive antidotal therapy with atropine and an oxime (see below). The assessment of victims of dermal nerve agent exposure should also be based upon the severity of their clinical cholinergic toxidrome. However, it is important to note that initial symptoms can be localized to the site of nerve agent exposure and that severe or fatal toxicity can develop up to 18 hours after exposure. All patients should be reassessed frequently for worsening, or resolution, of symptoms, the effectiveness of antidote administration, or the need for additional antidote.

The initial assessment of any suspected nerve agent victim should include airway, breathing and circulation. The clinical presentation of a child poisoned by nerve agent may differ from that of an adult. An effective response to a mass casualty incident includes rapid assessment, triage, and treatment of victims. However, the typical parameters used for assessing adult victims of a nerve agent attack may not be appropriate for assessing the pediatric victims of the same attack. Although there is no replacement for sharp clinical acumen in assessing and treating any patient, adult or pediatric, the Pediatric Assessment Triangle (PAT) is a tool developed for the assessment of pediatric patients. It uses only visual and auditory clues to develop a first impression of the severity of the child's condition and to identify physiologic instability. It offers a quick (30 to 60 seconds) standardized approach to triage, resuscitation, treatment and transport. The PAT includes assessment of: appearance, work of breathing, and circulation to the skin. Appearance is assessed by generally observing the child (e.g., alertness, age appropriate speech/behavior). Work of breathing is assessed by listening for abnormal breath sounds (e.g., wheezing) and looking for signs of increased work of breathing (e.g., grunting, retractions). Skin circulation is assessed by looking for signs of poor skin perfusion (e.g., pallor, mottling, cyanosis). The combination of all three components of the PAT should determine a child's degree of nerve agent poisoning and need for treatment.

TREATMENT

The most immediate concern in the treatment of acute nerve agent poisoning is to establish an airway and provide adequate ventilation and oxygenation, using advanced life support techniques including intubation and ventilation with supplemental oxygen. Mouth-to-mouth resuscitation is not recommended due to the high risk of rescuer contamination and poisoning. Note that intubation may be difficult due to trismus from muscular spasm and fasciculations and/or seizures (Sidell, 1973; Blank, 1952). Initial advanced life support measures should be accompanied by the earliest possible administration of nerve agent antidotes, including atropine, an oxime, and a benzodiazepine for the treatment of seizures. Initial ventilation may demonstrate marked airway resistance due to severe bronchoconstriction and bronchorrhea. Therefore, atropine should be administered as soon as possible by whatever route is available (e.g., IM, IV, endotracheal) to reverse the respiratory effects of the nerve agent.

Antidotes

The early administration of antidotes is critical in the treatment of nerve agent poisoning. Antidotal therapy for nerve agent poisoning includes atropine, an oxime, and a benzodiazepine (each is discussed in detail below). The decision to administer antidote(s) is based upon the severity of poisoning and route of exposure. Victims of an inhalational exposure that present with mild symptoms including miosis, eye pain, and rhinorrhea, but no other significant signs or symptoms, may be observed without the administration of antidote. Those with any complaints of respiratory distress, including shortness of breath, chest tightness, wheezing or dyspnea should be treated with a initial administration of atropine 2 mg and pralidoxime (600 mg via autoinjector IM injection or 500 to 1,000 mg/hr via IV infusion). If respiratory symptoms are significant (e.g., dyspnea, wheezing, shortness of breath), or the victim has additional symptoms such as weakness or vomiting, the initial doses of atropine and pralidoxime should be doubled to 4 mg via IM/IV injection, and 1,200 mg IM (i.e., two 600 mg autoinjectors), respectively. Victims with severe manifestations of nerve agent poisoning, including severe respiratory distress or apnea, seizures or coma, or significant skeletal muscle weakness, should receive initial doses of atropine and pralidoxime of 6 mg IM/IV and 1,800 mg IM, respectively, as well as a benzodiazepine to treat or prevent seizures.

Atropine

Atropine is a direct-acting competitive muscarinic receptor antagonist that reverses muscarinic-mediated smooth muscle contraction and exocrine hypersecretion. This clinical effect is most important in the lungs where excessive bronchorrhea and bronchoconstriction leads to hypoxemia, decreased ventilation, and respiratory arrest. As the acetylcholine receptors found at the neuromuscular junction are nicotinic, atropine does not reverse skeletal muscle paralysis. Atropine eye drops can be used to reverse nerve agent induced miosis and paralysis of accommodation (Nozaki, 1995). All patients who receive atropine should only be monitored for therapeutic improvement, and also for signs of anticholinergic effects. These include increased heart rate, drying of secretions, dilated pupils, loss of accommodation, and decreased sweating and other signs of an anticholinergic toxidrome.

The recommended adult dose of atropine is 2 mg, which can be administered intravenously, intramuscularly, endotracheally, as well as by autoinjector (e.g., Mark I kit). The autoinjector is an effective means of administering atropine in an expeditious and effective manner, as it can quickly deliver antidote through clothing (including PPE) and animal studies have shown that atropine administered by autoinjector was absorbed at a rate intermediate between intravenous administration and intramuscular administration with a conventional syringe (Sidell, 1974; Friedl, 1989). Atropine administration should be repeated in 2 mg doses every 5–10 minutes based on clinical response. The most critical indicator of antidotal response is pulmonary function (i.e., drying of bronchial secretions, decreased airway resistance, improved ventilation and oxygenation). This can be assessed by the patient's self-reported ease of breathing or by improved compliance if the patient is being artificially ventilated. There is no dose limit for the total amount of atropine administered and end of therapy should be determined by clinical stabilization. Patients who require continued antidotal treatment after initial improvement should be suspected of having ongoing dermal nerve agent absorption and undergo repeat decontamination.

Oxime Antidotes
Oximes are the second important antidote in the treatment of nerve agent poisoning (Grob, 1958). Their primary role is to reactivate acetylcholinesterase (the enzyme that breaks down acetylcholine in cholinergic synapses to decrease or stop acetylcholine binding to post-synaptic receptors) after it has been inhibited by a nerve agent by removing the nerve agent from its active site. Because atropine effectively antagonizes the muscarinic effects of nerve agent poisoning, oximes are clinically most important due to their ability to reactivate AChE in nicotinic synapse, restoring neuromuscular function and reversing skeletal muscle paralysis. In the United States, 2-pralidoxime chloride (2-PAM, Protopam®) is the only oxime currently approved by the Food and Drug Administration (FDA) for the treatment of organophosphate or nerve agent poisoning. If pralidoxime is administered IV, a dosing regimen consists of an IV bolus of 1 gram over 30 minutes followed by an infusion of 500 mg/h which should be continued until the patient's muscle weakness has resolved. Administration at a rate faster

than 1 gram over 30 minutes may cause hypertension. As a general rule, any victim that receives atropine should also receive an oxime antidote.

Benzodiazepines

Victims with severe nerve agent poisoning may also have seizures. The addition of a benzodiazepine has been shown to improve survival from nerve agent poisoning and to decrease the development of permanent brain damage (Rump, 2003; Martin, 1987). Diazepam is available in an auto injector. It is recommended that a benzodiazepine be administered for any seizure activity as well as for any moderate to severe manifestations of nerve agent poisoning (prior to the development of seizures). Although diazepam is most commonly recommended, other benzodiazepines can be used if diazepam is not available, as might be the case in a mass casualty incident.

Decontamination is a critical step in the care of nerve agent victims. Continued absorption of agent will significantly undermine the effectiveness of advanced life support measures and/or antidotes administered to nerve agent poisoning victims. Therefore, treatment plans and protocols should provide for decontamination taking place as early as possible. Briefly, victims with dermal exposure require thorough decontamination, including undressing and full body water decontamination. Large volume low pressure water is the preferred method of decontamination. Soap and water has not been found to offer significant benefit over timely and adequate water decontamination. Victims with only vapor exposure (i.e., no possible dermal contact with liquid agent) to nerve agent can be adequately decontaminated by removing them from the exposure and undressing them. Nerve agents form aerosols or vapors that can adsorb into victims' clothing, and then off-gas well after the victim has been removed from the site of exposure. It is estimated that removal of all clothing will provide approximately 80% of all possible decontamination after exposure to a nerve agent vapor. Victims of the 1995 Tokyo subway sarin attack were transported from the scene of the attack without any decontamination. Prehospital first responders quickly became symptomatic until ambulances were ordered to keep all windows open to maximize ventilation during transport. Hospital-based care providers also became symptomatic after exposure to off-gassing victims that were brought into the hospital without decontamination (Okumura, 1995; Ohbu, 1997).

Ideally, all victims would undergo adequate decontamination prior to leaving the incident scene. Historically, however, approximately 70–85% of victims of a mass casualty incident will self-evacuate themselves, and each other, from the incident scene and then self-triage to nearby healthcare facilities. This creates the need for decontamination plans and equipment at healthcare facilities. This was the case during the 1995 Tokyo sarin attack, where there was no field decontamination of victims at the incident scene. Secondary exposures occurred at the receiving hospitals with 23% of the Saint Luke's hospital staff developing signs and symptoms of sarin poisoning while treating the hundreds of victims that presented to the hospital. Forty-six percent of those working in a poorly ventilated hospital chapel became symptomatic. However, only one nurse was admitted, and no one required antidotal treatment (Okumura, 1995; Ohbu, 1997; Nozaki, 1995; Okumura, 1998). In summary, an inhalational exposure will likely be due to the use of a nerve agent aerosol or vapor, as in the Tokyo subway attacks. Victims exposed to nerve agent vapor will adsorb the agent into their clothing and will "off gas" the agent after they have been removed from the exposure. The risk associated with off-gassing is continued inhalational exposure for the patient, as well as medical care providers in close proximity to the patient, especially indoors and in confined spaces (e.g., ambulances). Hospital care providers became symptomatic due to off-gassing from patients brought into the hospital without decontamination.

Mustard

Mustard agent was developed as a chemical warfare agent during WWI and was responsible for the largest number of chemical casualties of the war. Lewisite, an arsenical vesicant, was also developed during WWI, but never deployed on the battlefield. It is mentioned here as the methods and formulas for its production are available on the open literature (Ledgard, 2003), making it a possible choice of terrorists for a chemical weapon attack. Mustard was also heavily used by Saddam Hussein in the 1980s, both during Iraq's conflict with Iran, and as part of his genocidal campaign against the Kurdish population of northern Iraq. Mustard was also synthesized in small quantities by the Aum Shinrikyo cult, but there is no evidence it was ever used.

Sulfur mustard is a liquid blister agent which is usually a yellowish, amber color. It evaporates about five times more slowly than water, and may persist for several months in cold conditions. Mustards received their name from their garlic-like, pungent smell. The mustard molecule cyclizes when dermally absorbed, forming a highly reactive intermediate that binds to tissue proteins, enzymes and DNA. This chemical action leads to cell death and tissue necrosis, causing characteristic skin burns and blisters. If inhaled, mustard agents can cause severe lung injury.

Treatment for mustard exposures includes decontamination to remove any residual product, followed by symptomatic treatment of the chemical burns and supportive care for any pulmonary injury. There are no antidotes for mustard, so treatment is primarily respiratory care and burn management. British Anti-Lewisite (BAL) is a specific chelating agent for treatment the arsenic component of Lewisite.

Other chemicals that individual HERTs should be prepared for will come from a good community hazard analysis.

Biological MCE

Biological warfare is considered the oldest of the nuclear, biological and chemical triad of weapons of mass destruction. There are references to the use of biological weapons over 2,000 years ago. The Assyrians poisoned their enemies' wells with ergot fungus, which contains hallucinogenic compounds. In the 14th century, the Tartars laid siege to the fortress city of Caffa when they invaded from Asia. They brought plague, which was endemic to continental Asia, with them. During the protracted siege, it became apparent that they were losing more soldiers to plague than they were to the battle. Therefore, a strategy was used to catapult dead plague victims into the city, thereby introducing plague into the city of Caffa. Eventually the city of Caffa fell, and plague spread to Europe leading to one of the great plague pandemics. There are many more examples of biological weapons being used throughout history, including the use of smallpox by the British during the French and Indian War and Japan's Unit 731 during World War II.

To date, the simple explosive device remains the number one weapon choice for terrorists. However, increasingly they have acquired biological weapon capabilities, as well. The Aum Shinrikyo cult released botulinum toxin and anthrax on multiple occasions but were unsuccessful in causing any casualties. The strain of anthrax used, was derived from the attenuated Sterne strain used for vaccines, was not virulent enough to cause illness. It is also known that they sent "humanitarian aid" to Zaire during the Ebola outbreak in 1995. This was purportedly an aid mission to help contain the epidemic but in reality it was an attempt to acquire samples of the Ebola virus to bring back to their laboratories in Japan for weaponization. Notably, this same strategy was used by the Soviets on multiple occasions to acquire pathogenic agents from various outbreaks around the world and to bring them back to the Soviet Union to incorporate into their own biological weapons programs. The largest biological weapons attack in the United States took place in 1984, in The Dalles, OR, sending 751 victims to local hospitals. This outbreak was caused by the intentional contamination of restaurant salad bars with Salmonella by members of a large local religious commune.

Due to the difficulty in determining the etiology of a patient(s) presenting with "flu-like" symptoms, timely use of PPE when appropriate will be a critical decision if the disease turns out to be contagious. Table 2.1 was developed to help guide this decision early in the contact (even by phone) with a symptomatic patient.

Table 2.1   D.O.C.T.O.R. Decision-Making Guide

Letter	Question	Interpretation of Results
D	**D**ifficulty Breathing	Difficulty breathing typically indicates higher patient acuity which is always wise to ascertain prior to arrival. New or worsening dyspnea raises the index of suspicion for utilization of appropriate respiratory and droplet protective equipment if a traumatic origin is ruled out. Respiratory distress brought on by illness may be the result of an organism residing in the respiratory tract which translates to aerosolzation of organism via coughing or sneezing. This places the care-giver at high risk for inoculation via the respiratory or mucus membrane route. Treatment may demand aggressive airway and/or ventilatory support, which places the care-giver at grave risk for inoculation, demanding appropriate respiratory and droplet protective equipment to be worn.
O	**O**ccupation	Certain occupations lend themselves to placing the employee at higher risk for disease exposure. The zoonotic feature of many organisms suggests wearing of appropriate respiratory and droplet protective equipment when caring for anyone ill who works around animals (e.g., zoo, veterinarian office, wildlife park), or a patient who has been around an ill animal. In addition, laboratory workers, personnel who may work in parks or urban settings around bird excrement, as well as workers disposing of road-killed animal carcasses are at higher risk.
C	**C**ontact History	If your patient has been around anyone or anything (see occupation) ill in the past two weeks, you should adopt a more aggressive posture of appropriate respiratory and droplet protective equipment. One or more patients ill at a site (ensure hazardous materials event is ruled out first) are highly indicative of a contagious organism that requires protection against.
T	**T**emperature	Patients exhibiting a fever suggest an infection until ruled out. Since the exact cause of the infection can not readily or reliably be assessed early in the patient contact, the care-giver should adopt appropriate respiratory and droplet protective equipment. If there are other close contacts of the patient on scene, it may be wise to assess them for subtle signs and symptoms of illness as well.
O	**O**ut of Country	Patients, who in the previous two weeks have traveled outside the country, or to an area inside the country where the care-giver knows an endemic disease of interest resides, may pose a higher risk of danger to the care-giver and they should adopt the appropriate respiratory and droplet protective equipment.
R	**R**ash	Rashes are always suggestive of a need to adopt a more aggressive stance of respiratory and droplet protective equipment.

Anthrax

Bacillus anthracis is a toxigenic, spore-forming, non-motile, aerobic, encapsulating, gram-positive bacillus that causes the disease anthrax. It is usually found as the spore form in the environment, and as the vegetative bacillus form when causing infection in an animal host.

The soil is the natural reservoir of *B. anthracis* spores resulting in areas of endemic anthrax. They are extremely stable in the environment, remaining viable for decades when protected from ultraviolet light. Anthrax most often exists as a zoonotic infection of herbivores such as sheep, cattle, and other domesticated livestock, as well as wild grazing animals. When introduced into the body of a susceptible host, the dormant spore will germinate into a vegetative bacillus and cause disease. Historically, humans become infected by contact with infected animals or contaminated animal products, such as wool, hides, and bones. Typically, there are a few zoonotic outbreaks of animal anthrax per year in the United States.

The spore form of the bacteria does not cause illness. For anthrax to cause illness the spore must germinate into a vegetative bacillus, which grows and causes infection. When a human is exposed to anthrax spores, either through an open wound, ingestion, or via an inhalational route, the germination of the spore into the bacillus form initiates the process that eventually leads to the clinical disease anthrax.

When considering anthrax as a biological weapon, the inhalational form of anthrax is the most worrisome threat because biological weapons are much more effective when disseminated by an aerosol route because a much larger number of victims may be infected. However, as exemplified by the anthrax attacks that took place in the United States in the fall of 2001, a significant number of cutaneous anthrax cases may be seen in conjunction with inhalational cases. Therefore, it is important to remember that even though the anthrax may be disseminated via an aerosol or inhalational route, one may find cases of cutaneous anthrax as well. These cutaneous cases are typically less severe and less life threatening. In summary, anthrax may appear in multiple clinical forms as the result of a single biological weapon attack.

Human anthrax infection occurs in three forms, classified by the organism's route of entry into the host: cutaneous, gastrointestinal (including oropharyngeal), and inhalational. Cutaneous anthrax is the most common naturally occurring form of the disease and is acquired by direct contact with anthrax spores, infected animals or animal products, or through an abrasion or open wound in the skin. After the incubation period, a small papule appears at the site of inoculation. These lesions are typically not painful, but may be pruritic and evolve into fluid-filled vesicles within a day or two. Gram stain of the vesicular fluid may demonstrate many *B. anthracis* organisms. These vesicles, in turn, rupture and ulcerate, leaving the characteristic black eschar of cutaneous anthrax that gives *B. anthracis* its name (*anthrakos*, Greek: coal, black). The surrounding tissue becomes markedly edematous, sometimes involving the entire limb. Tender, local lymphadenopathy may also be seen. Patients with cutaneous anthrax may develop systemic disease, including fever, lymphadenopathy, septic shock and death.

Inhalational anthrax's initial presentation is essentially that of a nonspecific febrile illness. This is a recurrent theme with most biological weapons, in that their initial presentation is not really specific enough to diagnose the cause of infection. This emphasizes the importance of recognizing cutaneous anthrax, as it may lead to the diagnosis of other victims with inhalational anthrax. It is important to note that in all workplaces where workers contracted anthrax in 2001 as a result of the anthrax letters, there were workers with cutaneous as well as inhalational anthrax.

The prodrome essentially resembles a viral-like illness. Patients will have of fever, respiratory symptoms, a non-productive cough later, shortness of breath, dyspnea (difficulty breathing), and chest pain. They may also complain of other more nonspecific symptoms such as muscle aches, fatigue, nausea, vomiting, abdominal pain, and malaise. As symptoms progress, more significant respiratory complaints develop, and patients may become significantly short of breath with complaints of air hunger (hypoxia). This is often the point at which they seek medical care.

The pulmonary form of anthrax results from inhalation of aerosolized anthrax spores and is the most severe clinical form of the disease. The median incubation period in the 2001 bioterrorism-related cases in the United States from known times of exposure in six cases was 4 days (range 4–6). This range is similar to that seen in the 1979 Sverdlovsk anthrax outbreak. However, at Sverdlovsk there were a significant number of cases that presented up to 43 days after the date of the release. Initially, patients will likely have relatively nonspecific symptoms including fever, fatigue, nausea, vomiting, muscle aches, abdominal pain, and sore throat, as well as shock and coma. However, respiratory complaints, including nonproductive cough, shortness of breath, chest pain, and dyspnea soon develop. This initial presentation is painfully nonspecific given the grave nature of the disease. Edema of the chest wall may also be seen with advanced cases of mediastinal anthrax. Approximately one-half of patients with inhalational anthrax will also develop hemorrhagic meningitis. These patients may present with fever, headaches, confusion, and mental status changes. The index case of inhalational anthrax from the U.S. bioterrorist attacks of 2001 initially presented with fever, confusion, vomiting, myalgias, malaise, and *without* any respiratory

(a)

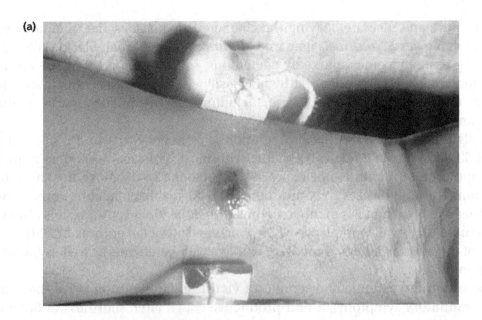

(b)

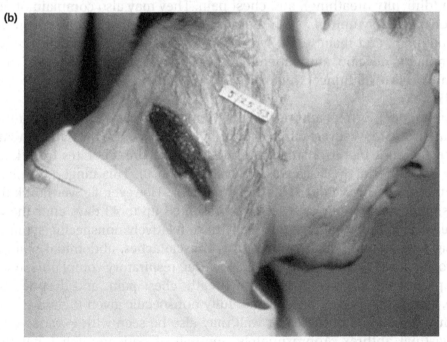

FIGURE 2.1 (a) Cutaneous Anthrax: Forearm lesion on Day 7—vesiculation and ulceration of initial macular or papular anthrax skin lesion. *Source: CDC.* (b) Eschar of the neck on Day 15, typical of the last day of lesion. From Binford CH, Connor DH, eds. *Pathology of Tropical and Extraordinary Diseases.* Vol 1. Washington DC: AFIP:1976:119. AFIP negative 71-1290-2.

complaints. The diagnosis was made by isolating *B. anthracis* from cerebrospinal fluid obtained by lumbar puncture to rule out meningitis.

Gastrointestinal anthrax is caused by the ingestion of insufficiently cooked contaminated meat. It is thought to occur as the result from the ingestion of vegetative bacilli rather than anthrax spores. It is a relatively rare form of human anthrax, but carries a high case fatality ratio (greater than 90%), and may be seen following the use of an anthrax bioweapon. It is found in two forms: oropharyngeal and abdominal. Oropharyngeal anthrax may produce significant edema of the soft tissues of the mouth, oropharynx, head and neck. Gastrointestinal anthrax involving the intestines presents with abdominal pain, nausea, vomiting, gastrointestinal hemorrhage, and ascites. As with the other clinical forms of anthrax, gastrointestinal anthrax will progress to fatal sepsis and toxemia if not treated early and aggressively.

DIAGNOSIS
It is critical to consider the possibility of a bioterrorism-related infection in the differential diagnosis of a patient with a febrile syndrome that includes clinical features of anthrax. As mentioned above, the clinical presentation of bioterrorism-related anthrax may be relatively nonspecific. Therefore, it is important to be alert to local epidemiological trends and patterns of febrile illness. The diagnosis of a bioterrorism-related illness is likely to be made by considering both the individual presentation (e.g., fever, dyspnea, confusion) as well as the situational presentation (e.g., multiple patients presenting to area hospitals with similar severe illnesses and a common history of attending a parade the preceding weekend) of ill patients. History regarding the patient's place and type of employment, recent travel, both local and distant, and all other information should be obtained in order to reconstruct the patient's activities and whereabouts for at least the previous two weeks. As multiple cases present with an undiagnosed febrile illness, either within a hospital, a hospital system, or a community, a careful review of their recent activities may reveal a pattern of common event(s) (e.g., recent sporting event, concert), or location(s) linking patients to the site where a bioweapon release took place days earlier (i.e., the incubation period of the agent).

The highly distinctive appearance of cutaneous anthrax lesions simplify their diagnosis. Characteristically, they are painless lesions that eventually ulcerate into a black eschar with associated tissue edema. If they are recognized early, these more visible cutaneous cases may lead to early detection of an anthrax bioterrorist attack. As discussed above, the clinical presentation of inhalational anthrax may be varied, but respiratory symptoms will likely be common. Pulmonary findings include chest wall edema, rhonchi, wheezing, pleural effusions, stridor, and hypoxemia. Other systemic symptoms include confusion, fever, headache, vomiting, diarrhea, abdominal pain, and fatigue.

TREATMENT

A high index of suspicion and rapid administration of antibiotic therapy are crucial for the timely and effective treatment of anthrax. Penicillin, doxycycline, and ciprofloxacin are the only antibiotics currently approved by the U.S. Food and Drug Administration for the treatment of inhalational anthrax. The U.S. Centers for Disease Control recommends using either ciprofloxacin or doxycycline as first line drugs in a multidrug regimen that includes at least one additional antibiotic until antimicrobial sensitivities are known. Once antimicrobial sensitivities are determined, antibiotic regimens can be adjusted appropriately. Although based on a very small series (n = 11), the survival rate for the U.S. bioterrorist-related inhalational anthrax cases treated with multidrug regimens (55%) is significantly higher than survival rates previously reported. Antibiotics that inhibit protein synthesis, such as clindamycin, can inhibit the production of anthrax exotoxins, lethal toxin and edema toxin, and are recommended as part of the multidrug regimen for the treatment of anthrax.

Genetic engineering by terrorists to create more virulent organisms with antibiotic resistance is a significant concern. Therefore, the possibility of a terrorist using multiple strains of a biological agent simultaneously, or a multi-drug resistant strain of *B. anthracis* as a bioweapon, also supports the use of a multi-drug antimicrobial regimen.

For patients exposed to anthrax, but without symptoms of illness, prophylaxis with antibiotics is indicated. Again, the drugs of choice are ciprofloxacin or doxycycline. These should be started as soon as exposure has been suspected and should not wait for symptoms to develop. Active immunity against anthrax infection has also been developed. The U.S. anthrax vaccine is a cell-free filtrate, including protective antigen (PA) as the primary immunogenic antigen, has been FDA approved for over 30 years. It is administered as a six-dose series over 18 months. Although not effective as monotherapy in the post-exposure treatment of inhalational anthrax, the anthrax vaccine adsorbed (AVA) prevented latent cases of anthrax after cessation of antibiotic treatment, and also protected against an anthrax rechallenge, in an animal model.

Smallpox

Historically, smallpox is responsible for more human deaths that any other single cause. It has affected nearly every culture, in all geographical regions of the world, over many centuries. The causative agent of smallpox, variola virus, makes an effective biological weapon because it is infectious via aerosol exposure. Smallpox vaccination has been discontinued, leaving the general population susceptible to infection. Clinical inexperience of healthcare providers, limited availability of vaccine, and lack of effective antiviral medications will unfortunately limit therapeutic options. Infection causes severe morbidity and mortality, and it is highly contagious. The last case of variola major was on Bhola Island, Bangladesh, 1975. The last case of variola minor was in Somalia, 1977. On August 24, 1978, the world's last known case of smallpox was diagnosed in a medical photographer who worked in the anatomy department of Birmingham University Medical School in England. Although never as common as in Asia and Africa, variola major was endemic in the United States until 1926, and variola minor persisted until the late 1940s. The last U.S. epidemic occurred in the lower Rio Grande valley of Texas in 1949.

As with many of the viral biowarfare agents, smallpox is difficult to weaponize in large quantities. However, the former Soviet Union's biological weapons program, *Biopreparat*, developed the capacity to produce 200 metric tons of smallpox per year. More concerning, however, is that the demise of the U.S.S.R., and *Biopreparat* with it, has made their weaponization expertise, and possibly even variola virus, potentially available to terrorist entities around the world. This is also in addition to the fact that because *Variola* is still very infectious in the natural form of smallpox, a terrorist can carry out his bioterrorist attack by infecting himself with *Variola* virus and simply be traveling, working, or living among his victims while spreading smallpox.

Variola virus is a member of the orthopoxvirus genus that also includes vaccinia virus, monkeypox, cowpox, ectromelia, rabbitpox, raccoonpox, camelpox, buffalopox, taterapox, and Uasin Gishu disease. Among this group, variola, vaccinia, cowpox, and monkeypox viruses can infect humans.

Variola virus strains have traditionally have been classified as variola major and variola minor. Major and minor strains typically produce case fatality rates of 30–40% and less than 1%, respectively. After many decades of a concerted worldwide effort to immunize the world's population against smallpox, the World Health Organization (WHO) declared smallpox eradicated in 1980. Smallpox is not a zoonotic disease. With the exception of a few animal models that have been developed to study the virus in the laboratory, smallpox is exclusively a disease of humans and has no known animal reservoir. Although its common name, chickenpox, suggests that varicella virus belongs in the poxvirus family, it is a herpesvirus.

EPIDEMIOLOGY

The predominant route of smallpox transmission is by aerosol. The principal route of entry is via the oropharynx, nasopharynx, occasionally the lower respiratory

(a)

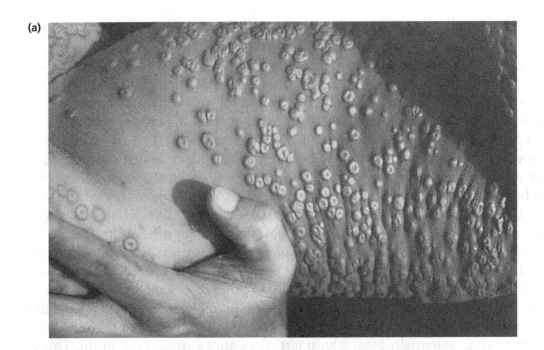

(b)

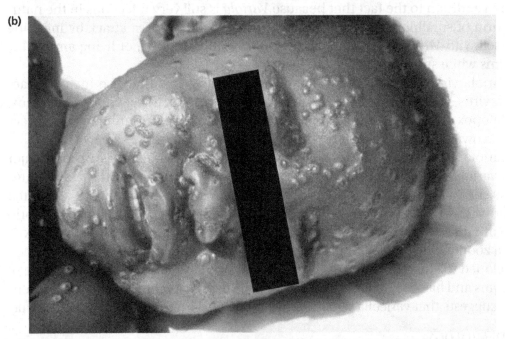

FIGURE 2.2 (a) Smallpox Lesions on Skin of Trunk. Picture taken in Bangladesh, 1973. Public Health Images Library (PHIL) ID # 284. *Source: CDC/James Hicks.* (b) Face Lesions on Boy with Smallpox. Public Health Images Library (PHIL) ID # 3. *Source: CDC/Cheryl Tyron.*

tract, and, very rarely, the conjunctiva. After an asymptomatic incubation period, clinical smallpox presents with an initial fever spike, followed by ulcerative lesions (enanthem) in the oropharynx. These lesions release large amounts of virus into oropharyngeal secretions, and spreading of variola virus occurs primarily by the aerosolization of these virus-laden secretions by coughing, sneezing, or simply talking. Human-to-human transmission usually occurs by inhalation of droplet nuclei of these secretions from an infected person. Variola virus in these airborne droplets infects the epithelial cells of the mucus membranes of a susceptible individual, who in turn becomes infected, repeats the cycle of virus aerosolization, which propagates spread of the virus among the population. Infection via the skin is rare and historically has been either by accidental inoculation with variola virus in certain occupations, such as healthcare providers or morticians, or by variolation (the intentional practice of dermal inoculation with a small amount smallpox scab material that contained viable variola virus). Although the recipient of variolation ran the risk of developing a fatal case of smallpox, the practice conferred lifelong immunity.

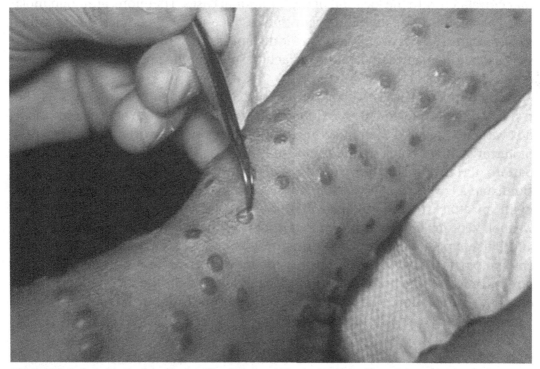

FIGURE 2.3 Left Ankle Region of a Brazilian Woman, Who in 1966 Manifested the Dermal Lesions Determined to Be Due to the DNA Virus, Variola Minor. *Source: CDC/Dr. Noble.*

There are three possible mechanisms of transmission: direct personal contact with an infected person, contact with contaminated fomites (e.g., patient bed linens), and airborne spread. Transmission of smallpox most often occurs as the result of direct face-to-face contact with an infected person. However, there have been smallpox outbreaks resulting from the dissemination of variola virus over considerable distance. Two well-documented hospital outbreaks, Monschau in 1961 and Meschede in 1969, were the result of airborne transmission of the virus. The outbreak at Meschede began when a 20-year-old male returned from Pakistan and, was initially diagnosed with typhoid fever and restricted to his hospital room. However, it became apparent that he had smallpox when he developed a rash 3 days after admission. This case resulted in 17 secondary cases and two tertiary cases of smallpox. One case occurred in a hospital visitor who spent no more than 15 minutes in the hospital lobby, well away from the index patient's room or any of the identified contacts. Several factors were identified that may have favored the airborne transmission of virus: the index patient had a densely confluent rash and severe cough; low humidity in the hospital (outbreak occurred in January); and smoke diffusion studies identified air current patterns within the hospital that correlated with the location of the additional cases. Therefore, although most cases of smallpox transmission occur due to "face-to-face" contact, it is possible to have transmission over much longer distances. This underscores the need for strict isolation practices at healthcare facilities to limit the possible dissemination of the virus.

Naturally occurring smallpox outbreaks often occur in communities as the result of a single infected person (index case) returning from an area where small-pox was endemic and then infecting multiple persons. However, in the case of a bioterrorist attack using smallpox, one may not see this "natural" epidemiological pattern of transmission. In June 2001, a table-top exercise entitled "Dark Winter" simulated a covert smallpox attack on the United States. The scenario was based upon an attack that simultaneously disseminated approximately 30 grams of weaponized smallpox in three separate shopping malls in Atlanta, Oklahoma City, and Philadelphia, causing 3,000 primary infections. The model utilized known epidemiological data, such as transmission rates, from naturally occurring small-pox outbreaks of the pre-eradication era, and allowed for the increased mobility of today's population. The worst-case scenario projected 3 million cases with 1 million deaths over a simulated 8 weeks.

DIAGNOSIS

The clinical presentation of smallpox will vary with which clinical type, and at what point in the illness, the patient presents. The incubation period is the time between implantation of infectious virus on the respiratory mucosa and the onset of fever. All patients experience an asymptomatic incubation period lasting 7 to 17 days (mean, 10–12 days). Its length can be affected by virulence of the variola virus strain, number of infectious particles received, and underlying health of the patient. The incubation period for ordinary-type smallpox is usually around 12 days, with a range of 7 to 19 days. After multiplying in the regional lymph nodes for 3 to 4 days, a brief asymptomatic viremia occurs, followed by an asymptomatic latent period during which viral replication continues.

The abrupt onset of a febrile prodrome marks the beginning of the second viremia and the end of the incubation period. The fever is often as high as 105°F. Other symptoms include severe malaise, chills, headache, backache, vomiting, pharyngitis, abdominal pain that is sometimes severe, and diarrhea.

Smallpox is divided into two major types: variola major and variola minor. Rao established 5 major clinical forms of variola major, based primarily upon rash characteristics: ordinary-type smallpox (OTS); modified type (MTS); flat type (FTS), also called malignant type; hemorrhagic type (HTS), which is subdivided into early and late forms; and variola sine eruption. These clinical distinctions have prognostic value for variola major with OTS having a case fatality rate (CFR) of approximately 30%, HTS and FTS have CFRs of greater than 90% and typically do not survive long after the development of the rash. Variola minor has relatively low fatality rate (<1%), and variola sine eruption and MTS are also rarely fatal.

The rash that follows the prodrome erupts in a characteristic pattern, although there is variation patient-to-patient, and a history without a classical rash evolution is not uncommon. Patients typically remain febrile throughout the development of the rash. The rash erupts in a synchronous pattern, with all lesions appearing within 24 hours. This is an important distinction from the rash associated with varicella, which typically develops in an asynchronous pattern, or in "crops," with lesions of varying ages present at a given point in time on a given anatomical area. The rash usually begins as macules on the face, often around the mouth and nares, although the appearance of "herald spots" or "herald lesions," especially on the forehead, have been reported. The rash then spreads to the trunk and proximal, then distal, extremities in a centrifugal pattern. The rash is denser on the extremities than the trunk. The pustular lesions of the rash are typically painful as they grow and expand. These lesions are more deeply embedded in the skin compared to the more superficial lesions of varicella (chickenpox). Loss of vesicular fluid and retraction of the fibrinous threads causes a dimpling at the apex of the lesion, referred as umbilication. In OTS the characteristic evolution of the rash is seen as a progression through an order of appearance of focal lesions: macules → papules → vesicles → pustules → umbilication → scabbing → scab separation and scarring. The complete course of evolution of the rash in OTS usually takes three to four weeks, and patients remain infectious until all scabs separate.

Clinical Manifestations and Pathogenesis of Smallpox and the Immune Response

The Centers for Disease Control have established criteria (**CDC Vesicular or Pustular Rash Protocol**) for determining the risk that a febrile illness associated with a rash is indeed smallpox:

High Risk for Smallpox (All 3 of the Following Major Criteria are Present)
- Febrile prodrome occurring 1 to 4 days before rash onset with fever >102°F AND at least one of the following:
  - Prostration
  - Headache
  - Backache
  - Chills
  - Vomiting
  - Severe abdominal pain
- Classic smallpox lesions:
  - Deeply embedded in the dermis
  - Firm/hard
  - Well-circumscribed
  - Round
  - May be umbilicated
  - May be discrete, semi-confluent, confluent
- Synchronous eruption; all lesions in the same stage of development

Moderate Risk for Smallpox
- Febrile prodrome AND one of the "High Risk for Smallpox" criteria listed above, **OR**
- Febrile prodrome and at least 4 of the 5 following *minor criteria*:
  - Centrifugal distribution
  - First lesions appear on the oral mucosa/palate, face, or forearms
  - Patient appears toxic or moribund
  - Slow evolution of lesions from macules to papules to pustules over several days
  - Lesions on the palms and soles

- Comparison between the characteristic rashes of smallpox and chickenpox (see Table 2.1): Smallpox's incubation period is 7–17 days, where chickenpox is longer, up to 3 weeks.
- Smallpox's prodrome is much more significant (sicker patient overall) than that of chickenpox.
- A very important characteristic is the distribution of the rash, being centrifugal (more on the extremities and head and neck) versus centripetal (more concentrated on the trunk) with varicella.
- An important characteristic that can distinguish these two rashes is the fact that the smallpox lesions all appear synchronously. That is, they all appear at the same time and they go through the progression at the same pace, such that they all appear relatively uniform. In contrast, chickenpox lesions appear in what we would term "crops" because they develop asynchronously, with new lesions appearing over time. On examination you would notice a large variability in the ages and appearance of chickenpox lesions.
- Scabs typically form after 10 days to approximately 2 weeks with chickenpox, whereas with smallpox they typically form within a week. Likewise, the scabs separate between 2–4 weeks with smallpox and usually are done separating within 2 weeks with chickenpox.

The most important distinction here is that the patient's smallpox remains infectious until the **separation** of the scabs of the healing lesions. A smallpox patient will no longer be infectious once all of their scab lesions **separate**. In contrast, chickenpox lesions are infectious until they have **scabbed**. The patient with chickenpox is no longer infectious and may still have lesions that are **scabbed** over on their skin. For smallpox, the patient is infectious from the onset of their enanthem until all scabs separate. Chickenpox is infectious from one day before the eruption of the rash until all vesicles scab.

Monkeypox is an orthopoxvirus closely related to variola and causes human illness that probably most resembles smallpox. Humans usually become infected through contact with infected animals, although studies have shown that monkeypox is infectious via the aerosol route. Monkeypox is considered a potential biological weapon as a surrogate for variola virus. Furthermore; outbreaks of human monkeypox continue to occur in Africa, providing a potential source of the infectious agent for modification and weaponization by bioterrorists. Its clinical presentation includes a vesiculopustular exanthem that erupts in a centrifugal, synchronous pattern, including the palms and soles, and an ulcerating enanthem. Monkeypox symptoms include fever, diarrhea, cough, sore throat, and prominent cervical lymphadenopathy (inguinal lymphadenopathy has also been reported), which are not typical of smallpox. Case fatality rates reported in several

Table 2.2   Differential Diagnosis of Smallpox and Chickenpox

	Variola Major (OTS)	Varicella (Chickenpox)
Incubation Period*	7–19 days (mean 12 days)	14–21 days
Prodrome	2–4 days with high fever, headache, backache, severe prostration, fever may persist	Minimal symptoms lasting one day or absent
Distribution of Rash	Centrifugal	Centripetal
	Involves palms and soles	No palm or sole involvement
	Enanthem present	Enanthem absent
	Synchronous eruption	Asynchronous (cropping)
Pock Characteristics	"Shotty"	Pleomorphic
	Deep dermally based	Superficial
	Painful	Pruritic
Lesion Evolution	Macules → papules → vesicles → pustules → umbilication → scabbing → scab separation → scarring	Macules → papules → vesicles → pustules → scabbing → scab separation
Scab Formation	10–14 days after rash onset	1–7 days after rash onset
Scab Separation	14–28 days after rash onset	Within 14 days of rash onset
Infectivity	From onset of enanthem to scab separation	From 1 day *before* rash eruption until scab formation

OTS—ordinary type smallpox.
*May vary with form of smallpox.

case series ranged between 1.5% and 11%. Given its similarity to smallpox, and the theoretical potential that it could be used as a biological weapon, it should be included in the differential diagnosis of smallpox.

> *Public health officials should be notified immediately of any suspected smallpox patient.*

   All patients should be vaccinated if they will be isolated with other suspected or confirmed cases of smallpox. This is done to prevent accidental transmission of smallpox virus to any *suspected* smallpox patients who have been misdiagnosed and placed in quarantine with "true" smallpox patients. However, vaccination with vaccinia virus is not without complications. In a normal healthy host there can be inadvertent autoinoculation (transferring the *vaccinia* virus from the vaccination site to another body site such as the eye), generalized vaccinia (overwhelming *vaccinia* infection), erythema multiforme, and *vaccinia* encephalitis.

Initial management of any suspected smallpox patient should include immediate isolation of the patient in a negative pressure room, strict contact and respiratory isolation, and immediate quarantine of all contacts. All protective clothing should be removed and disposed of into biohazard waste containers before leaving the isolation area and re-entering other areas of the hospital. All infectious waste and contaminated protective clothing should be properly disposed of in biohazard containers and/or sterilized in an appropriate manner.

Treatment for smallpox is largely supportive, as no effective antiviral therapies have yet been adequately tested as safe and effective. Insuring adequate fluid and nutrition intake is important, as the enanthem typically makes it impossible for severely ill patients to take sufficient amounts of liquids and/or food. Patients during the vesicular and pustular stages of smallpox are at high risk for hypovolemic shock due to fluid losses from fever, vomiting, decreased oral fluid intake due to painful enanthem, fluid shifts into the skin, and skin desquamation in patients with confluent lesions. Patients with HTS are at risk for additional blood loss due to hemorrhage. Control of pain and fever with appropriate analgesics and antipyretics is indicated. Keeping lesions clean and dressed and taking care to avoid rupturing vesicles and pustules can reduce risk of secondary infection of the rash lesions. Salves and/or ointments are not recommended. The desquamation sometimes seen with the severest forms of smallpox, such as HTS, may necessitate dressing changes and treatment comparable to those employed in the management of major burns. Secondary bacterial skin infections should be treated with appropriate antibiotics and guided by culture and sensitivity testing.

Plague

Plague has been a part of human history for thousands of years. It has been estimated that over time plague has been responsible for in excess of 200 million deaths and is referenced as far back as 1320 B.C. In the modern era, many countries, including the United States, the Soviet Union, and Japan, have studied the use of plague as a biological weapon (Zaucha, 2001). However, Japan holds the distinction of being the only country known to have actually used plague as a bioweapon. During World War II, Japan established Unit 731. At the height of the program, Unit 731 was able to produce 660 pounds of *Y. pestis* per month. Although unable to successfully weaponize isolated *Y. pestis*, Unit 731 did develop a plague-infected-flea weapon that was released in airborne attacks over Manchuria at least five times between 1940 and 1941, successfully causing localized plague outbreaks (Zaucha, 2001). Plague is arguably the first biological agent used as a weapon of war. Caffa, now Feodosia, Ukraine, was established in 1266 as a port city for trading between European merchants and the Asian Mongols. The Tartars laid siege to the city in 1345, but were forced to abandon their attack in late 1346 due to devastation of their troops by an epidemic of plague. As their losses due to plague mounted, the Tartar forces hurled the diseased cadavers of their dead comrades over the defensive walls of Caffa, and into the city. The task of removing the accumulating corpses from the city was likely a sufficient means to spread *Y. pestis* among the city's inhabitants, and Caffa became overwhelmed by the plague as well. The interested reader is referred to an historical review written by Mark Wheelis: Biological Warfare at the 1346 siege of Caffa, *Emerging Infectious Diseases*, September 2002.

A naturally occurring plague is a zoonotic disease that is maintained within a mammalian reservoir, particularly in wild rodents, in endemic foci worldwide, with the exception of Australia (Jezek, 1986). Plague is transmitted between rodents and to humans primarily by fleabite, which causes the most common form: the bubonic plague. A second important mode of plague transmission is the aerosol route. Aerosolization of infectious *Yersinia pestis* may occur two ways. In a natural outbreak, bubonic or septicemic cases will usually occur first. Some of these patients will develop pneumonic plague via spread of the infection to their lungs via the blood. These patients can then transmit plague directly from person to person by droplet infection due to coughing, causing additional cases of pneumonic plague. Alternatively, the intentional aerosolization of weaponized *Y. pestis* by a bioterrorist will produce the pneumonic form without any preceding cases of bubonic plague.

Over 200 species of rodents, including the common brown rat, *Rattus rattus*, and the Norwegian rat, *R. norvegicus*, are reservoirs for *Y. pestis*. In the United States, ground squirrels, rock squirrels, prairie dogs, chipmunks, bats, and rabbits, as well as domestic animals, may become infected.

Yersinia pestis is a small, gram-negative, non-motile, non-spore-forming, invasive, pathogenic coccobacillus, of the family Enterobacteriaceae (Jezek, 1986). Similar to infection with *Bacillus anthracis,* the clinical pathogenesis of *Y. pestis* infection varies with the route of infection. The plague bacillus gains entry by inoculation of the skin, either by fleabite or the introduction of *Y. pestis*-infected material, such as flea feces, into an open wound. The organism may also be inhaled due to exposure to a person with pneumonic plague and a productive cough or by the release of an aerosolized plague bioweapon. It is important to note that plague can either be in the bubonic form or the pneumonic form. The bubonic form is the form of plague that is acquired from the bite of a plague-carrying vector such as the flea. The bubonic form is much more common than the pneumonic form and is still endemic to a number of areas of the world including Asia and Africa. The pneumonic, or inhalational, form of plague is acquired via inhalation of aerosolized plague organisms. This is a naturally occurring form of plague but is also the likely form that will result from an aerosolized plague biological weapon.

Upon inoculation, or introduction of the plague organism into the human host, these plague bacterium are engulfed by macrophages that transport foreign organisms, such as bacteria and viruses, to regional lymph nodes. Once in the regional lymph nodes, *Y. pestis* creates a localized infection. These enlarged lymph nodes are usually in the groin or axilla, are extremely tender, may reach several inches in diameter, and are called buboes. The infection then spreads from these buboes via the blood to the rest of the body. When they reach the lungs, the plague organism will grow in the sputum and cause pneumonia. Therefore, when this patient coughs, he can aerosolize plague and spread the infection. This bubonic to pneumonic to aerosolization route that plague can follow is why it is extremely contagious.

In the United States, most patients (85–90%) with human plague present clinically with the bubonic form, 10–15% with the primary septicemic form, and 1% with the pneumonic form. Secondary septicemic plague occurs in 23% of patients who present with bubonic plague, and secondary pneumonic plague occurs in 9%.

Septicemic plague occurs in two forms: *primary*, which occurs due to direct introduction of *Y. pestis*, usually by fleabite, into the blood, and *secondary*, in which *Y. pestis* is introduced into the blood by hematogenous extension from either bubonic or pneumonic plague. Primary septicemic plague occurs without palpable lymphadenopathy or focal pneumonia. The incubation period for bubonic plague lasts 1 to 8 days after being bitten by an infected flea. The length of the incubation period varies with the size of inoculum, virulence of the organism, and underlying health of the patient. Ulcerating lesions at the site of the inoculation (fleabite) may develop, but are not common. Initial systemic symptoms are nonspecific, with sudden onset of fever, chills, generalized weakness and malaise, chest pain, cough, skin rash, nausea, vomiting, diarrhea, abdominal pain, myalgias, arthralgias, sore throat and headache. Fever develops very quickly and is present in virtually all cases. Patients are often tachycardic, hypotensive, and may be tachypneic if there is pulmonary involvement. Within a day and often within hours of the fleabite, the infection spreads from the inoculation site

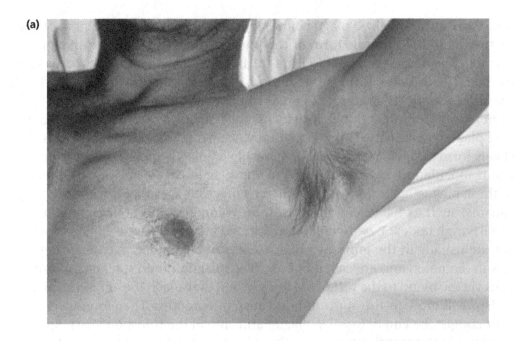

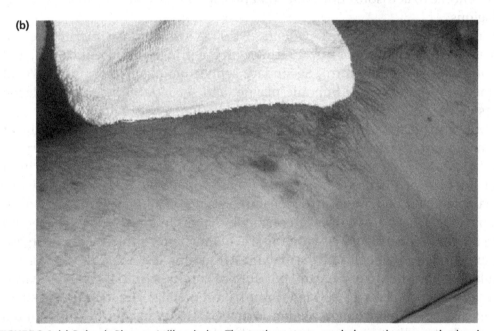

FIGURE 2.4 (a) Bubonic Plague: Axillary bubo. The erythematous, eroded, crusting, necrotic ulcer is located at the presumed primary inoculation site, which occurs in anywhere from 4–10% of bubonic plague patients, and is likely to be the primary inoculation site. (b) Bubonic Plague: Femoral bubo. (c) Bubonic Plague: Inguinal bubo—a patient with an enlarged right inguinal lymph node. This patient was likely bitten and infected on his right lower extremity. *Source: CDC.*

(c)

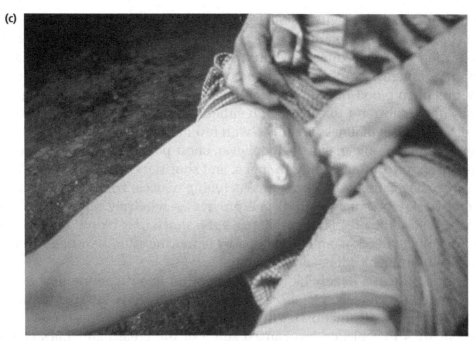

FIGURE 2.4 (Continued)

via the lymphatics to regional lymph nodes, which become swollen and painful (buboes). One may occasionally see cervical or submandibular buboes with plague pneumonia or plague pharyngitis. They are nonfluctuant, painful, warm, and extremely tender on palpation. They are often associated with a significant amount of surrounding edema and erythema, but rarely lymphangitis, and may point and drain spontaneously.

Gastrointestinal symptoms may be prominent in all forms of plague, and include nausea, vomiting, diarrhea, anorexia, and abdominal pain. The liver and spleen may be palpable and/or tender, and liver function tests may be abnormal. Intra-abdominal buboes may also develop, with severe abdominal pain mimicking an acute abdomen. Upper and lower gastrointestinal hemorrhages have also been reported.

If treated early and appropriately, the course of bubonic plague usually includes rapid defervescence and overall clinical improvement over 3 to 5 days. Buboes typically remain tender for about a week, becoming fluctuant as they resolve. Untreated bubonic plague has a mortality rate of approximately 60%. This mortality rate can be reduced to <5% with appropriate antibiotic treatment. However, if untreated, bubonic plague can rapidly progress to *septicemic plague*, causing fulminant gram-negative sepsis and death with 2 to 4 days.

Primary pneumonic plague results from the inhalation of plague bacilli. This may occur following the intentional release of weaponized plague bacilli, or the aerosolization of plague infected sputum by a person, or animal with plague pneumonia. Cough is productive of copious purulent sputum that is frothy, watery, and often blood-tinged. The incubation period for pneumonic plague is generally much shorter, 1 to 4 days, than either the bubonic or septicemic forms of the disease. Onset of illness is sudden with fever and chills. The primary manifestations of pneumonic plague include fever, chest pain, and productive cough of purulent sputum, often bloody, dyspnea, and shortness of breath. Patients are also likely to have additional symptoms including nausea, vomiting, abdominal pain, and weakness. Pneumonic plague progresses relatively rapidly, and may quickly be followed by respiratory failure, septic shock (low blood pressure due to overwhelming infection) and coagulopathy (abnormal blood clotting—usually leading to abnormal bleeding and bruising).

Anthrax, although a deadly biological weapon, it is not communicable between patients. Conversely, plague is extremely contagious between patients. This is a very critical distinction between plague and anthrax. This is one of the primary reasons that plague has caused some of the great pandemics of history. A single person can become infected with plague as a result of a biological weapons attack and go on to propagate that infection to many other individuals. Therefore, the public health measures needed to contain plague are much more important. Any healthcare provider that has suspicion of a plague outbreak anywhere should notify the appropriate medical and public health authorities immediately.

With severe plague infection, the cooler areas or parts of the body such as the fingers, toes, and nose may become gangrenous due to the lack of blood supply and develop into what is referred to as acral gangrene. Similar to the importance of noticing cutaneous anthrax amidst cases of inhalational anthrax, noticing such a pattern of gangrene, or diffuse bruising, on a patient should alert a HERT member that the patient may indeed be suffering from a septicemic form of plague.

Again, it is of paramount importance to identify anybody who is infected with plague or has been exposed to a person who is infected with plague. Early detection is the most important step of minimizing the spread of plague and preventing epidemics.

Differential diagnosis of large and tender lymph nodes includes diseases such as tularemia, cat scratch fever, and staphylococcal and/or streptococcal lymphadenitis. Cat scratch fever as well as lymphadenitis are relatively common and can be ruled out easily. Keep in mind that tularemia has also been weaponized as an effective biological weapon. It is highly contagious and communicable and should a tularemia outbreak be identified one should have a high index of suspicion that it may be the result of a biological weapons attack until proven otherwise.

The diagnosis of plague thus requires the recognition of the clinical syndrome by an astute HERT member. The most effective response to a bioterrorist attack includes rapid recognition of the event, identification of agent, treatment of the victims, and containment of the outbreak. However, empiric antibiotic treatment should not be delayed while awaiting laboratory results. Antibiotic options include gentamicin, doxycycline and ciprofloxacin. Recall that doxycycline as well as ciprofloxacin were recommended treatments for anthrax as well.

Viral Hemorrhagic Fevers

The viral hemorrhagic fevers (VHFs) are caused by a family of RNA viruses that have a predilection for the vascular system. In their natural form these viruses are contracted from an insect bite, or by contact with blood or body fluids from an infected individual.

The Filoviridae includes the causative agents of Ebola and Marburg hemorrhagic fevers. Marburg virus was first recognized in 1967 when a lethal epidemic of VHF occurred in Marburg, Germany, among laboratory workers exposed to the blood and tissues of African green monkeys that had been imported from Uganda. Subsequently, Marburg virus has been associated with sporadic, isolated, usually fatal cases, among residents and travelers in Africa.

Ebola viruses are related to Marburg viruses; they were first recognized in association with outbreaks that occurred almost simultaneously in 1976 in small communities in Zaire and Sudan. Significant secondary transmission occurred through reuse of unsterilized needles and syringes and nosocomial contacts.

As most viruses have a predilection for a certain cell type, viral hemorrhagic viruses have a predilection for the vasculature of a patient (i.e., the VHF viruses preferentially infect cells found in the blood and blood vessels, causing bleeding).

They are highly communicable (contagious) and may be spread by aerosol (such as when a person coughs up bloody sputum) or on fomites (furniture or contaminated medical equipment). Also they can be spread by bites from animals. Most human infections are typically due to contact with the blood or body fluids of patients with this illness.

VHF infection begins with fevers, muscle aches, and rapid onset of prostration and toxic illness. The cases rapidly evolve to have significant hypotension (shock), mucous membrane hemorrhage, as well as conjunctival injection and hemorrhage. The skin is notable for a maculopapular rash associated with petechial hemorrhages and confluent ecchymoses. Severe cases will evolve into shock and generalized mucous membrane hemorrhage with involvement of the respiratory, bone marrow, and central nervous systems.

Patients who develop evidence of significant liver damage or renal failure have a very poor prognosis. Mortality rates range between 50% and 80% for strains of Ebola and depends heavily on the underlying health of the host, as well as the availability of critical care medicine and supportive care such as blood products and transfusions.

The clinical characteristics of the various VHFs are variable. For Lassa fever patients, hemorrhagic manifestations are not pronounced, and neurological complications are infrequent, occurring only late and in only the most severely ill group. For the South American arenaviruses (Argentine and Bolivian hemorrhagic fevers), neurological and hemorrhagic manifestations are much more prominent. Rift Valley Fever virus is primarily hepatotropic; hemorrhagic disease is seen in only a small proportion of cases. Crimean-Congo hemorrhagic fever infection is usually associated with profound disseminated intravascular coagulation (DIC). Patients with Crimean-Congo hemorrhagic fever may bleed profusely. Since this occurs during the acute, viremic phase, contact with the blood of an infected patient is a special concern: a number of nosocomial outbreaks have been associated with C-CHV virus.

VHF should be suspected in any patient presenting with a severe febrile illness and evidence of vascular involvement (low blood pressure, petechiae, hemorrhagic diathesis, flushing of the face and chest, nondependent edema) who has traveled to an area where the VHF is known to occur, or where intelligence suggests a biological warfare threat. Signs and symptoms suggesting additional organ system involvement are common (headache, photophobia, pharyngitis, cough, nausea or vomiting, diarrhea, constipation, abdominal pain, hyperesthesia, dizziness, confusion, tremor), but they rarely dominate the picture. A macular eruption occurs in most patients who have Marburg and Ebola hemorrhagic fevers; this clinical manifestation is of diagnostic importance.

The treatment of a patient with viral hemorrhagic fevers is essentially critical care medicine. In the HERT setting, limiting any procedures (like intravenous lines and other injections) and minimizing movement will limit bleeding. Encourage oral fluid intake if patient is able to drink without vomiting. Supportive critical care medicine includes volume resuscitation (intravenous fluids to prevent dehydration) and blood products (such as blood and platelet transfusions and clotting factors) as needed. Medications to increase blood pressure (vasopressors and inotropes) can be used. Additional treatment includes pain medication and sedation, both to make the patient comfortable, as well as to limit movement and potential hemorrhages. Common sense interventions include minimizing, or avoiding, any kind of injections, or moving of the patient. Overall, the treatment goal for a viral hemorrhagic fever victim is to limit any further bleeding, ensure adequate fluid resuscitation, and supplement with transfusions as necessary.

Venezuelan Equine Encephalitis

Venezuelan equine encephalitis (VEE) belongs to the group of viruses called alpha viruses. They are spread primarily by mosquitoes and are endemic to Central and South America. However, VEE has been found in southern continental United States, including Florida and on the border with Mexico and has been weaponized in the past.

Venezuelan equine encephalitis is highly infectious with essentially 100% of exposed individuals developing the illness. Fortunately, its mortality rate is relatively low, with deaths usually due to central nervous system complications such as seizures. However, the low mortality rate is in naturally occurring disease. The fatality rate in a bioterrorist attack is unknown.

Clinical effects typically begin following an incubation period of several days to 2 weeks. However, the incubation period may be shorter (i.e., 1–5 days) with aerosol-acquired infections. Initial symptoms include fever, chills, headache, malaise, nausea, vomiting, abdominal pain, myalgias, and sore throat. Occasionally, photophobia or respiratory symptoms may be present. Since few cases of aerosol-acquired disease have been reported in humans, it is not currently known whether such victims are more likely to develop respiratory symptoms.

Physical examination during the prodromal phase usually reveals little more than pharyngeal erythema, conjunctival injection, or muscle tenderness. Viremia is greatest during this phase of the disease, and it generally follows the fever curve. In most patients, the viremia and symptoms begin to fade after several days and the illness resolves without further sequelae. In those who do not go on to develop encephalitis, improvement appears to correlate with a rise in antibody titers against the offending virus. Even in those patients who do go on to develop neurologic sequelae, antibody titers may still rise to similar levels.

The diagnosis of Venezuelan equine encephalitis is difficult and is usually done on clinical grounds in endemic areas. Laboratory testing includes viral culture or viral antigen immunoassay. Serological testing (testing for the presence of antibodies against VEE) is done in patients after they have developed the illness. Needless to say, the individual patient with Venezuelan equine encephalitis will be difficult to diagnose on a clinical basis. Therefore, the diagnosis of Venezuelan equine encephalitis will likely be based on an epidemiological pattern of a large number of patients presenting with the illness.

There are no specific treatments for the equine encephalitides or other alphavirus infections, and no antimicrobial agents have yet been shown to alter the clinical course. Management rests instead on aggressive supportive care, and monitoring for and treating complications. Airway management is important, especially if patients have significant alterations in mental state, and it should take precedence over all other measures. Seizures should be treated with benzo-diazepines or phenobarbital in the usual doses. However, anticonvulsants should not be given prophylactically as this may worsen clinical outcome. Corticosteroids do not appear to be helpful and may lead to complications. Fluid and electrolytes should be monitored closely and corrected if necessary.

Botulinum Toxin

Clostridium botulinum is a spore-forming bacteria (like *B. anthracis*). *C. botulinum* spores are often found in the environment (e.g., soil). When the spores are exposed to an anaerobic environment (very little or no oxygen, e.g., canned vegetables) they sporulate into vegetative bacilli and produce botulinum toxin. It is this toxin that is weaponized as a biological weapon. Therefore, botulinum toxin causes a poisoning, NOT an infection. There is a lag time between the time of exposure and the onset of symptoms. However, this is not an incubation time; this is simply the time necessary for the toxin to exert its effect.

Botlinum toxin acts at the neuromuscular junction (the site that the nervous system interacts with muscles), where the motor neuron secretes the neurotrans-mitter acetylcholine from the presynaptic nerve ending (the end of the motor nerve where acetylcholine is released into the synapse (gap between nerve cell and muscle cell). Acetylcholine binds to receptors on the muscle cell making up the other half of the neuromuscular junction to trigger muscular contraction. Botulinum toxin blocks the release of acetylcholine effectively cutting communi-cation between the nervous system and the muscles, causing paralysis.

Botulinum toxin is 15,000 times as toxic as the nerve agent VX, and 100,000 times more toxic than sarin. However, note that this toxicity is via ingestion of the toxin. The inhalational route is thought to be 1,400 times less toxic than the inges-tion dose. Botulinum toxin is the most lethal toxin yet discovered.

The most important characteristic feature of botulism is a descending paralysis (head to toe) and bulbar palsies (a bulbar palsy is a loss of function in the nerves that originates from the upper part of the spinal cord where it attaches to the brain). This leads to dysfunction of the cranial nerves that control all the muscles of the face, the eyes, and swallowing. Symptoms include: blurred vision, dilated pupils (mydriasis), double vision (diplopia), drooping eyelids (ptosis), light sensi-tivities (photophobia); difficulty swallowing (dysphagia); and problems speaking.

Soon, the skeletal muscles become weak, starting in the upper body and progressing downwards in a symmetrical fashion until involvement of the diaphragm and accessory breathing muscles results in respiratory failure.

Botulism is usually a rapidly progressing illness, therefore early treatment is essential. The descending paralysis is so characteristic of botulism, that any illness that includes such a pattern of paralysis should always raise botulism as a possible diagnosis. Paralysis also affects the cranial nerves, including the nerves that control the muscles of facial expression and swallowing. Patients may also have dry mouth and throat (and may complain of sore throat), and dizziness. Onset of botulism is usually over 24 to 36 hours, but may be longer if exposure is inhalational. Botulinum toxin is not dermally active and is not absorbed through the skin.

Treatment of botulism includes the use of antitoxins. There are several preparations of antitoxin available, including a trivalent (A,B,E). However, antitoxin is of limited help unless given early in the course of the disease. A human immunoglobulin is also available. Many patients become paralyzed, requiring long-term mechanical ventilation. Typically, motor nerves require 2 to 3 months to regenerate the cellular machinery irreversibly inhibited by botulinum toxin.

Whether the result of a bioterrorist attack or a naturally occurring case, efforts must be made to identify anyone who may have ingested the same food as the patient, and to notify the department of public health. Once again, early recognition by HERT members will be key in initiating this epidemiological investigation. Remember, once the patient is paralyzed, he/she will not be able to provide this history. Furthermore, the insidious onset of the illness, and poorly recognized presentation, means that most patients are diagnosed well into their course.

Ricin

Ricin is a toxin produced by the castor bean *Ricinus communis*. Approximately 5% (by dry weight) of castor bean mash (pulverized castor beans after they have been crushed to extract castor bean oil) is ricin. Although not nearly as toxic as botulinum toxin, it is still considered many times more toxic that the most lethal nerve agents. The toxin blocks cellular protein synthesis, leading to cell death and tissue necrosis. If ricin is inhaled, the patient will develop airway necrosis and bleeding, severe inflammation of the trachea, bronchi, and distal airways (alveoli). Pneumonia and pulmonary edema develop with widespread necrosis of lung tissue. If ingested, ricin produces predominantly gastrointestinal symptoms first, including bloody stools, vomiting blood, and abdominal pain. Ricin can also be injected, and has been used in this fashion for assassinations (the interested reader is referred to the story of Georgi Markov's assassination by ricin). However, all these routes of exposure can culminate in systemic toxicity and death. As there is no antitoxin or antidote for ricin poisoning, treatment is purely supportive.

Radiological and Nuclear Devices

Terrorist use of radioactive materials or a nuclear device could occur in one of several ways. The medical consequences will be dependent on the type of device used.

Simple Radiological Device

The simplest would be spreading radioactive material without the use of an explosive device. An example would be the placement of a highly radioactive source in a public place, exposing numerous individuals to radiation. Although the easiest methods of using a radioactive weapon, it is not likely to cause large numbers of casualties or widespread radioactive contamination.

Radiological Dispersal Device

This device (commonly referred to as a dirty bomb) uses a conventional explosive device combined with radioactive material. The intent is to disperse the radiological material over a wide area, causing contamination of people as well as the area surrounding the blast. Most immediate injuries are due to the blast itself, while any radiation injuries are delayed.

Explosive Nuclear Device

Although perhaps the most catastrophic of all weapons of mass destruction, a nuclear device is also considered the most unlikely due to the difficulty of obtaining one. Although considered unlikely, it is thought that if terrorists are be able to obtain nuclear weapon technology and fissile material, they may be able to construct a more rudimentary "partial yield" device.

Ionizing Radiation

Ionizing radiation is a form of electromagnetic radiation that is carried by any of several types of particles and rays given off by radioactive material and nuclear reactions. When ionizing radiation impacts a molecule, it knocks electrons off the molecules, thus creating ions. Non-ionizing radiation, such as infrared (thermal) radiation, is different because it does not create ions when it interacts with matter, but dissipates energy. The three main types of ionizing radiation are alpha particles, beta particles, and gamma rays.

Alpha radiation is made up of alpha particles, which consist of two protons and two neutrons and is identical to the nucleus of a helium atom. An alpha particle has a short range (several centimeters) in air, and can be shielded by a thin layer of paper or clothing. Because alpha particles are unable to penetrate through the outer dead layers of skin to reach the lower layers of living cells, they generally will not cause any skin damage. However, if an alpha-emitting radioactive material is internalized through inhalation, ingestion, or through a wound, the emitted alpha particles can cause ionization that results in damage to tissue. Therefore, alpha radiation is an internal hazard only.

Beta radiation is made up of beta particles, which are electrons ejected from the nucleus of a radioactive atom. Beta particles are smaller and more penetrating than alpha particles, but their range in tissue is still limited. Beta radiation can travel several meters in air and is only moderately penetrating in other materials. Some beta radiation can penetrate human skin to the layer where new skin cells are produced (germinal layer). If beta-emitting material is allowed to remain on the skin for a prolonged period of time, it may cause skin injury ("beta burns"). Beta-emitting contaminants may be harmful if deposited internally.

Gamma rays and x-rays (photons) are electromagnetic wave radiation given off by an atom as a means of releasing excess energy, have no charge or mass, and can travel up to great distances through air. They readily penetrate most materials. Thick layers of dense materials (e.g., lead) are needed to shield against gamma radiation. A gamma ray can pass through a body without hitting anything, or it may hit an atom, ionizing it, and setting off a cascade of ionization reactions that result in molecular damage, tissue injury, and if DNA is damaged, the development of cancer. Radioactive materials that emit gamma radiation constitute both an external and an internal hazard to humans; x-rays are primarily external hazards since they are usually machine-produced.

Neutrons are particles emitted from the nucleus of an unstable atom. Neutrons lose most of their energy through collisions with other atomic nuclei. Neutrons can be captured by a stable nucleus, making the nucleus radioactive and potentially very penetrating.

Radiation Doses

Radioactivity exists in the earth's crust, in building materials, in the food we eat, the air we breathe, and in virtually everything that surrounds us. Radiation from these materials, as well as cosmic radiation from the sun and universe, makes up the natural background radiation to which we are constantly exposed.

Most individuals are exposed to about 360 millirems per year from natural (80%) and manmade (20%) sources. Smoking 1.5 packs of cigarettes a day for one year produces an accumulative radiation dose of 16 rem to the bronchial epithelium. If an individual is exposed to more than 100 rads at one time, predictable signs and symptoms will develop within a few hours, days, or weeks, depending on the dose.

Three types of radiation-induced injuries can occur: external irradiation, contamination with radioactive materials, and incorporation of radioactive material into body cells, tissues, or organs. Radiation exposure/contamination may also be complicated by trauma. These three types of events (external irradiation, contamination, and incorporation) can happen in combination and can be complicated by physical injury or illness.

External Exposure without Contamination (Irradiation)

External irradiation occurs when all or part of the body is exposed to penetrating radiation from an external source. During exposure, this radiation can be absorbed by the body or it can pass completely through. Following external exposure, an individual is not radioactive and can be treated like any other patient.

Contamination

External contamination is radioactive material on external surface of the body, such as the skin. External radioactive material will continue to irradiate the body and therefore should be decontaminated as soon as possible. Decontamination procedures must be sure not to increase internal contamination, either through reaerosolization of radioactive particulates into the victim's breathing zone or by ingestion of contaminated runoff. If radioactive materials get inside the body through the lungs, gastrointestinal tract, or wounds, the contaminant can become deposited internally. This is extremely important for alpha emitter radioactive material, as it is very ionizing and causes significant injury once internalized.

Incorporation

Radionuclides, although radioactive, behave chemically like non-radioactive atoms of the same element, and are metabolized by the body in the same fashion as the nonradioactive element. Incorporation refers to the uptake of radioactive materials by body cells, tissues, and target organs such as bone, liver or thyroid.

Because radiation exposure is not immediately life-threatening, HERT personnel should treat life-threatening problems first (e.g., airway, trauma), while at the same time taking measures to limit the radiation dose to both victim and personnel and control the spread of radioactive contaminants. Serious medical problems (e.g. airway management or trauma) always have priority over concerns about radiation.

There are three methods for reducing radiation exposure: time, distance, and shielding.

Time The shorter the time exposed to the radiation source, the less the radiation exposure. Rotating team members, and working efficiently can keep individual radiation exposures to a minimum. The longer a person is exposed to a radiation source, the higher will be the dose received. To minimize the dose, reduce the time of exposure to the radiation.

Distance HERT members can further reduce exposure by taking advantage of distance. Radiation dose rate falls off very quickly as the distance between the radiation source and the individual is increased. The farther a person is from a source of radiation, the lower the radiation dose. Do not handle or touch radioactive materials. Use long surgical instruments to remove radioactive material from victims or any other device that will allow you to maintain the maximum distance from the source of radiation.

Shielding Another method of minimizing dose is through the use of shielding. Leaded aprons are not recommended and usually provide little shielding protection from the types of radiation expected from contaminated patients. Although not always practical in emergency situations, shielding can reduce radiation exposure.

Quantity Limit the amount of radioactive material (e.g. contaminated clothing, waste water) in the working area to decrease exposure. Remove as much radioactive material as possible from the work area, either place away from patients and/or personnel (increasing distance) or placing it in a shielded container (if available).

Acute Radiation Syndrome (ARS)

Acute radiation syndrome (ARS) is the name given to a group of signs and symptoms that develop after total body (or large body volume) irradiation at doses greater than 100 rads delivered over a short period of time. The severity of ARS is primarily related to the total dose, dose rate, region and amount of the body irradiated, type of radiation, age, and health status.

Depending on radiation dose, specific systems in the body are affected. At doses greater than 100 rads, the bone marrow (hematopoietic system) is affected, leading to infection and bleeding; at doses greater than 600 rads, the gastrointestinal system becomes affected, leading to severe (and often continuing) nausea, vomiting, diarrhea, electrolyte imbalance, and sepsis; at doses greater than 1,000 rads, the central nervous system is affected.

The acute radiation syndrome follows a predictable course over a period of time ranging from a few hours to several weeks.

The severity of the syndrome increases with dose, amount of the body exposed (whole body vs. partial body exposure), and the penetrating ability of the radiation.

The severity is also affected by patient factors such as age, gender, medical conditions, etc. The signs and symptoms that develop in the ARS occur in four distinct phases: prodromal, latent period, manifest illness stage and recovery or death.

Prodromal phase Depending on the dose of radiation, patients may experience loss of appetite, nausea, vomiting, fatigue, and diarrhea. After extremely high radiation doses, additional symptoms such as prostration, fever, respiratory difficulties, and increased excitability may develop. This is the stage at which most victims seek medical care.

Latent period In this phase many of the initial symptoms partially or completely resolve. It may last for a few hours or up to a few weeks depending on the radiation dose. During this time, critical cell populations (leukocytes, platelets) are decreasing as a result of bone marrow damage. Monitoring of these cell counts is helpful in estimating doses and predicting outcome. The latent period shortens as the initial dose increases.

Illness stage This stage is characterized by the predominant syndrome and/or organ systems involved.

Recovery phase or death This may be protracted (weeks or months) depending on the severity of initial injury and the development of long term medical complications (e.g., cancer).

The NCRP Report No. 65, *Management of Persons Accidentally Contaminated with Radionuclides* is an excellent source for treatment information.

Protecting HERT Staff from Contamination

Hospital staff are accustomed to protecting themselves and their work areas from microbiological contamination through the use of universal precautions. The same techniques can be used effectively to protect personnel and the work area from contamination by radioactive materials. Most radioactive material can be detected easily and in very small quantities with the use of a simple instrument such as a GM survey meter (Geiger counter). However, due to its very low penetration and/or travel through air, detection of alpha radiation requires careful use of an alpha meter.

Frequent use of the GM survey meter can alert personnel to the need to change their gloves or clothing when they become contaminated or to tell them when contamination is being spread to the work area so that cleanup and extra precautions can be implemented.

Blast Injuries

Blast injury is usually classified into four types: primary, secondary, tertiary and quaternary.

Primary blast injury results from the impact of the overpressurization wave with body surfaces. Gas-filled organs such as the lungs, GI tract, and ear structures, are most susceptible. Any injury to the ear that presents with hearing loss, tinnitus, ear pain, vertigo, bleeding from the external canal, tympanic membrane (eardrum) rupture, or drainage from the ear should be considered a marker for primary blast injury. Tympanic membrane rupture is a sensitive indicator that the victim was exposed to significant blast overpressure and is more likely to have other significant blast injuries. Significant primary blast injury to the lungs may cause air emboli in the circulatory system. These patients may present with symptoms of respiratory distress, as well as symptoms of stroke if the air emboli travel to the brain. Primary blast injury may also directly cause traumatic brain and eye (globe) injuries. "Blast lung" is characterized by the clinical triad of apnea, bradycardia, and hypotension. It is usually present at the time of initial presentation, but may be delayed many hours after the explosion. Blast lung should be suspected for victims with dyspnea, hemoptysis, or chest pain following blast exposure. The incidence of pulmonary blast injuries increases with increasing blast overpressure. Blasts that occur within a closed space (e.g., bus, room) have a higher incidence of pulmonary blast injury as blast overpressure is multiplied when reflected by stationary surfaces (e.g., walls, ceilings). It the most common fatal primary blast injury among initial survivors and should be treated aggressively. Primary blast injuries to the abdomen include bowel perforation, solid organ laceration or rupture, and internal bleeding. Signs of primary abdominal blast injury may be delayed and therefore should be sought out on physical exam. They include abdominal pain, vomiting, gastrointestinal bleeding, rectal pain, testicular pain or unexplained shock.

Secondary blast injury results from flying debris and/or bomb fragments (shrapnel). Many terrorist bombs have additional material, such as nails or ball bearings, added to the exterior of bombs to increase secondary blast injury. These injuries typically take the form of penetrating ballistic injuries similar to gunshot wounds, although they may be numerous. Secondary blast injury would also include injuries from falling debris.

Tertiary blast injury results from individuals being thrown by the blast wind of the explosion. They may have blunt trauma similar to that from a significant fall, including head injuries, fractures, traumatic amputations and occult intra-abdominal injuries.

Quaternary blast injury refers to all blast-related injuries not encompassed in the first three types listed above. These include burns, toxic gas inhalation, smoke inhalation, crush injuries and exacerbation of pre-existing medical conditions.

Treatment of blast injuries should be based upon established trauma management principles and methods with additional consideration for the unique blast-related injuries described above. Management of airway and breathing is the first priority followed by treatment for shock if present. Additionally, when managing victims of bomb blast, HERT members should continually be vigilant for signs and/or symptoms of unique complications of blast injury, such as air emboli, occult blunt trauma, toxic inhalation injuries and crush injuries.

Summary

The HERT is a critical part of a healthcare facility's response to an MCE. Its special function as part of a hospital's surge response to an MCE is largely founded on its training in the concepts reviewed in this chapter, including hospital emergency response organization, use of hospital resources, planning and preparation for all types of MCEs, as well as those that are of high likelihood and/or high consequence. Also reviewed in this chapter is material about specific types of MCEs, including those resulting from chemical, biological, radiological and explosive events, both accidental and those that are the result of deliberate acts of terrorism. It is important to emphasize that the material reviewed in this chapter should not be considered a "list" of events that a HERT should prepare for, or the limit of education and/or training that a HERT should pursue. All readers and HERT members are encouraged to use this material as an introduction and to continue to improve their knowledge base as part of their ongoing HERT training.

References

Altered Standards of Care in Mass Casualty Events. Prepared by Health Systems Research Inc. under Contract No. 290-04-0010. AHRQ Publication No. 05-0043. Rockville, MD: Agency for Healthcare Research and Quality. April 2005.

Anonymous. Cyanide arsenal stirs domestic terror fear. January 30, 2004. Available at www.cnn.com/2004/US/Southwest/01/30/cyanide.probe.ap/index.html. Accessed 9 February 2004.

Anonymous. "Cyanide plotters" face terror charges. Available at http://new/bbc/co/uk/1/hi/world/europe/1833646.stm. Accessed 26 January 2004.

Anonymous: Human monkeypox in Kasai Oriental, Democratic Republic of Congo (former Zaire). *Wkly Epidemiol Rec* 72:369–372, 1997.

Anonymous: Human monkeypox in Kasai Oriental, Zaire (1996–1997). *Wkly Epidemiol Rec* 72:101–104, 1997.

Anonymous. M15 foils al-Qaeda's London cyanide plot. Sunday Herald, 17 November 2002. Available at: www.sundayherald.com/print29314. Accessed 26 January 2004.

Bioterrorism-Related Inhalational Anthrax: The First 10 Cases Reported in the United States, *Emerging Infectious Diseases*, vol.7, no. 6, 2001.

Blank IH, Griesemer RD, Gould E: The penetration of an anticholinesterase agent (sarin) into skin. *J Invest Dermatol* 29:299–309, 1957.

Borron SW, Baud FJ. Toxicity, cyanide. February 2003. Available at: www.emedicine.com/emerg/topic118.htm. Accessed 13 January 2004.

Borron SW, et al. *Intensive Care Medicine* 1997;23:S181.

Breman JG, Henderson DA: Poxvirus dilemmas—monkeypox, smallpox, and biologic terrorism *New Engl J Med* 339(8): 556, 1998.

Cleri DJ, Vernaleo JR, Lombardi LJ, et al: Plague pneumonia disease caused by Yersinia pestis. *Sem Resp Infections* 12(1):12–23, 1997.

Cloud DS. Long in US signs, a young terrorist builds grim resume. Tuesday, February 10, 2004. The Wall Street Journal, Dow Jones & Company, 2004.

Crandell RA, Casey HW, Brumlow WB: Studies of a newly recognized poxvirus of monkeys. *J Infect Dis* 119(1):80–88, 1969.

Craig FN, Cummings EG, Sim VM: Environmental temperature and the percutaneous absorption of a cholinesterase inhibitor, VX. *J Invest Dermatol* 68:357–361, 1977.

Cushman JG, Pachter HL, Beaton HL. Department of Surgery, New York University School of Medicine, New York, New York, USA.

Dennis DT, Gage KL, Gratz N, et al: World Health Organization Plague Manual: Epidemiology, distribution, surveillance, and control. WHO/CDS/CSR/EDC/99.2. Geneva, World Health Organization.

Dennis DT, Inglesby TV, Henderson DA, et al: Plague as a biological weapon. *JAMA* 283(17): 2281–2290, 2000.

Friedl KE, Hannan CJ, Schadler PW, et al: Atropine absorption after intramuscular administration with 2-pralidoxime chloride by two automatic injector devices. *J Pharm Sci* 78(9): 728–731, 1989.

Grob D, Johns RJ: Use of oximes in the treatment of intoxication by anticholinesterase compounds in normal subjects. *Am J Med* 24:497–511, 1958.

Hall AH, et al. *Journal de Toxicologie Clinique et Expérimentale* 1989;9:3–9.

Hall A, Rumack BH. *Ann Emerg Med* 1986;15:1067–1074.

Heddurshetti R, Pumpradit W, Lutwick LI: Pulmonary manifestations of bioterrorism. *Curr Infect Dis Reports* 3:249–257, 2001.

Hull HF, Montes JM, Mann JM: Plague masquerading as gastrointestinal illness. *West J Med* 145:485–487, 1986.

Hutin YJF, Williams RJ, Malfait P, et al: Outbreak of human monkeypox, Democratic republic of Congo, 1996–1997. *Emerg Infect Dis* 7(3):434–438, 2001.

Jezek Z, Mutombo M, Dunn C, et al: Four generations of probable person-to-person transmission of human mokeypox. *Am J Epidemiol* 123:1004–1012, 1986.

Jezek Z, Szczeniowski M, Paluku KM, et al: Human monkeypox: clinical features of 282 patients. *J Infect Dis* 156(2):293–298, 1987.

John A, Jernigan, et al. Bioterrorism-Related Inhalational Anthrax: The First 10 Cases Reported in the United States, *Emerging Infectious Diseases*, Vol. 7, No. 6, November–December 2001, pages 933–944.

Leibovici, D, *Ann Emerg Med* August 1999; None of 142 pts with isolated TM rupture developed blast lung injury. 18 of 31 pts with evidence for blast lung injury had intact TM's bilaterally.

Leibovici D, et al. Blast injuries: bus versus open-air bombings—a comparative study of injuries in survivors of open-air versus confined-space explosions. *J Trauma*; 1996, Dec; 41 (6): 1030–5.

Ledgard J: The preparatory manual of chemical warfare agents. Columbus, OH, The Paranoid Publications Group, 2003.

Martin LJ, Doebler JA, Shih T-M, et al: Protective effect of diazepam pretreatment on soman-induced brain lesion formation. *Brain Res* 325:287–289, 1987.

Mégarbane B, et al. *J Chin Med Assoc* 2003;66:193–203.

National Institute of Occupational Safety and Health Emergency Response Card. Available at: www.bt.cdc.gov/agent/cyanide/erc74-90-8pr.asp

Neitlich HW: Effect of percutaneous GD on human subjects. CRDL Technical Memorandum 2–21, DTIC AD471794, 1965.

Nozaki H, Aikawa N, Shinozawa Y, et al: Sarin poisoning in Tokyo subway. *Lancet* 345:980–981, 1995.

Nozaki H, Hori S, Shinozawa Y, et al: Secondary exposure of medical staff to sarin vapor in the emergency room. *Intensive Care Med* 21:1032–1035, 1995.

Ohbu S, Yamashina A, Nobukatsu T, et al: Sarin poisoning on the Tokyo subway. *South J Med* 90(6):587–593, 1997.

Okumura T, Nobukatsu T, Ishimatsu S, et al: Report on 640 victims of the Tokyo subway sarin attack. *Annals Emerg Med* 28:129–135, 1995.

Okumura T, Suzuki K, Fukuda A, et al: The Tokyo subway sarin attack: Disaster management, part 2: Hospital response. *Acad Emerg Med* 5:618–624, 1998.

Opulski A, MacNeill E, Rosales C, et al: Plague pneumonia—Arizona, 1992. *MMWR* 41(40): 737–739, 1992.

OSHA Best Practices for Hospital-Based First Receiver of Victims from Mass Casualty Incidents Involving the release of Hazardous Substances, OSHA, January, 2005.

O'Toole T, Inglesby T, Larsen R, DeMier M: Dark Winter: A bioterrorism exercise. Johns Hopkins Center for Civilian Biodefense, Center for Strategic and International Studies, Analytic Services, Inc., and Memorial Institute for the prevention of Terrorism, 2001. Available at: http://www.hopkins-biodefense.org/index.html

O'Toole T, Mair M, Inglesby TV: Shining light on "Dark Winter." *Clin Infect Dis* 34:972–983, 2002.

Phillips SJ, Knebel A, eds. *Mass Medical Care with Scarce Resources: A Community Planning Guide.* Prepared by Health Systems Research, Inc., an Altarum company, under contract No. 290-04-0010. AHRQ Publication No. 07-0001. Rockville, MD: Agency for Healthcare Research and Quality 2007.

Rengstorff RH: Accidental exposure to sarin: Vision effects. *Arch Toxicol* 56:201–203, 1985.

Rickett DL, Glenn JF, Beers ET: Central respiratory effects versus neuromuscular actions of nerve agents. *Neurotoxicology* 7(1):225–236, 1986.

Rubin LS, Goldberg MN: Effect of sarin on dark adaptation in man: Threshold changes. *J Appl Physiol* 2:439–444, 1957.

Rubin LS, Krop S, Goldberg MN: Effect of sarin on dark adaptation in man: Mechanism of action. *J Appl Physiol* 2:445–449, 1957.

Rump S, Kowaczyk M: Management of convulsions in nerve agent acute poisoning: A Polish perspective. *J Med Chem Def* 1:1–14, 2003.

Sauer SW, Keim ME. *Ann Emerg Med* 2001;37:635–641.

Sidell FR, Markis JE, Groff W, et al: Enhancement of drug absorption after administration by an automatic injector. *J Pharmacokinet Biopharm* 2(3):197–210, 1974.

Sidell FR: Sarin and Soman: Observations on accidental exposures. *Edgewood Arsenal Technical Report 4747*, DTIC AD769737, 1973.

Torok TJ, et al: A large community outbreak of salmonellosis caused by intentional contamination of restaurant salad bars. *JAMA* 6;278(5):389–95, 1997.

Tu AT: Anatomy of Aum Shinrikyo's organization and terrorist attacks with chemical and biological weapons. *Arch Toxicol Kinetics Xenobiotic Metabolism* 7(3):45–82, 1999.

Tu AT: The first mass chemical terrorism using sarin in Matsumoto, Japan. *Arch Toxicol Kinetics Xenobiotic Metabolism* 9(3);65–93, 2001.

Two New York City hospitals' surgical response to the September 11, 2001, terrorist attack in New York City, J Trauma. 2003 Jan;54(1):147–54.

United States Coast Guard, *Record of Proceedings of Board of Investigation Inquiring into Losses by Fires and Explosions of the French Steamship Grandcamp...* Retrieved from http://www.uscg.mil/hq/cg5/docs/boards/grandcamp.pdf

Waselenko, JK., MacVittie, TJ., Blakely, WF., Pesik, N, Wiley, AL., Dickerson, WE., Tsu, H; Confer, DL., Coleman, C, Seed, T, Lowry, P; Armitage, JO., and Dainiak, N. "Medical Management of the Acute Radiation Syndrome: Recommendations of the Strategic National Stockpile Radiation Working Group." *Annals of Internal Medicine* 140, no. 12 (2004):1037–1051.

Wright PG: An analysis of central and peripheral components of respiratory failure by anticholinesterase poisoning in the rabbit. *J Physiol* 126:52–70, 1954.

Zaucha GM, Jahrling PB, Geisbert GW, et al: The pathology of experimental aerosolized monkeypox virus infection cynomolgus monkeys (*Macaca fascicularis*). *Lab Investigation* 81(12):1581–1600, 2001.

3

Personal Protective Equipment (PPE)

CHAPTER OBJECTIVES

- Describe the process for identifying the hazards personnel at a medical facility may be exposed to.
- Describe the sites or locations where hazards may be present that may impact medical facility operations.
- Describe the process for determining the appropriate PPE in the medical facility setting.
- Identify the levels of personal protective equipment as indicated by OSHA and the NFPA.
- Describe the components of a personal protective ensemble for medical facility use.
- Identify the human sensory organs that are limited by the use of personal protective equipment.
- Describe the effect on individuals when using personal protective equipment.
- Describe the term "shelf life" for the storage of personal protective equipment.
- Identify a suitable storage location inside a medical facility for personal protective equipment storage.
- Describe the term "sustainment" as it applies to the medical facility setting.
- Identify issues that may be addressed as part of a sustainment program.
- Describe the availability of PPE worldwide.
- Describe the international impact a CBRN incident may have on medical facilities.

Introduction

Personal protective material technology has been both a friend and a foe to humans: a friend in providing advanced materials that offer protection from the harsh elements of outer space and against materials posing a toxic threat to the unprotected human; a foe in the physical and environmental restrictions and hazards posed just by wearing the protective ensemble. The ability to protect ourselves has been an evolutional trail since the beginning of mankind; first to shield ourselves from the harsh environmental elements of the planet and later evolving into today's sophisticated personal protective equipment. As humans we aspire to create material and equipment that will offer personal protection, even under the most severe situations, in order to help us explore new worlds or protect us during disasters. In the medical facility arena we have created equipment that protects us from potentially hazardous materials and provides life-saving services to patients or victims of a significant incident. The technology of advanced molecular material design and application has played a critical role in keeping medical facility responders safe even when faced with the unknown.

Local Hazard Assessment and Selection Criteria

To better prepare and ensure adequate response capability, a medical facility should always start by completing a local hazard assessment. This assessment will provide a realistic picture of the hazards the medical facility may face during significant events. For many medical facilities the assessment might be completed as part of a government requirement or in conjunction with a preparedness program. Regardless of the reason for the assessment, an essential part of the process is the creation of community partnerships. Valuable information can be gained by contacting associated agencies or committees who have already produced similar documents as part of their own local area planning assessment. Likewise, local police, fire and emergency disaster responders or agencies may have local hazard information that can be incorporated into a medical facility's assessment.

During the assessment process there are a number of factors to consider to ensure you produce a comprehensive picture of the hazards your personnel and patients may face. The first factor is the overall size and scope of operations occurring within the medical facility on a 24-hour basis. Most facilities have internal all-hazards response plans that address chemical, biological, radiological and explosive incidents. These plans generally focus on internal releases or incidents. While these plans may address reception of a patient with hazardous materials, they generally do not encompass the full scope of external scenarios a facility might face. A clear picture of the overall local hazards should include a thorough assessment of the hazards beyond the front door of your facility.

When creating your assessment, there is a simple yet valuable technique that can produce a thorough picture of hazards. Place your medical facility at the center of a grid and work outwards in all directions at preset intervals, plotting the potential hazards closest to you. Using the medical facility as ground zero, determine all the hazards within a one mile radius and then rate them on a scale of 1 to 10 for their potential medical facility impact risk. Risk factors should include current hazardous materials located on commercial/industrial properties, types of processes the hazardous materials are used in, risk if you were to receive

(a)

(b)

(c)

FIGURE 3.1 (a) Industry photo showing large silos, a potential source of hazards in a community. (b) Hospital emergency entrance. (c) Railroad tank cars, derailed in an accident, may create a hazmat incident. Photos (a), (b), and (c) are by Don Birou.

potentially contaminated patients/victims, and potential downwind exposure for your medical facility should the release of a chemical, biological, radiological, or nuclear (CBRN) material occur. Perform the same assessment for five, ten, and twenty mile radii. This grid approach produces the highest risk potential for a given area and allows for pre-planning of the most likely hazards your facility may face. It does not, however, include the possibility of terrorist or intentional acts in which an unknown hazardous material, substance or agent is released, posing a threat to your employees, the medical facility and your patients.

Next, you should identify possible transportation routes for CBRN materials, e.g., highway, railroad, pipeline, air, and waterways. It is generally difficult to predict what cargo may be transported on any of the above transportation routes at a given time on any given day. You may find some data on the types of CBRN materials in transit, but it is generally limited to the number and type of CBRN materials transported annually in a national or regional area. It may be possible to create a picture of the most frequently transported CBRN materials in your area, but this will require both diligent work and access to sensitive information. Proper contacts and associations related to CBRN materials transportation will likely provide the most accurate information for completing the assessment.

The next risk factor to include on the list is commercial or industrial businesses which utilize or store CBRN materials. These are easier to track than transportation routes, as these businesses are in fixed locations with known CBRN materials and quantities. It is likely that these companies will have the nearest medical facility listed as the hospital of choice for employee emergency care during an exposure or release. Anticipating the CBRN response necessary for these businesses allows for improved decision-making concerning protective equipment and locations for rapid response based on the hazard assessment.

Selection Criteria

Selecting the proper personal protective equipment (PPE) for a hospital setting requires a thorough understanding of the different types of PPE. The selection process can be tedious and time-consuming, as the specifications for PPE are technical and require some knowledge of the construction, materials, design features and testing requirements.

Any serious look into the best possible PPE for use in the medical facility environment is sure to arouse debate and disagreement. However, the ultimate goal should be a well-prepared and well-equipped medical facility. Completion of a local hazard analysis and risk assessment, coupled with a thorough review of the facility's capability to respond to significant incidents, will form the rationale for creating a state of PPE readiness.

CRITICAL THINKING

The first step in the PPE selection process will be to ask several questions that, while they may not provide absolute answers, will provide a path to follow that allows for decision-making.

- Question 1—What hazards were revealed through completion of the hazard assessment?
- Question 2—What grouping or highest level of hazard(s) did the hazard assessment indicate?
- Question 3—What level of personal protection equipment will be required to address the hazards indicated in the hazard assessment?
- Question 4—What level of personal protective equipment will be required to address an unidentified or unknown hazard?

The following questions are designed to address a medical facility's PPE needs regarding level of coverage and available staff. This section does pose some serious questions that a medical facility will have to address. The answers will depend on the capabilities of those staff members who are obligated to meet federal agency requirements for hazardous environments and emergency situations (i.e., FEMA). The final result of the discussion here may only produce options, not definitive answers. You may find that various levels of PPE are required to address the potential hazards for your medical facility. One must consider the funding that is available to acquire and maintain the equipment. Purchasing the necessary PPE is only the beginning, as all equipment will incur maintenance costs to ensure it is functional and safe for operations when needed. An additional consideration is the shelf life of the equipment purchased. Virtually all PPE has a shelf life as indicated by the manufacturer, along with recommended storage conditions. These details cannot be overlooked as this equipment is vital to ensuring the health and safety of your medical facility employees. The failure of a single component of any of the personnel protective equipment items would provide an opportunity for a hazardous material, substance or agent to contaminate an employee. Hazardous material exposure is a serious situation that could lead to acute or chronic medical issues for the employee and loss of a critical staff member to the response team.

The following questions may provide guidance in achieving a workable PPE selection list.

Question 1—Can staff members meet the basic physical demands of the type of work anticipated at significant all hazards incidents? Are they able to adapt to the limitations of the protective equipment, including limited dexterity, vision, sense

CHOOSING THE RIGHT TEAM MEMBERS FOR YOUR HOSPITAL EMERGENCY RESPONSE TEAM "HERT"!

No one medical facility will have a hard and fast system for choosing who among the staff should be on the hazards team. Generally, medical staff personnel tasked with forming a team will seek out individuals using a common sense approach. No agency or government entity has created or proposed a checklist or questionnaire for determining who would best fit the hospital response team positions and what considerations may influence the selection process. Therefore, you may want to use the following information to create your own checklist to help determine who may best fit your team needs.

Supervisory personnel tasked with selecting individuals for their response team may follow a questionnaire type format such as the one below:

Skill Set Checklist:

What skill sets will absolutely be required for the Hospital Emergency Response Team?

- Physician(s)—as the health and medical leaders
- Physician(s), Nurses, Paramedics—used in the treatment and triage area, safety officer
- Security Officer(s)—enforcement and control elements
- Maintenance Engineers—facility support items
- Public Information Officer—liaison to media
- Technicians, General Staff—decontamination team

Other positions needed to complete the hospital emergency response team include:

Incident Commander: Provides overall command and control of the incident with full authority to direct and institute the strategy for responding to incidents of significant impact.

Safety Officer: Provides oversight for all safety aspects during incidents and has authority to halt unsafe operations or actions at any time.

Public Information Officer: Provides pertinent information to all entities regarding the incident and directs, organizes and delivers media press releases as needed.

Employees with additional skill sets: As part of your review of potential employees for your HERT, seek out those who have knowledge and skills from previous or current professions or activities that will benefit the team. Examples include employees who volunteer or hold part-time jobs with fire departments with HazMat teams, law enforcement and security agencies, or emergency medical services. You should also consider individuals with any of the following: prior experience in the chemical industry sector, military experience, multi-lingual language capabilities, hearing-impaired skills, lip-readers, fluency in ASL, and veterinary or animal training background.

A general sector of the questionnaire should include questions that help to inform and prepare the potential team member for some of the anticipated physical and mental stressors they may face while functioning in a HERT environment with PPE.

Potential HERT member questions:
HERT members are required to wear personal protective equipment to protect against potentially hazardous or toxic materials and substances. The protective equipment will restrict visual acuity, and will reduce dexterity, hearing, and sense of touch. It will also be confining, constricting and hot to work in. The protective equipment may also create or intensify a feeling of claustrophobia and/or aggravate any medical issues you may have.

- Question 1—Considering the above statement do you believe you can learn to work in such an environment?
  - Yes
  - No
  - Unsure

- Question 2—Would working in PPE during very hot or very cold atmospheric conditions present an issue for you physically?
  - Yes
  - No
  - Unsure

- Question 3—Would working in PPE under stressful conditions where a potential for hazardous or toxic materials may exist present any psychological barriers for you?
  - Yes
  - No
  - Unsure

of touch, and hearing as well as exert themselves under extreme environmental conditions such as intense heat and humidity?

Question 2—Do staff members have personal physical attributes such as facial hair or eyeglasses which would interfere with the use of an Air Purifying Respirator (APR)? This question needs to be addressed *only* if use of APRs will be part of your Standard Operating Procedure. It will be necessary to conduct fit-testing for each member of the response team who will be expected to use an APR in a hazardous environment. If the use of a hooded powered air purifying respirator (PAPR) will be the respirator protection of choice by your medical facility then facial hair, eyeglasses and other facial issues will not have to be addressed as the hooded PAPR resolves those concerns.

NOTE

The Occupational Safety and Health Administration (OSHA) has a specific Code of Federal Regulation that outlines the necessary requirements that must be met for the use of APRs by employees when such equipment is necessary to protect their health.

   As a reference I will provide you with the overview of the major requirements for the OSHA Respiratory Protection Standard 29 CFR 1910.134. In no way will this overview cover every aspect or detail of the standard; you are encouraged to consult the OSHA 29 CFR 1910.134 Standard in its entirety by accessing the OSHA web page (http://www.osha.gov/pls/oshaweb/owadisp.show_document?p_id=12716&p_table=standards) or other source for the complete text.

Major Requirements of OSHA's Respiratory Protection Standard 29 CFR 1910.134

Introduction:

   Standard applies to General Industry (Part 1910)

- Permissible Practice
  This section establishes OSHA's hierarchy of controls by requiring the use of feasible engineering controls as the primary means to control air contaminants. Respirators are required when "effective engineering controls are not feasible, or while they are being instituted." It requires employers to provide employees with respirators that are "applicable and suitable" for the purpose intended "when such equipment is necessary to protect the health of the employee."

- Definitions
  This paragraph contains definitions of important terms used in the regulatory text.

- Respiratory Protection Program
  States that facilities must designate a "qualified program administrator" to oversee the program. The program must also provide respirators, training and medical evaluations at no cost to employees.

- Selection of Respirators
  Facilities must select a respirator certified by the National Institute for Occupational Safety and Health (NIOSH) which must be used in compliance with the conditions of its certification.

    Facilities must also identify and evaluate the respiratory hazards in the workplace, including a reasonable estimate of employee exposures and identification of the contaminant's chemical state and physical form.

    Where exposures cannot be identified or reasonably estimated, the atmosphere shall be considered immediately dangerous to life and health (IDLH).

- Respirators for IDLH atmospheres:

  - Full-face pressure demand self-contained breathing apparatus (SCBA) certified by NIOSH for a service life of thirty minutes or
  - Combination full facepiece pressure demand supplied-air respiratory (SAR) with auxiliary self contained air supply
  - All oxygen-deficient atmospheres (less than 19.5% oxygen by volume) shall be considered IDLH.

- Respirators for non-IDLH atmospheres:

  - Employers must use the assigned protection factors (APFs) listed in table 1 to select a respirator that meets or exceeds the required level of employee protection.
  - Employers must select a respirator for employee use that maintains the employee's exposure to the hazardous substance, when measured outside the respirator, at or below the maximum use concentration (MUC).
  - Employers must not apply MUCs to conditions that are IDLH
  - The selected respirator shall be appropriate for the chemical state and physical form of the containment.

- For protection against gases and vapors, the employer shall provide:

  - An atmosphere-supplying respirator, or
  - An air-purifying respirator provided that: (1) the respirator is equipped with an end-of-service-life indicator (ESLI) certified by NIOSH for the contaminant, or (2) if there is no ESLI appropriate for the conditions of the employer's workplace, the employer implements a "change schedule" for canisters and cartridges that will ensure that they are changed before the end of their service life and describes in the respirator program the information and data relied upon and basis for the change schedule and reliance on the data.

For protection against particulates, the employer shall provide:

An atmosphere-supplying respirator, or

An air-purifying respirator equipped with high efficiency particulate air (HEPA) filters certified by NIOSH under 30 CFR Part 11 or with filters certified for particulates under 42 CFR Part 84, or

An air purifying respirator equipped with any filter certified for particulates by NIOSH for contaminants consisting primarily of particles with mass median aerodynamic diameters of at least 2 micrometers.

- Medical Evaluation
  Employers must provide a medical evaluation to determine employee's ability to use a respirator, before fit testing and use.

  Employers must identify a physician or other licensed health care professional (PLHCP) to perform medical evaluations (information required is contained in mandatory appendix C).

  Employers must obtain a written recommendation regarding the employee's ability to use the respirator from the PLHCP.

  Additional medical evaluations are required under certain circumstances—see detailed document for examples.

  Annual review of medical status is not required.

- Fit Testing
  All employees using a negative or positive pressure tight-fitting facepiece respirator must pass an appropriate qualitative fit test (QLFT) or quantitative fit test (QNFT).

  Fit testing is required:

  Prior to use
  Whenever a different respirator facepiece is used
  At least annually thereafter

An additional fit test is required whenever the employee reports, or the employer or PLHCP makes visual observations of, changes in the employee's physical condition that could affect respirator fit—examples include:

Facial scarring
Dental changes
Cosmetic surgery
Obvious change in body weight

The fit test shall be administered using an OSHA-accepted QLFT or QNFT protocol as contained in the mandatory Appendix A.

- Use of Respirators
  Tight-fitting respirators shall not be worn by employees who have facial hair or any condition that interferes with the face-to-facepiece seal or valve function.
      Personal protective equipment shall be worn in such a manner that does not interfere with the seal of the facepiece to the face of the user.
      Employees shall perform a user seal check each time they put on a tight-fitting respirator using the procedures in mandatory Appendix B-1 or equally effective manufacturer's procedures.

- Maintenance and Care of Respirators
  Employers must clean and disinfect respirators using the procedures in Appendix B-2, or equally effective manufacturer's procedures

- Breathing Air Quality and Use
  This section refers to compressed air requirements for self contained breathing apparatus and supplied air respiratory systems. See Type 1-Grade D breathing air requirements in ANSI/CGA.

- Identification of Filters, Cartridges, and Canisters
  All filters, cartridges, and canisters used in the workplace must be labeled and color coded with the NIOSH approval label.
      The label must not be removed and must remain legible.

- Training and Information
  Employers must provide effective training to respirator users—this section lists specifics to be met.
      Training is required prior to initial use, unless acceptable training has been provided by another employer within the past twelve months.

      Retraining is required annually and when:
      Workplace conditions change
      New types of respirator are used
      Inadequacies in the employee's knowledge or use indicates need

- Program Evaluation
  Employers must conduct evaluations of the workplace as necessary to ensure proper implementation of the program and consult with employees to ensure proper use.

- Recordkeeping
  Records of medical evaluations must be retained and made available per CFR 1910.1020
  A record of fit tests must be established and retained until the next fit test.
  A written copy of the current program must be retained.

As you can see, the overview alone is lengthy and only covers the essentials of what will be needed to meet the requirements. If the hazard assessment for your medical facility indicates a need to protect employees through use of an APR then a serious look at this standard will be required.

CRITICAL THINKING

If your facility is planning on using APRs as part of an overall emergency response plan, then a quick look at the general outline and resources may be helpful in creating an APR program.

An APR program will have a general outline as follows:

- Title
- Introduction
- Organization
- Purpose
- Administration
- Definitions
- Respirator Selection
- Instruction and Training
- Cleaning and Storage
- Maintenance, Inspection and Repair
- Medical Evaluation for Personnel
- Use and Limitations
- Fit Testing
- Forms

Each section should encompass detailed information and be routinely updated. If you prefer not to reinvent the wheel, then numerous resources are available that provide guidance and examples of APR programs. Some examples of resources that may assist you are:

- The Centers for Disease Control and Prevention "CDC" Emergency Preparedness and Response Site
- The Occupational Safety and Health Administration "OSHA" Respiratory Protection 29 CFR 1910.134

- Industrial Hygienists: Industrial Hygienists may provide a host of information and guidance on APR programs.
- Universities: Local universities may have established APR programs and provide guidance.
- State and Government agencies: Numerous agencies such as health departments, law enforcement and environmental response agencies may have APR guidelines and programs.
- Local Fire Departments with HazMat teams: Your local fire department may provide assistance and guidance for APR programs.

Meeting the OSHA standard will also involve addressing issues that are not in the standard directly but are typical of everyday operations at any medical facility, such as naturally occurring personnel changes (e.g., retirement, promotion, transfer, resignation). What does it take in time and money to train and equip new personnel in order to meet the standards for respiratory protection? This may seem like an odd section to ask this question but it addresses the overall complexity of formulating a PPE program and the resources you will need to allocate to both create and maintain it. At the end of this chapter I will discuss these issues and provide an overview.

There are other standards, regulations, requirements, laws or ordinances which may play a part in developing an acceptable PPE program, not only in the United States but in other countries as well. The following is a list of standards (here "standards" is a general reference to any and all requirements, regulations, laws, ordinances or any document that refers to meeting a prescribed directive or statement that is applicable in your country) broken down by geographic region or country and only provides the standards that are currently available. I will also provide a list of standards under development as additional information ("under development" does not mean the standard will be become effective or adopted; only that it exists).

Personal Protective Equipment—Respiratory Protection Equipment

United States Standards

OSHA's Respiratory Protection Standard 29 CFR 1910.134

NIOSH's 42 CFR Part 84 Respiratory Protective Devices, Final Rules and Notice

NFPA's 1981 Standard on Open-Circuit Self-Contained Breathing Apparatus for Fire and Emergency Services

NIOSH's Chemical, Biological, Radiological and Nuclear (CBRN) Standard for Open-Circuit Self-Contained Breathing Apparatus (SCBA)

NIOSH's Standard for Chemical, Biological, Radiological and Nuclear (CBRN) Full Facepiece Air Purifying Respirator (APR)

NIOSH's Standard for Chemical, Bilogical, Radiological and Nuclear (CBRN) Air-Purifying Escape Respirator and CBRN Self-Contained Escape Respirator

ASTM's F2101-01 Standard Test Method for Evaluating the Bacterial Filtration Efficiency (BFE) of Medical Face Mask Materials

European Standards

89/656/EEC—Personal Protective Equipment, European Commission

EN 136—Respiratory Protective Devices. Full Face Masks. Requirements, Testing, Marking.

EN 140—Respiratory Protective Devices. Half Masks and Quarter Masks. Requirements, Testing, Marking.

EN 141—Respiratory Protective Devices. Gas Filters and Combined Filters. Requirements, Testing, Marking.

EN 143—Respiratory Protective Devices. Particle Filters. Requirements, Testing, Marking.

EN 149—Respiratory Protective Devices. Filtering Half Masks to Protect against Particles. Requirements, Testing, Marking.

EN 405—Respiratory Protective Devices. Valved Filtering Half Masks to Protect against Gases or Gases and Particles. Requirements, Testing, Marking.

Canadian Standards

CSA Z180.1—Compressed Breathing Air Systems

CSA Z94.4—Selection, Use and Care of Respirators

Australian/New Zealand Standards

AS/NZS 1715: 1994—Selection, Use and Maintenance of Respiratory Protective Devices.

AS/NZS 1716—Respiratory Protective Devices

NZ 13.340.30—Respiratory Protective Devices

ISO—International Organization for Standardization

TC 94/SC 15 Respiratory Protective Devices

Published Standards

ISO/TS 16976-1:2007—Respiratory Protective Devices—Human Factors—Part 1: Metabolic Rates and Respiratory Flow Rates

Standards under Development

ISO/DIS 16900-1—Respiratory Protective Devices—Methods of Test and Test Equipment—Part 1: Determination of Inward Leakage.

ISO/DIS 16900-2—Respiratory Protective Devices—Methods of Test and Test Equipment—Part 2: Determination of Breathing Resistance.

ISO/DIS 16900-3—Respiratory Protective Devices—Methods of Test and Test Equipment—Part 3: Determination of Particle Filter Penetration.

ISO/DIS 16900-4—Respiratory Protective Devices—Methods of Test and Test Equipment—Part 4: Determination of Gas Filter Capacity.

ISO/CD 16900-9—Respiratory Protective Devices—Methods of Test and Test Equipment—Part 9: Carbon Dioxide Content of the Inhaled Air (dead space).

ISO/DIS 16972—Respiratory Protective Devices—Terms, Definitions, Graphical Symbols and Units of Measurement.

ISO/CD TR 16974—Respiratory Protective Devices—Marking and Information.

ISO/CD 16975—Respiratory Protective Devices—Selection, Use and Maintenance.

ISO/TS 16976-2—Respiratory Protective Devices—Human Factors— Part 2: Anthropometrics.

ISO/TS 16976-3—Respiratory Protective Devices—Human Factors— Part 3: Physiological Responses and Limitations of Oxygen and Limitations of Carbon Dioxide in the Breathing Environment.

It should be obvious at this point that deciding on the appropriate PPE for use at your medical facility is a major undertaking and requires due diligence in reviewing available materials, design features, capabilities, compatibilities, chemical resistance, functionality, durability, shelf life, maintenance, flexibility, dexterity and vision restrictions. At this point, most individuals will actively search out an expert in the PPE field and ask for assistance with this complex task. Indeed, I highly recommend that you reach out and discuss the PPE selection process with a knowledgeable individual who can guide you through the steps. They may provide a wealth of information that helps you in choosing the most appropriate PPE.

Due to the increase in international acts of intentional contamination and terrorism, medical facilities have become acutely aware of the need to protect their staff, patients and facility should a contaminated victim arrive at their door. Likewise, these acts have necessitated that accrediting agencies develop standards that mandate the need to provide for, respond to, and mitigate potential hazards prior to them reaching the inner workings of facility and harming others.

In the past, medical facilities did not consider hiring staff based on their capabilities concerning chemicals, biological, radiological or nuclear materials. At most, medical facilities had small internal response teams designed for a specific hazard such as lab chemicals or medical radiation materials. Few facilities were ready for a major event involving mass casualties with chemical contamination. Today, medical facilities are updating and modifying emergency response plans to address these issues; to adequately respond to, provide employee protection from, and properly treat victims of a CBRN incident.

In order to create relevant PPE emergency preparedness plans, medical facility staff members have historically reached out to local fire or police departments (and possibly chemical production facilities) for guidance on proper CBRN incident response. However, specialized hazardous materials response teams require a different level of PPE preparedness than do medical facility personnel; a level that is too stringent and too impractical for a medical facility to achieve. In order to bridge this gap, agencies responsible for standards and accreditation of medical facilities modified the accepted PPE guidelines to allow for the use of powered air purifying respirators (PAPR). This adoption paved the way for hospital medical facilities to accommodate current medical staff and future hires who could not meet the respiratory protection standards as set forth for industry and emergency responders. In 2005 OSHA produced a document titled "Best Practices for Hospital-Based First Receivers of Victims from Mass Casualty Incidents Involving the Release of Hazardous Substances" (http://www.osha.gov/dts/osta/bestpractices/html/hospital_firstreceivers.html). In 2008 the American Hospital Association (AHA), as part of the Joint Commission for Emergency Management, produced a best practice document for medical facility hospitals to follow. This document details the options a medical facility has in selecting appropriate PPE. It does not, however, provide definitive PPE answers or identify one particular PPE item that is appropriate for all potential hazards. Instead, it recognizes the unique position that medical facilities are faced with considering they may be the first receivers of victims exposed to hazardous substances.

An overview of these documents may provide some guidance on what best suits your medical facility based on your hazard assessment. The OSHA best practices document stresses due caution and reinforces that the "employee's role and the hazards that an employee might encounter dictate the level of training that must be provided to any individual first receiver. PPE selection must be based on a hazard assessment that carefully considers both of these factors" (OSHA, 2005). With that in mind, the first PPE selection criteria for the medical facility (hospital) setting should be based on the employee's role for response during a hazardous substance incident. The second PPE selection criteria will be based on the hazards the employee may be faced with (known or unknown).

The OSHA document also provides a statement concerning unknown substances which reads:

OSHA specifies PPE that hospitals could use to effectively protect first receivers assisting victims contaminated with *unknown substances*, provided the hospital meets certain prerequisite conditions designed to minimize the quantity of the substance to which first receivers might be exposed. This PPE for first receivers includes: a PAPR with an assigned protection factor of 1,000, a chemical-resistant protective garment, head covering if it is not already included in the respirator, a double layer of protective gloves, and chemical-protective boots.

The document also adds this statement as a reminder to be prepared for anything:

As part of OSHA's required hazard assessment process, each hospital also must consider the specific hazards first receivers might reasonably be expected to encounter. The hospital must then augment OSHA's PPE selection when necessary to provide adequate protection against those specific identified hazards.

Finally, this document cautions that a "higher level of protection" may be necessary for medical facilities that anticipate "providing specialized services" at the incident site.

The document also provides defining statements to clarify who first receivers are. In the document it states: "Healthcare workers at a hospital receiving contaminated victims for treatment may be termed *first receivers*" (Koenig, 2003). The document continues with an explanation of the basis for creating a subset to the term "first responder" which generally refers to firefighters, law enforcement, HazMat teams and ambulance service personnel. The first responder is typically at the incident site (location of the primary release); the medical facility is considered remote from the primary release site and "thus, the possible exposure of first receivers is limited to the quantity of substance arriving at the hospital as a contaminant on victims and their clothing or personal effects" (Horton et al., 2003).

In defining hazardous incident roles at a medical facility (hospital), the document makes this statement: "First receivers typically include personnel in the following roles: clinicians and other hospital staff who have a role in receiving and treating contaminated victims (e.g., triage, decontamination, medical treatment, and security) and those whose roles support these functions (e.g., emergency treatment area set up and patient tracking)." The importance of fully identifying the personnel who will respond to incidents at your facility and providing adequate PPE for them should not be overlooked. The first medical facility personnel to encounter the contaminated victims may be security personnel or emergency room staff, particularly if little or no notice of their arrival was provided. Ensuring these personnel are properly prepared and afforded PPE in order to meet their dual role of protecting themselves and caring for their patients is paramount.

The best practices document also highlights the need to augment your PPE when necessary and provides the following: "The best practices presented in this document indicate the minimum PPE that OSHA anticipates generally will be needed to protect first receivers faced with a wide range of unknown hazards." "When a hospital determines that first receivers could reasonably anticipate encountering a specific known hazard, the hospital also must determine whether this generalized protection must be supplemented to more fully address that specific hazard." "The Joint Commission requires that hospitals also consider their anticipated roles and coordinate activities with other emergency response agencies and hospitals within the community. When these sources point to a *specific* substance or situation from which the hospital should protect its first receivers, the hospital must confirm that PPE selection provides effective protection against that hazard."

The best practices document does provide recommendations and/or practical choices when selecting PPE for use by first receivers, yet it includes stipulations that are conditional and must be met prior to utilizing the recommended minimum PPE. Tables 3.1 and 3.2 identify prerequisite conditions that hospitals must meet to allow for the use of the minimum first receiver PPE found in Table 3.3.

As part of the document, OSHA does provide a statement concerning helmet/hood PAPR's which states: "OSHA concludes that PAPRs with helmet/hoods are a practical choice for first receivers. Helmet/hood PAPRs require no fit testing, can be worn by employees with facial hair and eye glasses, and are generally considered by most workers to be more comfortable than negative pressure APRs."

The above information provides guidance on the selection of PPE and assists in formulating a PPE plan that will address your needs. What the document does not specify is which garment material should be utilized, and with good reason. Not only are there numerous garments available, but there is a plethora of data for each—from technical information supplied by the manufacturers to independent studies on performance—that should be reviewed before deciding what is most appropriate for your needs. An additional concern is of course the constant advancement in garment material technology and value. The OSHA Best Practices document does mention protective garment types by product name but makes the disclaimer that "OSHA does not test, endorse, or recommend specific products." The same will hold true for this book, as new protective garments are routinely brought to market and have superior capabilities and/or features. The OSHA document states that "Manufacturers produce a variety of suit fabrics and designs, and several commercially available broad-spectrum protective fabrics might be appropriate, depending on the situations and hazards that the hospital anticipates first receivers reasonably might be expected to encounter."

Table 3.1 Hospital Decontamination Zone

Conditions Necessary for Hospitals to Rely on the Personal Protective Equipment (PPE) Selection Presented in Table 3.3 [A, B]

1. Thorough and complete hazard vulnerability analysis (HVA) and emergency management plan (EMP), which consider community input, have been conducted/developed, and have been updated within the past year.
2. The EMP includes plans to assist the numbers of victims that the community anticipates might seek treatment at this hospital, keeping in mind that the vast majority of victims may self-refer to the nearest hospital.
3. Preparations specified in the EMP have been implemented (e.g., employee training, equipment selection, maintenance, and a respiratory protection program).
4. The EMP includes methods for handling the numbers of ambulatory and non-ambulatory victims anticipated by the community.
5. The hazardous substance was not released in close proximity to the hospital, and the lapse time between the victims' exposure and victims' arrival at the hospital exceeds approximately 10 minutes, thereby permitting substantial levels of gases and vapors from volatile substances time to dissipate.[C]
6. Victims' contaminated clothing and possessions are promptly removed and contained (e.g., in an approved hazardous waste container that is isolated outdoors), and decontamination is initiated promptly upon arrival at the hospital. Hospital EMP includes shelter, tepid water, soap, privacy, and coverings to promote victim compliance with decontamination procedures.
7. EMP procedures are in place to ensure that contaminated medical waste and wastewater do not become a secondary source of employee exposure.

And

8. The decontamination system and pre-decontamination victim waiting areas are designed and used in a manner that promotes constant fresh air circulation through the system to limit hazardous substance accumulation.[D] Air exchange from a clean source has been considered in the design of fully enclosed systems (i.e., through consultation with professional engineer or certified industrial hygienist) and air is not re-circulated.

So what PPE should one purchase to fit the needs of a medical facility? It depends on your responses to the information above and your review of currently available garments, suits, fabrics, materials and the design features they offer. As a general recommendation you may want to look for the following:

Protective Garment—A broad spectrum chemical, biological, radiological, nuclear (CBRN) rated and certified garment with liquid/splash resistant closure design features.

Gloves—Options here are less definitive as multiple layering and glove thickness (mm thickness) are part of the deciding factors. A least two gloves designed from different materials should be worn simultaneously, as multiple layers of different CBRN-resistant materials will repel the broadest range of chemicals. Generally

Table 3.2 Hospital *Post*-decontamination Zone

Conditions Necessary for Hospitals to Rely on the Personal Protective Equipment (PPE) Selection Presented in Table 3.3 [E, F]

1. Emergency management plan (EMP) is developed and followed in a way that minimizes the emergency department (ED) personnel's reasonably anticipated contact with contaminated victims (e.g., with drills that test communication between the hospital and emergency responders at the incident site to reduce the likelihood of unanticipated victims).
2. Decontamination system (in the Hospital Decontamination Zone) and hospital security can be activated promptly to minimize the chance that victims will enter the ED and contact unprotected staff prior to decontamination.
3. EMP procedures specify that unannounced victims (once identified as possibly contaminated) disrobe in the appropriate decontamination area (not the ED) and follow hospital decontamination procedures before admission (or re-admission) to the ED.
4. Victims in this area were previously decontaminated by a shower with soap and water, including a minimum of 5 minutes under running water. Shower instructions are clearly presented and enforced. Shower facility encourages victim compliance (e.g., shelter, tepid water, reasonable degree of privacy).
5. EMP procedures clearly specify actions ED clerks or staff will take if they suspect a patient is contaminated. For example: 1) do not physically contact the patient, 2) immediately notify supervisor and safety officer of possible hospital contamination, and 3) allow qualified personnel to isolate and decontaminate the victim.

And

6. The EMP requires that if the ED becomes contaminated, that space is no longer eligible to be considered a Hospital Post-decontamination Zone. Instead, it should be considered contaminated and all employees working in this area should use PPE as described for the Hospital Decontamination Zone (see Table 3.3).

the inner glove is of nitrile material, followed by a butyl or foil-based glove. The number of gloves worn simultaneously is an individual hospital preference, with two being the expected minimum. The outer layer material and stacking design is also up to the individual hospital. The general concept is to provide an inner protective glove with dexterity followed by a CBRN-resistant glove and perhaps an outer glove with CBRN resistance and grip. Millimeter (mm) thickness is the other concern here, as it determines the dexterity an individual may have in performing tasks and may vary from 4 to 14 mm, It is highly recommended that you try different glove thickness combinations to determine the most acceptable layered design for your hospital personnel.

Boots—A similar situation occurs here as with the gloves; numerous boots that meet CBRN-resistant certification are available. Also, the material should match the capabilities of the garment and the gloves. Along with the CBRN resistance

Table 3.3 Minimum Personal Protective Equipment (PPE)

For Hospital-based First Receivers of Victims from Mass Casualty Incidents Involving the Release of Unknown Hazardous Substances

Scope And Limitations	
This Table Applies When	
• The hospital is not the release site.[G] • Prerequisite conditions of hospital eligibility are already met (Tables 3.1 and 3.2).	• The identity of the hazardous substance is unknown.[H]

Note: This table is part of, and intended to be used with, the document entitled *OSHA Best Practices for Hospital-based First Receivers of Victims from Mass Casualty Incidents Involving the Release of Hazardous Substances.*

Zone	Minimum PPE
Hospital Decontamination Zone[I] • All employees in this zone (Includes, but not limited to, any of the following employees: decontamination team members, clinicians, set-up crew, cleanup crew, security staff, and patient tracking clerks.)	• Powered air-purifying respirator (PAPR) that provides a protection factor of 1,000.[J] The respirator must be NIOSH-approved.[K] • Combination 99.97% high-efficiency particulate air (HEPA)/organic vapor/acid gas respirator cartridges (also NIOSH-approved). • Double layer protective gloves.[L] • Chemical resistant suit. • Head covering and eye/face protection (if not part of the respirator). • Chemical-protective boots. • Suit openings sealed with tape.
Hospital Post-decontamination Zone[M] • All employees in this zone	• Normal work clothes and PPE, as necessary, for infection control purposes (e.g., gloves, gown, appropriate respirator).

CRITICAL THINKING

Numerous hospital emergency response teams have developed techniques for glove configurations that will work during HERT operations.

One technique is to wear multiple layers of gloves and number them. As each set of gloves is used and becomes contaminated it can be removed and a new pair will be ready for the next patient. By numbering the gloves the team member can quickly ascertain how many he or she has left. The drawback to this technique is the bulk of multiple layers and loss of dexterity. A second technique is to re-glove as needed to prevent cross contamination. This technique requires readily accessible clean gloves and consistency in changing out the gloves.

rating you should consider the design features of the boot as they apply to durability, flexibility, non-slip tread design, ease of access and closure, and sizing.

Respiratory—The current consensus and OSHA statement concludes that PAPRs with helmet/hoods are a practical choice, but not the only choice. The highest level of respiratory protection is a Self-Contained Breathing Apparatus (SCBA) or Supplied Air System but these are generally heavy and bulky, with the SCBA having a limited working time frame. Air Purifying Respirators (APRs) require full compliance with standards for respiratory protection, which is obtainable but more intense. A full facepiece PAPR is another option but requires fit testing and meeting the respiratory protection standards. An option here is the PAPR with a disposable helmet/hood, which may be a good choice so long as the hooded garment material meets the CBRN certifications and ratings.

Tape Adhesive—No medical facility PPE ensemble is complete until you cover those openings and gaps normally found where one item meets another (e.g., the wrist, ankle, and neck areas). Chemically resistant, adhesive-backed tape designed for the purpose of closing those gaps are available. Ensure that the tape is designed and certified for CBRN materials and compatible with the ensemble materials you have chosen. Also ensure that the adhesive is compatible with the design features of the ensemble and will not degrade or alter the CBRN capabilities of the gloves, boots or respiratory protection equipment.

Personal Protective Equipment—Protective clothing standards are listed below and include other country and international standards. Some standards are under revision or development and thus may change. Routinely check these standards to stay abreast of changes that might affect your response plan.

Personal Protective Equipment—Protective Clothing U.S. Standards/ Canadian Standards

> OSHA 29 CFR 1910.120—HAZWOPER, Hazardous Waste Operations and Emergency Response.
>
> EPA Regulation 40 CFR Part 311—Worker Protection (This regulation mirrors the OSHA 29 CFR 1910.120 for U.S. States that do not have an OSHA approved State Plan).
>
> OSHA 29 CFR 1910.132—Personal Protective Equipment
>
> NFPA 1991—Standard on Vapor-Protective Ensembles for Hazardous Materials Emergencies.
>
> NFPA 1992—Liquid Splash-Protective Ensemble for Hazardous Materials Emergencies.
>
> NFPA 1994—Standard on Protective Ensembles for Chemical/Biological Terrorism Incidents.

NFPA 1999—Standard on Protective Clothing for Emergency Medical Operations.

European Standards

CEN/TR 15419:2006—Protective Clothing. Guidelines for Selection, Use, Care and Maintenance of Chemical Protective Clothing.

EN 14126:2003—Protective Clothing. Performance Requirements and Test Methods for Protective Clothing against Infective Agents.

BS 7184:2001—Selection, Use and Maintenance of Chemical Protective Clothing.

Guidance

BS 8467:2006—Protective Clothing—Personal Protective Ensembles for Use against Chemical, Biological, Radiological and Nuclear (CBRN) Agents. Categorization, Performance Requirements and Test Methods.

EN 13034:2005—Protective Clothing

IS EN 340:2004—Protective Clothing, General Requirements

BS EN 943:2002—Protective Clothing against Liquid and Gaseous Chemicals, Aerosols and Solid Particles.

EN ISO 13982-1:2004—Protective Clothing against Liquid Chemicals

Australian/New Zealand Standards

SAA HB9—1994—Occupational Personal Protection

AS 3765.1—1990—Clothing for Protection against Hazardous Chemicals. Part 1: Protection against General or Specific Chemicals.

AS/NZS ISO 13994:2006—Clothing for Protection against Chemicals. Determination of the Resistance of Protective Clothing Materials to Penetration by Liquids under Pressure.

AS/NZS 4501.1:2008—Occupational Protective Clothing—Guidelines on Selection, Use, Care and Maintenance of Protective Clothing.

NZ 13.340.10—Protective Clothing

ISO—International Organization for Standardization

13.340.10—Protective Clothing

Published Standards

ISO 6529:2001—Protective Clothing—Protection against Chemicals— Determination of Resistance of Protective Clothing Materials to Permeation by Liquids and Gases.

ISO 8194:1987—Radiation Protection—Clothing for Protection against Radioactive Contamination—Design, Selection, Testing and Use.

ISO 13688:1998—Protective Clothing—General Requirements

ISO 13982-1:2004—Protective Clothing for Use against Solid Particulates—Part 1: Performance Requirements for Chemical Protective Clothing Providing Protection to the Full Body against Airborne Solid Particulates (Type 5 Clothing).

ISO 16602:2007—Protective Clothing for Protection against Chemicals—Classification, Labeling and Performance Requirements.

ISO17491-4:2008—Protective Clothing—Test Methods for Clothing Providing Protection against Chemicals—Part 4: Determination of Resistance to Penetration by a Spray of Liquid.

ISO 22612:2005—Clothing for Protection against Infectious Agents—Test Method for Resistance to Dry Microbial Penetration.

Standards Under Development

ISO/AWI 13688—Protective Clothing—General Requirements.

ISO/DIS 17491-1—Protective Clothing—Test Methods for Clothing Providing Protection against Chemicals—Part 1: Determination of Resistance to Inward Leakage of Gases (Internal Pressure Test).

ISO/DIS 17491-2—Protective Clothing—Test Methods for Clothing Providing Protection against Chemicals—Part 2: Determination of Resistance to Inward Leakage of Aerosols and Gases (Inward Leakage Test).

Components of Protective Ensembles

Descriptions of protective equipment seem somewhat unnecessary, as PPE simply consists of suit, boots, gloves and PAPR. But in actuality these items are highly sophisticated materials that are constructed and manufactured for specific purposes. It is only when you take a closer look at them that you realize the balance between the complex structural materials that offer protection and the components that integrate garment with human interface. Sounds a little out there, but it's true; the materials we use to protect ourselves come from years of research and development by companies you may have never heard of. That research and development has resulted in some of the most advanced materials you can find that work under the most adverse conditions we can imagine.

In case you don't believe the complexity involved, consider the magnitude of what we are asking. We have asked the chemical engineers and manufacturers to design a material that will protect us from toxic and corrosive liquids, solids and gases, as well as radiological materials, biological agents, and flammable and combustible products. We have demanded that the material be flexible so we can move freely. It must be functional in every environmental condition we can expect to find ourselves in: rain, heat, cold, dust and dirt, wind, ultraviolet rays, direct sunlight and artificial light. It must also be able to withstand and resist abrasion, punctures and penetration and be flame retardant as well. And finally, it must be able to sit in storage for months on end and be ready to work on a moment's notice.

Indeed, we are asking a great deal of the product and yet our expectations are met by engineers and scientists who spend their careers formulating the right substance to accomplish the task. More recently, we have added chemical and biological warfare materials to the list of CBRN materials these suits are designed to protect against. Still, the engineers have answered this demand and there are now a host of certifications and ratings that indicate a material's ability to resist warfare products and be considered "CBRN compliant."

The commercial industry companies have responded with products that meet our demands and continue to evolve even better products for the future. So the question may not be how many components make up a protective ensemble, but how do the components work together and what are the areas of weakness? To address the components we will need to look at the different levels of protection and point out some features. To remain consistent here I will utilize the OSHA guidance for levels of protection 29 CFR 1910.120 and refer you to the NFPA standards 1991, 1992, 1994 and 1999. Other standards may apply depending on your location and should be reviewed. The following list of standards is by no means comprehensive and the reader is encouraged to check for current versions, updates, and any new standards produced.

Levels of Protection are generally referenced as Level "A," Level "B," Level "C" and Level "D" and include both the level of risk and the level of protection required to meet that assigned level. Starting with Level "A" we can break the components down and identify their function or purpose.

Level A: Selected when the greatest level of skin, respiratory, and eye protection is required.

Components:

- A positive pressure, full face-piece self-contained breathing apparatus (SCBA), or positive pressure supplied air respirator with escape SCBA, approved by the National Institute for Occupational Safety and Health (NIOSH).
- A totally encapsulating chemical-protective suit.
- Coveralls (optional).
- Long underwear (optional).
- Gloves, outer, chemical-resistant.

- Gloves, inner, chemical-resistant.
- Boots, chemical-resistant, steel toe and shank.
- Hard hat (under suit) (optional).
- A disposable protective suit, gloves and boots (depending on suit construction, may be worn over totally encapsulating suit).

Level B: The highest level of respiratory protection is necessary but a lesser level of skin protection is needed.
Components:

- Positive pressure, full face-piece self-contained breathing apparatus (SCBA), or positive pressure supplied air respirator with escape SCBA (NIOSH approved).
- Hooded chemical-resistant clothing (overalls and long-sleeved jacket; coveralls; one or two-piece chemical-splash suit; disposable chemical-resistant overalls).
- Coveralls (optional).
- Gloves, outer, chemical-resistant
- Gloves, inner, chemical-resistant
- Boots, outer, chemical-resistant steel toe and shank
- Boot-covers, outer, chemical-resistant (disposable) (optional).
- Hard hat (optional).
- Face shield (optional).

Level C: The concentration(s) and type(s) of airborne substance(s) is known and the criteria for using air purifying respirators are met.
Components:

- Full-face or half-mask, air purifying respirators (NIOSH approved).
- Hooded chemical-resistant clothing (overalls; two-piece chemical-splash suit; disposable chemical-resistant overalls).
- Coveralls (optional).
- Gloves, outer, chemical-resistant
- Gloves, inner, chemical-resistant.
- Boots (outer), chemical-resistant steel toe and shank.
- Boot-covers, outer, chemical-resistant (disposable) (optional).
- Hard hat (optional).
- Escape mask (optional).
- Face shield (optional).

Level D: A work uniform affording minimal protection: used for nuisance contamination only.

Components:

- Coveralls.
- Gloves (optional).
- Boots/shoes, chemical-resistant steel toe and shank.
- Boots, outer, chemical-resistant (disposable) (optional).
- Safety glasses or chemical splash goggles (optional).
- Hard hat (optional).
- Escape mask (optional).
- Face shield (optional).

A legitimate item to discuss here is the integration of multiple components into a functional protective suit. For the Level A ensemble (totally encapsulating protective suit), you would not need to address the integration of multiple components, but the chemical protective materials of the Level A ensemble do require protection from a harsh working environment, specifically—abrasion, puncture and penetration. Boots provide protection from rough surfaces and sharp objects that you may have to walk on, outer gloves provide the same protection and should offer additional grip for working with tools or griping handrails. Both the outer gloves and the boots have dual functions: first is chemical resistance, the second is protection from abrasion, puncture and penetrating objects or materials. The same will hold true for all four levels of protection and components should address those specific issues.

The remaining items used with the Level A suit are found inside the totally encapsulating suit. These items are designed to address functionality inside a confining garment and the ability to access them if a need arises. Having the SCBA inside the suit is a plus for protecting the SCBA from exposure to CBRN substances or materials. It also places all the control and safety devices inside the suit and makes accessing those controls somewhat difficult. Communicating to others through a face-piece and then through the garment material is virtually impossible. Two options are available to address this: one is to use hand signals that allow for easy interpretation of what you wish to communicate, the second is an electronic intrinsically safe two-way radio system. The second option is obviously best for direct verbal communications. This system may also be designed for hands free communications, eliminating the need to push a button or switch.

Level A suits are rarely utilized in the medical facility hospital setting due to the restrictive nature of the totally encapsulating design and the limited amount of available air in the breathing tank if SCBA is used.

For Levels B and C the same issues apply to protecting the suit material, so no further mention of those items is needed. Level B suits can be similar to Level A suits in design and appearance: the suit covers and encloses the individual and all the associated equipment including the SCBA, but the suit will have a small opening that allows atmospheric air to enter the suit. This small opening is covered to reduce the possibility of liquids making an entry, but is otherwise open to the atmosphere. A second type of Level B suit is one in which the SCBA is on the outside of the garment and is exposed to the elements, including the hazard you are facing. For Level B suits, integrating the suit, gloves, boots and SCBA or supplied air face-piece is important. The points of integration here will be the same for Level C suits with the exception of helmet/hood PAPR use. Starting at the top of the head and moving down, the first piece to integrate will be the face-piece to the hood of the garment (this is not the hood from the PAPR but the hood attached to the Level C garment). Generally you can overlap the stretchable part of the hood onto the outer edge of the face-piece. This will be followed by taping the hood to the face-piece (use a chemically resistant tape only, designed and certified for CBRN resistance). Start at the bottom and work your way up with the last piece at the center top area; this allows for overlapping of the tape so that liquids will flow down and over the seams (the same pattern as used on home roof shingles). The next area is the neck and front closure seam—use the same pattern. The wrist and ankle areas both need to be integrated, so that the glove mates with the sleeve and the boot mates with the leg section. A single piece of tape is needed to cover the circumference of each location. Place a folded tab at the end of the tape to make it easy to remove when desired. Some Level B and C suits come with a boot flap cover which will eliminate the need to tape the boot to the suit.

The components of the personal protective ensembles have primarily remained the same for some time now and generally are classified as:

- Respiratory Protection—SCBA, Supplied Air Systems, PAPRs, APRs or masks
- Skin Protection—encapsulating suits, splash-protective and coveralls
- Gloves—chemical protective and high grip
- Boots—chemical protective and non-slip
- Tape—chemically resistant and strong bonding
- Communications—radio or hand signal

When using the helmet/hooded PAPR system, one only needs to integrate the hood to the suit if a secondary internal hood piece is part of the hood design. If this is the case, then the internal hood is generally layered inside the suit at the neck area to add protection to the wearer. The PARP itself is attached around the waist in a belt type system with the intake cartridges/filter canisters located on the wearer's lower back. Integration here consists of ensuring the PAPR components are securely attached to the system and that they remain attached to the wearer even when leaning over objects.

An additional component that may be desired is a cooling vest system. This will only be necessary if the atmospheric temperature and humidity could be detrimental to the individual's ability to accomplish tasks while in personal protective equipment. Cooling vest systems come in a range of options and careful evaluation of these options should be considered prior to acquiring the system. A cooling vest system can be a double-edged sword: the benefit is that the wearer keeps their chest area cooler and can function better under elevated temperature and humidity conditions. The drawback is the additional weight the individual will have to bear during the work time frame. Clearly, the climate conditions your facility will face will dictate whether there is a need for cool vest systems.

The overall picture on components for a personal protective equipment system should be one of meeting standards and ensuring that the associated components enhance the suit capabilities and functionality while negating any detrimental aspects that may be inherent in the design.

The following is a list of manufacturing companies (in alphabetical order only) who produce personal protective ensembles. The list is not all inclusive but does represent most of the manufacturers in this field.

Dupont, E.I. du Pont de Nemouirs & Co.	Delaware, United States
Draeger Safety Inc.	Luebeck, Germany
Geomet Technologies LLC	Maryland, United States
Kappler Inc.	Alabama, United States
Lakeland Industries	Alabama, United States
Lion Apparel	Ohio, United States
Microgard LTD.	Kingston Upon Hull, United Kingdom
MSA	Pennsylvania, United States
New Pac Safety AB	Habo, Sweden
Paul Boye' Technologies	Le Vernet, France
Remploy Frontliner	Mersceyside, United Kingdom
Respirex International Limited	Surrey, England
Saint-Gobain Performance Plastics ChemFab	New Hampshire, United States
Sigmon Group LLC	Virginia, United States
Texplorer Gmbh	Nettetal, Germany
Tex Shield Inc.	North Carolina, United States
Trelleborg Viking Inc.	Norway, Sweden

I recommend the following guideline as an excellent source of technical information for the selection of PPE by first responders. The guide is comprehensive and informative:

The National Institute of Standards and Technology for the United States Department of Homeland Security. *Guide for the Selection of Personal Protective Equipment for Emergency First Responders*, 2nd Edition, Guide 102–06.

Hazards Associated with Utilization of PPE

Advancements in technology have saved numerous individuals around the world and yet the act of placing yourself inside a protective cocoon may place you at risk. From birth, we learn and advance our knowledge by interacting with the world around us; the ability to touch, see and hear are critical assets by which we navigate the hazards of, and enjoy the wonders of, life. The use of PPE to protect us during CBRN incidents comes with restraints that affect our useful tools: those of our senses. The loss or reduction of any sense is disturbing and difficult, the reduction or limitation of several human senses simultaneously is even more difficult to overcome, but not impossible.

Starting with the obvious, we can appreciate the hazards presented by the loss of touch or skin sensation. The medical community has become accustomed to using gloves as a level of protection in virtually all aspects of medical care and hospital operations. Yet the goal is to design the thinnest glove possible to afford the closest approximation to the sensation of human touch. The idea, of course, is to allow the healthcare worker to sense their actions as closely as possible to actual physical contact, which in turn allows for better skills. The idea of a physical barrier as a level of protection has proven to be the best option and has become a standard of practice in the medical community.

So what does it mean when workers have to wear two or three pairs of gloves simultaneously? It means sense of touch is drastically reduced, actions are more difficult, and the work requires greater concentration. If we expand this sensory reduction to include all of our skin, such as when we are in a Level C protection ensemble, it becomes obvious that normal sensory indicators are drastically reduced or lost altogether. Our sense of touch is a valuable asset in daily life and work, the reduction of that ability while wearing PPE will require the wearer to refocus and concentrate on their actions to ensure safe operations in the CBRN environment.

The next issue to address is reduction or loss of hearing. First, placing a material barrier (the suit) over your ears greatly reduces, if not almost entirely stops, sounds from making their way to your ear. Add ambient noises from the PARP blower motors and general background noises and a difficult task has just been made harder. Communicating while wearing PPE remains a struggle even under the best conditions. When communication is misunderstood there is a good chance an error will occur. This hazard remains at the top of list of problems to resolve; currently the best solution is to use two-way radio systems.

Wearing face-pieces and hoods as part of your PPE will limit your vision. Advances in high tech polymers have greatly improved the clarity of these clear protective barriers, but we are still faced with distortion and limited fields of vision. Compensating for individuals who wear glasses adds another level of complexity. Even those who can comfortably wear their glasses inside the hooded PAPR may still have the issue of fogging. Visual limitation by far causes the most frustration and requires wearers to exercise caution as they work. Safety issues such as trips, falls and unseen objects are a never-ending concern. Options for improving vision are limited; accommodations for wearing contact lenses or glasses will certainly aid in making the PPE wearer more comfortable, but does not resolve the distortion found in the clear barrier face-pieces and hoods. Face-pieces, by design, offer limited peripheral vision; hoods offer larger visual areas but may display distortions from flexibility and curvature of the clear shield. Most face shields will scatter light, especially at night, thus impeding visual acuity. Numerous products are on the market to help resolve shield or eyeglasses fogging, and trying different ones for hot or cold conditions will allow you to determine the best product for your facility. The nighttime light scatter currently has no resolution and remains problematic.

PPE brings with it another hazard: heat and heat dissipation. Once inside the PPE ensemble, the wearer is now faced with the issue of dissipating body heat. The garment material is designed to act as a barrier against CBRN substances, but it also acts to retain the heat your body produces. This, of course, leads to environmental heat factors inside the suit that place you at risk of heat stress, heat exhaustion, and if unattended, heat stroke or exacerbation of any number of medical issues. The main options available here are using a cool vest system if available and limiting the duration of work in PPE, based on the atmospheric conditions you will be exposed to.

A final consideration should be one of a personal nature. Confining and restricting PPE can make individuals feel uneasy at best and claustrophobic at worst. Individuals should be prepared to use such confining and stressful PPE and be aware of their own limitations.

As part of any PPE program there should be a pre and post medical evaluation conducted on each individual who will be in PPE during an incident. In fact, OSHA's Best Practices for Hospital-Based First Receivers of Victims requires this be accomplished.

Patience and diligence are the name of the game here. The wearer should routinely practice wearing and working in PPE to become skilled in using the equipment, know their limitations while wearing it, and learn which adjustments must be made to compensate for those limitations.

Logistical Considerations

The equipment you will utilize for response in the CBRN setting is highly specialized and requires proper storage and preparation to ensure functionality at the time of use. The first consideration starts even before you purchase the item. This step requires that you review the manufacturers' documentation and instructional information and take note of the recommended storage and maintenance section. PPE manufacturers all provide specific storage and maintenance requirements to ensure the PPE functions as warranted and provides the level of protection you had anticipated when you purchased the item.

Manufacturers also indicate the "shelf" life for the PPE you purchase, which describes the time a PPE item may remain in its original packaging before deterioration, degradation or material breakdown occurs and the PPE no longer meets the original standard for which it was manufactured. Shelf life includes product storage conditions as indicated by the manufacturer, otherwise the shelf life cannot be considered a valid time frame. If an item's shelf life expires, then it will be necessary to replace that item. Relegating the outdated garment for use in training is one way to obtain additional value from your purchase.

Another manufacturing term found in the PPE technical data sheet is the phrase "limited use." If this term is noted, then the inferred reference is that it is a "single use" item. PPE items with a limited use indication should be considered disposable and should not be used again following a onetime exposure during a CBRN incident. There are many reasons why a manufacturer may label a garment as having limited use. One reason is the risk that a contaminant may pose at the molecular level of the garment, if removal by typical onsite decontamination processes fail. This can pose a serious contamination risk and often disposal of the garment is the best option. The cost of having the PPE item cleaned by a professional company and then certified as clean and free of any contamination is generally cost-prohibitive as compared to purchasing a new PPE item. It is also highly likely that the PPE item received wear and tear while being worn, resulting in damage of the PPE protective material, thus allowing for a failure point in the material.

In general, the PPE items you purchase should be considered single use items and use should be viewed similarly to the common practice of only using gloves once in the hospital setting. The exception will be the respiratory protection item you choose. For APRs, the cartridge/canister/filter is the only single use item and must be properly disposed of following its use; the remaining components must be properly decontaminated and certified clean prior to reuse. For the PAPR, the cartridge/canister/filter and disposable hood is a single use item and must be properly disposed of following its use; the remaining components must be properly decontaminated and certified clean prior to reuse. If a SCBA is utilized then it will need to be properly decontaminated and certified clean prior to reuse unless it was inside the protective envelope of an encapsulating suit.

Another consideration if using a PAPR is the battery that powers the unit. These batteries require charging, battery cycling, and exercise. The manufacturer's instruction sheet will provide the necessary procedures to follow to ensure full functionality of the battery. PAPRs and APRs both require the use of cartridges/canisters/filters, which come with an instruction sheet that notes the expiration date and explains proper storage requirements. Cartridges/canisters/filters are shipped sealed for protection from the atmospheric elements and should remain sealed until needed; this ensures maximum functionality when the cartridge/canister/filter is needed.

A final point to think about is the storage location of the PPE. A location that is central to the expected patient/victim receiving area may be most advantageous for responding team members and may be an optimum site as it allows for quick retrieval of all equipment, staging and dress-out of personnel. It may take some effort to locate and create such a site, but it is well worth the effort when the time comes to deploy the team.

Sustainment Considerations

Many factors come into play when you describe what it will take to sustain an emergency operation such as a CBRN event. The first is personnel: how many qualified and trained members do you have on staff? How many individuals do you have available as backup? The answers to these questions are unique to your medical facility and the size of your work force. The size and scope of your response team will have a direct impact on your facility's ability to initiate, support and sustain the PPE program.

PPE program sustainment includes accommodating variations in height and weight, as PPE will need to fit and allow functionality for a wide range of individuals. Replacement of stocked PPE items whose expiration or shelf life has passed is an important consideration, as is having backup PPE on hand, should an item tear, break or become unusable at any point.

To summarize, there are several issues to consider when creating a maintenance and sustainment program.

- Ensure that extra equipment is available and meets the size requirements of all individuals.
- Create a staggered expiration/shelf life program to allow for ready use of items at any given time.
- Create a maintenance schedule for battery cycling and peak performance.
- Locate a suitable location for storage that meets the recommendations of the manufacturer.

Related Worldwide Considerations— International Look

On an international scale, the type of available PPE is generally similar, if not the same from country to country. The number of manufacturers who produce these highly specialized items is limited and thus the choices are relatively limited. This by no means indicates that these companies are not competitive and constantly developing new and improved PPE and features. A quick look at the manufacturers I've listed in the "Components of Protective Ensembles" section provides an indication of the worldwide market they encompass (nine of those companies are headquartered in the United States and seven in the United Kingdom). Their reach is vast as well, with affiliated offices in the Russian Federation, Norway, South East Asia, the United Arab Emirates and Lithuania.

On a global scale the use and type of PPE varies greatly within an organized emergency response team associated with or as part of the medical facility hospital setting. Countries, cities and towns who have faced terrorist/criminal attacks or who may have large scale chemical industrial complexes would have been acutely aware of the need to protect their facilities and have formulated response teams. Many others may not see the need to prepare or feel they are less likely to have to deal with a CBRN event. The economic and social climate of a country may also play a part in the capability of a medical facility to address supporting a CBRN team, if basic medical care is their primary focus. A push to better prepare and respond to CBRN incidents has been internationally supported through regulations, standards and guidelines, all of which have moved many a medical facility to improve their response capabilities or face a devastating hazardous incident. Many medical facilities have been aggressive in purporting and creating the means and equipment to accomplish this task, while others have been reluctant and pessimistic about moving forward on this issue, leaving them vulnerable should an incident occur. I believe the incident orchestrated by the Aum Shinrikyo Cult and its leader Shoko Asahara provides a classic example of the consequences when we are unable to readily identify the substance involved and are unprepared to respond and protect our personnel and facility.

Case Study—The Tokyo Subway Chemical Agent (Liquid Sarin) Attack

March 20, 1995. Tokyo, Japan. 07:00–08:10 am, Monday
Tokyo Metro, Commuter Transport Systems (subway).
Morning rush hour on one of the world's busiest subway systems.

The main perpetrators of the attack were ten individuals who had been partnered together as a getaway driver and a human chemical agent delivery device. They belonged to the cult group Aum Shinrikyo, an apocalyptic philosophy group led by Shoko Asahara. The attack sites were five subway trains that passed through Kasumigaseki and Nagatacho, centers of the Japanese government. Five individuals each carrying plastic bags wrapped in newspaper and carrying an umbrella with a sharpened tip boarded their assigned train in the middle of Monday morning rush hour and then punctured the bags carrying liquid sarin. The resulting release of the liquid sarin onto the floors of the commuter trains and the vaporization of liquid to gas in ambient temperature in the crowded trains affected thousands of commuters.

Of the 5,510 patients seen at hospitals, 688 were transported by ambulance; the remaining reached a hospital by other means. Of those 5,510 patients, 17 were critical, 37 were severe and 984 were indicated to be moderately ill with vision problems. There were 12 recorded deaths attributed to the attack.

In a lessons learned report from "Pre-hospital Disaster Medicine 2000;15(3):s30, Department of Acute Medicine, Kawasaki Medical School Hospital, Kurashiki-City, Okayama, Japan" two major lessons, one developed team and one created office are cited in the summary.

- The absence of decontamination
  - In total 1,364 EMTs were dispatched, and among them 135 were secondarily affected.
  - At St. Luke's hospital, 23% of the medical staff complained of symptoms and signs of secondary exposure.
  - The religious cult used a 30% sarin solution. If they had used a 100% sarin solution, the outcome would have been much more tragic—secondarily exposed prehospital and medical staff would have been killed.

- • This is the reason for the development of decontamination facilities and the use of personal protective equipment (PPE) in the pre-hospital and hospital setting.
- A confusion of information and lack of coordination among related organizations—Japan is a highly vertically structured society. Fire departments, police, metropolitan governments, and hospitals acted independently without coordination. After the attack, the Japanese government developed the Severe Chemical Hazard Response Team.
- Following the attack the Prime Minister's office created a National Security and Crisis Management Office that calls for realistic desktop hazmat drills involving the concerned organizations and specialist.

Tokyo is far away from many other cities and countries, yet there were ripple effects from the impact of this attack that were felt around the world. As a medical first responder, your immediate concern is to properly protect yourself from the hazard, as you are of no assistance if you're the next victim due to secondary exposure. Properly attending to victims and protecting your medical facility is your next concern, and none of this can be accomplished safely without Personal Protective Equipment (PPE).

PPE—Top Three Things to Do
- Complete a through Hazard Assessment for your area, include all possibilities.
- Review and determine the standards that you must meet to establish a functional response team.
- Practice, exercise and train with all aspects of the PPE you intend to utilize during a realistic response.

PPE—Top Three Things to Avoid
- Underestimating the need to prepare for a CBRN incident.
- Acquiring mismatched equipment and/or non-certified CBRN items.
- Limited or no intra-organization communications during a CBRN incident.

References

Horton D. K. Berkowitz, W.E. Kaye. 2003. Secondary contamination of ED personnel from hazardous materials events, 1995–2001. *American Journal of Medicine* 21:199–204, May.

Koenig, 2003, The duck and cover for the 21st century, Strip and Shower, *Annals of Emergency Medicine*, 42(3) 391–394, September.

OSHA—Occupational Safety and Health Administration, OSHA Best Practices for Hospital-Based First Receivers of Victims from Mass Casualty Incidents Involving the Release of Hazardous Substances, January 2005, U.S. Department of Labor.

OSHA—Best Practices for Hospital-Based First Receivers of Victims from Mass Casualty Incidents Involving the Release of Hazardous Substances, January 2005, U.S. Department of Labor, Occupational Safety and Health Administration.

U.S. Department of Labor, Occupational Safety & Health Administration, Major Requirements of OSHA's Respiratory Protection Standard, 29 CFR 1910.134.

OSHA—Personal Protective Equipment General Requirements, 29 CFR 1910.132, U.S. Department of Labor, Occupational Safety and Health Administration.

ISO—International Organization for Standardization, ISO Standards, 13 Environmental, Health, Protection, Safety, Section 13.340.10 Protective Clothing, Published Standards and Standards under Development.

The Medical Journal of Australia, Clinical Update, Chemical-Biological-Radiological (CBR) Response: a template for hospital emergency departments, Gim A Tan and Mark C B Fitzgerald, MJA 2002 177 (4): 196–199.

Standards SAA HB9-1994, Occupational Personal Protection, 2nd edition, Sydney: Standards Australia, 1994.

Standards AS 3765.1-1990, Clothing for Protection against Hazardous Chemicals, Part 1: Protection against general or specific chemicals. Sydney: Standards Australia, 1990.

Standards AS/NZS 1715: 1991, Selection, use and maintenance of respiratory protective devices, Sydney: Standards Australia, 1994.

Standards AS/NZS 4501.1: 2008, Occupational Protective Clothing—Guidelines on Selection, Use, Care and Maintenance of Protective Clothing, Sydney: Standards Australia.

Standards AS/NZS ISO 13994:2006, Clothing for Protection against Chemicals—Determination of the Resistance of Protective Clothing Materials to Penetration by Liquids under Pressure. Sydney: Standards Australia,.

EN 13034: 2005+A1, Protective Clothing against Liquid Chemicals—Performance requirements for Chemical Protective Clothing Offering Limited Protective Performance against Liquid Chemicals (Type 6 and Type PB [6] Equipment). European Standard, CEN European Committee for Standardization.

EN ISO 13982-1: 2004, Protective Clothing against Solid Particulates—Part 1: Performance requirements for chemical protective clothing providing protection to the full body against airborne solid particulates (type 5 clothing). European Standard, CEN European Committee for Standardization.

EN 374-1: 2003, Protective Gloves against Chemicals and Micro Organisms, Terminology and Performance Requirements. European Standard, CEN European Committee for Standardization.

EN 6530:2005, Protective Clothing—Protection against Liquid Chemicals—test method for Resistance of Materials to Penetration by Liquids. European Standard, CEN European Committee for Standardization.

Hospital Response to Chemical Terrorism: Personal Protective Equipment, Training and Operations Planning. Panos G. Georgopoulas, PhD, Paul Fedele, PhD, Pamela Shade, MS, Paul J. Lioy, PhD, Michael Hodgson, MD, MPH, Atkinson Longmire, MD, Melody Sands, MS, Mark A. Brown, PhD. 2004.

CSA Standard Z94.4-02, Selection, Use and Care of Respirators, Canadian Standards Association.

ATSDR 2000, Managing Hazardous Materials Incidents: Hospital Emergency Departments—A planning guide for the management of contaminated patients, Volume II (revised). Agency for Toxic Substances and Disease Registry, U.S. Department of Health and Human Services, 2003

ATSDR 2000, Managing Hazardous Materials Incidents: Medical Management Guidelines (MMG's) for unidentified Chemical, Volume III. Agency for Toxic Substances and Disease Registry, U.S. Department of Health and Human Services, 2003.

NFPA 472—Standard for Professional Competence of Responders to Hazardous Materials/ Weapons of Mass Destruction Incidents, 2008. National Fire Protection Association.

NFPA 473—Standard for Competencies for EMS Personnel Responding to Hazardous Materials/Weapons of Mass Destruction Incidents, 2008. National Fire Protection Association.

NFPA 1991—Standard on Vapor-Protective Ensemble for Hazardous Materials Emergencies, 2005. National Fire Protection Association.

NFPA 1992—Standard on Liquid Splash-protective Ensemble and Clothing for Hazardous Materials Emergencies, 2005. National Fire Protection Association.

NFPA 1994—Standard on Protective Ensemble for Chemical/Biological Terrorism Incidents, 2007. National Fire Protection Association.

NFPA 1999—Standard on Protective Clothing for Emergency Medical Operations, 2008. National Fire Protection Association.

JCAHO—Standing Together, An Emergency Planning Guide for America's Communities, 2005. Joint Commission on Accreditation of Healthcare Organizations.

JCAHO—Standard EC.4.10, The Organization Addresses Emergency Management, 2008, Comprehensive Accreditation Manual for Hospitals, Joint Commission on Accreditation of Healthcare Organizations.

CA EMSA 223—Patient Decontamination Recommendations for Hospitals, The Hospital and Healthcare System Disaster Interest Group and the California Emergency Medical Services Authority, 2005.

ATSDR—Managing Hazardous Materials Incidents: Hospital Emergency Departments— A Planning Guide for the Management of Contaminated Patients, Volume II. Agency for Toxic Substances and Disease Registry, U.S. Department of Health and Human Services, 2001.

HSC 1998/197: Planning for Major incidents the NHS Guidance Fully Revised and Updated Guidance. Health Service Circular, Department of Health, U.K., 1998.

The Decontamination of People Exposed to Chemical, Biological, Radiological or Nuclear (CBRN) Substances or Material, Strategic National Guidance, First Edition, 2003. U.K. Home Office.

Public Health Response to Deliberate Release of Biological and Chemical Agents, Planning for Major Incidents, The NHS Guidance, 2000. U.K. Department of Health.

NIOSH/OSHA—Chemical—Biological—Radiological—Nuclear (CBRN) Personal Protective Equipment Selection Matrix for Emergency Responders. Interim Guidance (April 2005). U.S. Department of Labor, Occupational Safety & Health Administration, National Institute for Occupational Safety and Health.

NIOSH—Recommendations for the Selection and Use of Respirators and Protective Clothing for Protection against Biological Agents. Publication No. 2009-132. U.S. Department of Labor, Occupational Safety & Health Administration, National Institute for Occupational Safety and Health.

NIOSH—Guidance on Emergency Responder Personal Protective Equipment (PPE) for Response to CBRN terrorism Incidents. Publication No. 2008-132. U.S. Department of Labor, Occupational Safety & Health Administration, National Institute for Occupational Safety and Health.

Industrial Fire World, Hazardous Exposure, St. Louis ER's Face HazMat Crisis, Volume 23, No. 6 November-December 2008, by Anton Riecher/IFW Editor.

Lessons Learned from the Tokyo Subway Sarin Attack, PreHospital Disaster Medicine 2000;15(3):s30, Tetsu Okumura; Kouichiro Suzuki; Shinichi Ishimatsu; Nobukatsu Takasu; Chiiho Fuiji; Akitsugu Kohama, Department of Acute Medicine, Kawasaki Medical School Hospital, Kurashiki-City, Okayama, Japan.

Sarin Gas Attack on the Tokyo Subway, Japan-101, Information Resource, Japan's Culture, 2003-2005, Japan-101.com. Details derived from Murakami Haruki's book on the attack titled "Underground" and Wikipedia—"Sarin Gas Attack on the Tokyo Subway" the page was last modified on January 11, 2009, all text is available under the terms of the GNU Free Documentation License (see copyright for detals), Wikipedia Foundation, Inc.

4 ⚏

Emergency Treatment Area

CHAPTER OBJECTIVES

- Understand the purpose of an Emergency Treatment Area
- Know and define the four categories of initial patients
- Understand and detail the need for site control and security
- Describe how to effectively demobilize an ETA

Introduction

Hospitals and health facilities are obviously about much more than steel, bricks and mortar, and high-priced bills. They are home to critical health services such as public health laboratories, blood banks, rehabilitation facilities and pharmacies. They are the setting in which healthcare workers labor diligently to ensure the highest level of service. Their importance extends far beyond their role in saving lives and safeguarding the public's health in the aftermath of disasters. Health facilities have a symbolic social and political value and contribute to a community's sense of security and well-being. As such, they must be protected from the avoidable consequences of disasters, emergencies and other crises.

From a disaster management perspective, all disaster preparedness plans should contain provision of healthcare as a critical resource. Many community emergency plans lump hospitals in with public health resources and likewise many public officials consider hospitals as part of their infrastructure, when in fact about two-thirds of U.S. hospitals are operating as private businesses. Damage or interruption to hospitals or healthcare systems has an effect on every part of society and on nations as a whole. As such, hospitals' operational resiliency should be a national concern, as should a commitment to ensure that hospitals and healthcare facilities are prepared against foreseeable hazards. Awareness and commitment are the major ingredients of successful disaster preparedness: awareness of the need for vigilance and commitment from both policy makers and the public at large to demand and enable hospitals to enhance their preparedness posture.

FIGURE 4.1 After a disaster, patient capture areas and capacity of healthcare resources may be dramatically altered, necessitating the ability to be self-sufficient in service delivery. A well-thought-out HERT may be all that remains between additional morbidity and mortality post-disaster.

As news of a disaster or emergency reaches us, our thoughts turn immediately to the human consequences and at the forefront of those thoughts are concerns for the health and well-being of those suffering in times of crisis. One way in which we can be prepared for these unexpected but predictable events such as floods in the Pacific Northwest as seen in Figure 4.1, is by strengthening the capacity and resilience of healthcare facilities and systems, which in turn assists the community at large to mitigate and manage the effects of disasters.

Purpose of the Emergency Treatment Area (ETA)

The mission of establishing a HERT to staff an ETA is clear: when hospitals, healthcare facilities, or systems fail in disaster and emergency situations, the result is the

Hospitals tend to fall into an abyss between the public's perception of them as part of the Critical Infrastructure and Key Resources (CIKR) when it comes to seeking sanctuary during times of disaster, and federal funding dollars which tend to shy away from significant enhancement of private industry other than the banking or auto industry. In order for hospitals to achieve a statistically significant jump in preparedness, the public will have to campaign for dedicated funding either from the hospitals themselves or the government. Perhaps healthcare reform could include hospital performance criteria during times of disasters assuming they are putting up the money to build such capacity.

Protecting and ensuring the continuity of all the critical infrastructure and key resources of the United States—including hospitals—are essential to the nation's security, public health and safety, economic vitality, and way of life.

- Critical Infrastructure are the assets, systems, and networks, whether physical or virtual, so vital to the United States that their incapacitation or destruction would have a debilitating effect on security, national economic security, public health or safety, or any combination thereof.
- Key Resources are publicly or privately controlled resources essential to the minimal operations of the economy and government.

In 2003, Homeland Security Presidential Directive 7 (HSPD-7) established U.S. policy for enhancing CIKR protection by establishing a framework for National Infrastructure Protection Plan (NIPP) partners to identify, prioritize, and protect the nation's CIKR from terrorist attacks. The directive identified 17 CIKR sectors and designated a federal Sector-Specific Agency (SSA) to lead CIKR protection efforts in each. The directive allows for the Department of Homeland Security to identify gaps in existing CIKR sectors and establish new sectors to fill these gaps. Under this authority, the Department established the Critical Manufacturing Sector in March 2008.

same: they are not available to treat the victims at precisely the moment they are most needed.

The Emergency Treatment Area (ETA), staffed by members of the Hospital Emergency Response Team (HERT), is a cornerstone of any healthcare facility's disaster preparedness plan; a first line of defense if you will. The overall objectives of the healthcare facility are to protect the lives of patients and healthcare workers by ensuring the integrity of healthcare facilities; to make sure healthcare facilities and healthcare services are able to function in the aftermath of emergencies and disasters (when they are most needed); and to mitigate risk to healthcare workers and institutions, thus supporting disaster response entities and local emergency management authorities.

Location of the Emergency Treatment Area

It is important to note that the ETA is not an extension of a hospital's Emergency Department (ED) or a service whose primary function is triage and treatment of patients arriving after some emergency. The ETA is much more than a simple outdoor decontamination and treatment area, and considerable thought must go into its placement on the medical facility footprint, let alone what function it will serve. It is conceivable that location and function of the ETA may vary from event to event (or catastrophe to catastrophe). If the ETA is considered to be a physical extension of the ED, any slip-up in decontamination or access control would potentially compromise the safety of patients and personnel in the ED, as well as create an impediment to ED operations. However, if the ETA is properly located, any breach of its perimeter should not result in operational impact on any of the hospital's critical functions. There are several issues for consideration when establishing an ETA, as well as important ramifications of decisions you might make.

Disaster epidemiology has taught us that the closest hospital to a sudden major event is the hospital where the bulk of the patients will end up. We also know that the majority of early triage is actually done by the public, with a good deal of patients being transported by private automobile, taxis, buses, police cars, or even walking to the nearest healthcare facility. This knowledge about the aftermath of disasters shows us the importance of ETA placement and staffing. It is a reasonable assumption that the initial patients arriving at the closest facility, which could be yours, will fall into one of the following four categories:

- First to arrive are those who are injured or ill to some extent, but who are not transported by any organized EMS system. A majority of these will have minor injuries, some moderate, and a few may be severely injured. Of the severely injured, some will require life-saving care/stabilization, while others may be stable and require transport to a suitable tertiary facility.
- The second category of patients are not injured or ill but are brought to the facility because someone thought they needed "to be checked out."
- The third category comprises those who are emotionally or psychologically damaged.
- Finally, there are those patients without injury who believe they should go to the hospital to get checked out anyway.

Obviously, if all of these patients were to be welcomed directly into the ED, collapse of the department would be imminent and predictable. Functional collapse, not structural damage, is the primary reason for hospitals being put out of service during emergencies. Functional collapse occurs when the elements that allow a hospital to operate on a day-to-day basis are unable to perform because a disaster has overloaded the system. Your ETA must prevent this predictable cascade of events.

One important consideration when thinking about potential ETA locations is the issue of access. For instance, you may need to ask: How many roadways lead into or out of the reception area? If the answer is one, and it must carry traffic both for both ingress and egress, then problems with congestion are inevitable. This kind of set-up is prone to bottlenecks which will not only become frustrating, but may lead to people overstepping their bounds and ignoring the authority of the HERT. If the answer is two, one for ingress and one for egress, the location may be more amenable to traffic flow. However, if traffic is stopped in one lane and people are in a hurry, they may choose to simply go around the bottleneck, into the other lane of traffic. A better arrangement is to turn this two-lane road into a one-way access point, and use an alternative road on the backside to allow for egress. If you have additional roadways, you can establish separate points of ingress and egress for arriving patients and staff as a component of your disaster plan.

The reception area of your ETA will be the point where anyone approaching your facility footprint will be funneled, challenged to stop, and assessed. The assessment will be to determine their disposition, which informs where they will be directed to next. Selection of qualified personnel for this position is important, as their job will be to determine which of the following five routes each patient should take.

1. Referral of patient/s to the appropriate place within the healthcare facility per your disaster plan.
2. Referral of patient/s to tertiary healthcare facilities following stabilization at your facility.
3. Referral of patient/s to tertiary healthcare facilities directly by EMS without any additional stabilization at your facility.
4. Referral through your ETA for life-saving care and/or initial stabilization and then disposition as above in #1.
5. If appropriate, referral through the decontamination corridor of your ETA, prior to additional medical assessment.

As you can see, if you are to have any hope of bringing organization to the chaos moving toward your facility following a major event, there must be a clear plan in place for assessing where and how to best treat people who are arriving. Your facility will benefit from an established and well-marked location and well-trained personnel, for channeling arriving patients, conducting a methodical sorting, and then ensuring a logical disposition for each one. The general public is unaware of the strain a major disaster can put on a facility's resources. They are coming to you confident that they will be well taken care of, as they have been in the past. Yet you only have the time it takes for people to travel from the incident site (and maybe an additional 10–15 minutes) to prepare, before the masses begin arriving. If your facility performs well during a disaster, you essentially increase your facility's "stock" and community confidence. However, if your facility performs poorly, you inadvertently invite intense scrutiny and possibly litigation, by failing the public when they needed you most.

Site Control and Security

To ensure traffic patterns are quickly established, people must be assigned to key intersections, with well-marked signage that provides direction for those seeking care. As part of your plan, consider whether these staff members will require appropriate personal protective equipment (PPE). It can be challenging and downright hazardous to ask non-uniformed staff members to stop vehicles entering your access roadways. Using vehicles to block roadways, or if available, uniformed security personnel, sworn police officers, or members of the military, may yield better results.

Keep in mind that the personnel required to establish the ETA and for ingress and egress control must come from your existing personnel pool. Most hospital disaster plans have staff assigned to security and crowd-control of the facility itself. One could make an argument that shifting these personnel to rapid and robust resourcing of the ETA and pre-planned access control routes will mitigate some of the challenges associated with controlling the flow of people entering the health facility.

Another question to consider is: Can the perimeter of the facility, reception area and ETA be adequately secured against possible external attack? Remember that even a simple gang shooting can lead to retaliation. A hard perimeter, one that can protect critical areas, could be composed of an uninterrupted ring of anti-ram barriers, generally in the form of rated bollards, which will prevent vehicles from penetrating a building's prescribed standoff distance for bomb blasts. If possible, new construction designs should incorporate decorative soft perimeters, such as concrete planters. If such soft perimeter devices are used, proper engineering should be undertaken to ensure that a bomb blast will not turn the planter into a stack of lethal fragments. Depending on the circumstances, it may also be appropriate for existing buildings to install hard perimeters.

Regardless of the type of physical security barrier solution decided upon, it is recommended that hospitals use current roadway designs and other traffic-calming measures to minimize potential vehicle congestion, as well as velocity when approaching access control points, such as the initial reception area of the ETA. If it becomes second nature to establish robust perimeter security on a regular basis, your employees will perform better when the stakes are higher.

Operational Considerations

Be aware that your local environment may play an unexpected role in times of disaster by creating situations that cause more injuries. For instance, when flood waters rise, certain species of animals such as venomous snakes are displaced and may end up in close proximity to humans, increasing dangerous interactions (snake bites, in this case). If injuries from falls and sprains are predictable after an ice storm, why not apply the same logic to predicting injuries or illness that may follow potential hazards in any hospital capture area? Flood plains, tsunami inundation zones, elevated areas or valleys, and proximity to earthquake fault lines are all factors to consider when conducting a hazard analysis and injury matrix. Do this in conjunction with a gap analysis of your capabilities to address the injuries you identify and are most likely to encounter. Your local emergency management agency is likely to have a complete hazard vulnerability analysis available and would allow you to review a copy. This is a great place to start the path to preparedness: assess your ETA's ability to treat patients suffering illnesses or injuries derived from the previously identified threats in your facility's capture area.

What kind of healthcare infrastructure exists in your patient capture area? If there are multiple facilities, you may still find yourself hit with an initial influx of patients, but you can identify outlets for the overflow if you plan appropriately. If you are the only healthcare facility in the area, don't plan that another facility will be able to help (they may, but don't plan for it). Pre-existing public health issues will be exacerbated in times of emergency; if you have a high retirement age population, expect increased demand for services compared to a bedroom community near an industrial area.

Is there an industrial area or firm within your health facility's catchment area such as seen in Figure 4.2? If so, how far away is it from the facility? It is likely that your facility was named in the firm's emergency plan as the destination for any employees exposed to materials on site (regardless of having confirmed beforehand your facility's ability to care for them). If your facility is near a roadway that is used by vehicles transporting potentially hazardous substances to or from the industrial site, it is likely that sooner or later an accident will occur that at the very least places employees at risk of exposure, if not your entire facility if you are situated downwind of the release. It could be argued that such an event would be considered a predictable hazard (in that you can assume there is a likely chance an accident will occur at some point). You need to prepare, properly train, and equip your employees for just such a disaster, both to properly handle the event and to mitigate any potential legal negligence. If an antidote exists for the hazardous material in question, it is best to have it on site, as it will take far too long to have it transported in from a remote location.

It will take some time and effort to answer these questions, but the results will be invaluable in times of emergency. As previously mentioned, events produce predictable injury or illness patterns, and these in turn drive the performance capability requirements in the emergency treatment area.

FIGURE 4.2 Potential for disaster (either accidental or intentional) resides in most communities and in some cases quite close to significant medical resources. Not being prepared to safely and efficiently respond to a chemical release of these known hazards could be considered negligent.

Logistical Considerations

If the event is such that decontamination operations are deemed prudent, a whole new set of challenges in planning and preparedness emerge. The chapter on decontamination will give details on decisions necessary to conduct a safe and efficient decontamination operation, so here we will only look at ETA site selection as it applies to meeting the objective of protecting the facility and its normal operations.

How far is the decontamination area from the main treatment facility, and are there alternate locations based upon wind direction or weather considerations? As seen in Figure 4.3, gathering storm clouds indicate the operating conditions on the ground will change soon. Distance adds a measure of protection for reduced accessibility but leads to logistical and personnel challenges depending upon the expected duration of operations. A simple decontamination operation in the middle of a parking lot in 60 degree weather is dramatically different than one in 90 degree weather without shade of any kind.

FIGURE 4.3 Determining where to establish your ETA, decontamination corridor or other HERT should take into consideration current and anticipated weather conditions, patient loads and how long your operation may run. Having to relocating or adjusting your operations once underway can detract from their efficiency and effectiveness.

It is outside the scope of this chapter to cover all aspects of detection and monitoring equipment, but one strategy that may save your facility some frustration is the early deployment of skilled technicians from your facility, who can conduct rapid radiologic surveys of incoming patients and of the facility itself in order to detect possibly harmful radiologic contamination. If radioactive material is present, you can take appropriate measures to protect the staff, prevent cross-contamination, and be fairly confident that your facility will not become contaminated. Placing portal detectors near key hospital entrances carries an initial burden of expense, but eliminates the guesswork on when to deploy radiation detection equipment.

Proper development of the ETA requires a complete system designed to receive potentially contaminated patients, triage and process those patients, provide them with medical treatment, and infuse them into the hospital setting or facilitate their transportation to other medical facilities. The ETA is a complex system relying on its numerous team members to orchestrate emergency procedures, utilize self-protection, function with specialized equipment, and provide medical treatment on short notice. Coordination among the entire hospital staff in completing these important functions is paramount to successfully achieving the goals of providing medical care to the injured, protecting hospital personnel, and protecting the hospital itself.

Operational Components

OSHA's Best Practices for the Protection of Hospital-Based First Receivers has broken up the ETA into three sections as seen in Figure 4.4. The patient reception/receiving area provides triage and control procedures. This first area is also considered a potentially contaminated zone and self-protection should be a priority. The second section is the decontamination corridor, which handles ambulatory and non-ambulatory patients for the purpose of removing contaminates. The third section is the clean treatment and transport area, which provides medical care, secondary triage, and transport functions.

Activation and Incident Assessment

Hospital emergency plans may vary, but common triggers to establish the ETA are mass casualty incidents, hazardous materials incidents, or sudden severe events that create casualties. Employees noticing television "breaking news" alerts may be one of your best notification triggers.

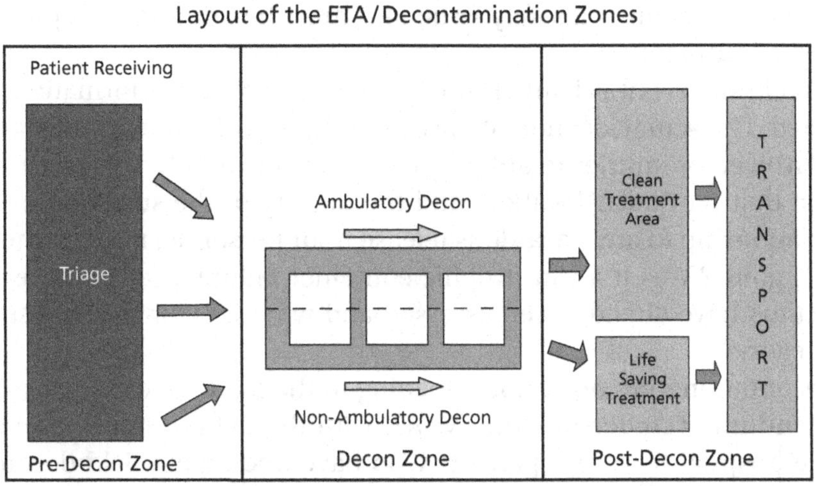

Layout of the ETA/Decontamination Zones

FIGURE 4.4 A big part of efficiency in your ETA is having everything in the same place every time it is activated. Just as important is focusing on the function of an area and not becoming obsessed with specific tools to carry out the function.

Obviously, the more warning time the facility has, the easier it will be to establish its ETA. Unfortunately, protocols should be based upon more realistic parameters—in the event of a disaster, it is likely the facility will literally only have minutes to establish perimeter security, mark traffic flow routes, and funnel incoming patients to a rapidly established ETA reception area. The only way to ensure that the ETA can be quickly and efficiently set up is through training. The ideal solution is to adopt triggers which are sensitive enough to allow for HERT activation to occur several times a year. This keeps interest amongst the team members and allows them to hone their skills.

If the determination is made to activate the HERT, it is important to collect as much information as possible on the nature of the event. It may be helpful to delegate an employee whose task is to establish contact with an on-scene liaison; monitor radio, TV and Internet reports; determine the size, scope, and nature of the event; and if possible, confirm early reports with on-scene responders. As critical information is received, it must be communicated to all team members. The more details ETA team members have, the better they will be able to select appropriate PPE, understand hazards that may be present, be prepared for anticipated injury patterns, prepare antidotes if available, and go into the operation with more confidence. Hospitals should always be prepared for a no-notice situation, as it is a realistic possibility, but as soon as pertinent information is collected and confirmed it should be disseminated to ETA team members. Effective and timely communication is a safety issue and must be addressed in pre-planning protocol development.

Once an initial event briefing is provided, more specific information needs to be collected. The actual location of the event can provide clues to substances that may be involved or injuries to anticipate, the capacity of workers or citizens that may be in that particular location, and the density of the surrounding population in relationship to any hazardous release. Your personnel need to know: Is the release on going? Was it a catastrophic container failure or a "puff event"? How many victims have already been assessed and what is their medical status and triage category?

Are decontamination operations ongoing in the field? Does the hospital have a memorandum of understanding (MOU) with the field response agencies that allows the hospital to accept patients who have undergone field decontamination as suitably clean to bypass the hospital decontamination corridor? Time spent cross-training with field personnel before an event to ensure confidence in decontamination thoroughness will be well worth the effort at this point. Decontamination operations will tax hospital personnel resources and hospitals should work with local response agencies to support each other in avoiding duplication of effort.

Continuous dissemination of collected information is a crucial task in establishing a prepared Emergency Treatment Area (ETA). A timely and concise briefing to the ETA members provides for a well-prepared and well-informed team. Throughout the pre-arrival time frame, information should be collected and disseminated. The utilization of outside technical assistance agencies (CDC, Poison Control, local HazMat Teams and ATSDR) and reference documents can only improve the facility's overall response.

The ETA has many components that must be set up and completed in order to be fully prepared to receive patients. Mobilization of these assets based on accurate incident information results in an efficient and effective ETA and plays a key role in ensuring protection of all team members, staff and the hospital itself. Practicing mobilization of personnel and equipment is the only sure way to measure the facility's ability to respond.

Perimeter control zones are designed to layer access to the hospital; they help ensure a safe and reliable environment for employees to function, allow for identifying persons who should not be within a secured area, and provide a positive image of organization and effectiveness in patient care. The seriousness of maintaining control during major events cannot be overstated, as an uncontrolled site will lend itself to chaos, which will ultimately compromise the hospital, your patients and your employees.

The perimeter can be separated into three areas: (1) controlled access to the grounds, parking and hospital buildings, (2) facility security from human intrusion and (3) decontamination corridor protection to prevent contamination intrusion into the facility. Many techniques can be used to create the control zones, from a simple barricade to electronic security access control. The number and type of systems utilized varies from facility to facility. A realistic review of a facility's campus layout, topography, natural barriers and capabilities can provide a blueprint for improving and enhancing the perimeter control aspects during worst case scenarios.

ETA Decontamination Zone

This section does not specifically address hospital decontamination zones or procedures, as they are detailed in Chapter 6. This section will focus on activities and actions within the decontamination corridor and outline its relationship to the ETA as a whole.

The Pre-Decontamination Zone or "Hot Zone" is the reception or receiving area at the hospital for potentially contaminated patients and is where the triage process initiates. This work area requires employees to wear personal protective equipment. Activities that may occur in this zone include interviewing patients to better understand the event, hospital scene control, assessing contamination on patients, patient triage, immediate treatment versus decontamination issues, transfer to other facilities, and ambulatory versus non-ambulatory designations.

A critical task requiring appropriately trained personnel is observation of possible exposure syndromes and communicating suspected findings through the appropriate chain of command. Notifications should be made to ETA team members and may include field command posts, the local Emergency Operations Center (EOC), or even health department representatives.

The Hospital Decontamination Zone provides for the actual decontamination of patients and acts as a barrier between the contaminated victims and the hospital itself. It is in this area that medical teams may struggle over weighing the risk of expediting a patient through decontamination to improve the chances of that patient receiving timely life-saving care versus committing to a thorough, yet timely decontamination process. Hospitals may choose the option of being prepared to offer simple life saving care in the decontamination zone, in order to temper decisions to bypass decontamination efforts. As discussed in Chapter 6, the characteristics of the contaminant will dictate how easily the product may be removed. When weighing the risk of bypassing the decontamination process, numerous variables come into play. These can include: type of hazardous substance suspected or known to be involved; biological agent or radiological material suspected; length of exposure for each individual victim; age, history and medical condition of the patient; current stage of decontamination (has a gross decontamination been accomplished?); location of exposure; wind direction; temperature; humidity and other relevant environmental factors.

When you add safety of personnel, patients, and facility as the factor of highest priority, it's obvious why complete decontamination may be the safest option. You may find that situations exist in which the correct call is for a modified decontamination procedure that significantly reduces risk of cross-contamination, yet critical medical care is provided. No hard and fast doctrine exists to answer the question in favor of one choice or the other; instead a reasonable judgment call must be made based on the facts known at that point in time. Providing personnel with the ability to perform critical life-saving procedures, while utilizing subject matter experts to offer guidance on weighing priorities, may prove invaluable in both protecting the facility from preventable contamination and ensuring the best outcomes for those seeking care.

Based on the dynamics above, it is clear that whether to medically intervene prior to complete decontamination is a difficult decision. Yet, no one wants to see "untimely medical care" listed as a contributing cause of a patient's death, both for legal and ethical reasons. The best tools you can give your staff members to increase their confidence in themselves and the functions of the ETA, are education and training, in order to replace fear with knowledge as seen in Figure 4.5 where medical personnel are training to take care of a patient in a hazardous area. As staff members become better adept at separating real versus potential risk from a particular contaminant, you will see that efficiency and effectiveness increase.

Activities within the decontamination zone include all patient-related actions. This starts when ETA team members direct or conduct cut-out operations to remove patient clothing and collect the patient's personal items. The process may then include directing the patient through the rinse, wash, rinse procedure; redressing; basic medical care; and containment and control techniques for wash/rinse solutions. If it has not been established as a separate component, the decontamination zone may also provide a decontamination corridor for team members working in this zone and includes containing and/or disposal of residual contaminants, neutralization or disposal of substances, routine change-out of gloves and splash shielding and other actions to ensure the decontamination system remains functional.

The Post-Decontamination Zone or "Cold Zone" is the area where medical treatment and secondary triage happen in earnest. This area is considered the support zone of the ETA and is the last zone the patient will proceed through prior to

FIGURE 4.5 Realistic training allows the medical team member to focus on applying life saving medical skills and remain as safe as possible while doing so in rare but predictable situations.

admittance into the hospital or transfer to tertiary care sites per protocol. The Post-Decontamination Zone has historically been positioned near or next to the hospital's ED so as to be near enough to access further medical care for patients if necessary.

Two issues that bear noting at this point are the security and the control elements between the ED and Post-Decontamination Zone. Absolute respect of security issues and one-way movement restrictions are a must with these areas as seen in Figure 4.6. Your facility must build a self-protection capacity and practice securing critical areas. Integrity of the facility, particularly the ED, is paramount and takes priority over the needs of any one patient. Any loss of perimeter security and access control would be detrimental to the other patients and staff. We feel the ETA decontamination corridor is best placed separate from the ED, far enough away so as not to breach the invisible line between clean and dirty. This allows for normal operation of the ED and separation of "clean" (non-contaminated) patients and staff from the turmoil outside the walls. Post decontamination, the patients are transported to the appropriate designated location. Transfer may be to any of various locations within the hospital, or to other facilities as part of continued or specialized care.

Personnel Requirements

In this section we will take a look at personnel requirements. For our estimates we are only looking at the ETA, not the perimeter security needs of the facility footprint or personnel needed for access and egress control.

Pre-Decontamination Zone—Two personnel are required to perform initial assessment for decontamination needs, triage, and deployment of detection equipment. A minimum of one uniformed security officer is necessary for safety of staff and to help ensure compliance by patients.

Decontamination Zone—Two personnel are required for clothing removal and evidence/personal property preservation, at least four to staff the decontamination line itself, one person for medical assessment and life-saving interventions, and two people for drying, redress (if part of your protocol) and passing patients off to the clean side of the line.

If we estimate that the influx of patients will continue for greater than one hour, we will need to rotate those personnel in PPE as seen in Figure 4.7. Based upon the author's experience, 20 minutes of working time for personnel dressed in Level C PPE is a good rough estimate. This may vary somewhat based upon actual environmental conditions, personnel fitness and acclimatization to the PPE, and workload. Time must be allotted for personnel to be processed through the technical decontamination line themselves and a medical screening and rehabilitation period prior to resuming activities in the ETA. This means a facility needs

FIGURE 4.6 Medical facilities are typically soft targets and medical providers rarely think about perimeter and security issues. Risk assessment and capability analysis will help determine how to best meet your facility's security needs in times of disaster. Security may come in the form of mutual aid agreements with local police departments, contracts with private security firms, or cross-training of medical staff to help protect your facility.

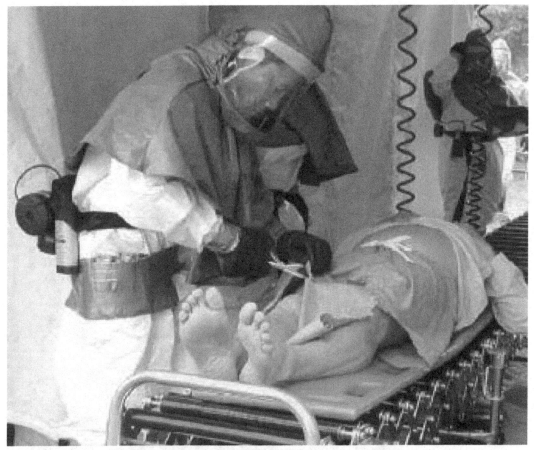

FIGURE 4.7 When PPE goes on for decontamination operations, safety issues associated with heat stress require the utmost attention.

three times the base number of ETA staff. In our example here, we have 11 staff engaged in ETA activities, requiring an additional 22 staff to form two additional teams to rotate in the following manner. Team A—20 minutes work, while Team B is getting ready, Team B deploys while Team A heads for technical decontamination and rehabilitation, Team C then is preparing to deploy to replace Team B, and Team A comes back on line in 45–60 minutes to relieve Team C.

This example may seem overwhelming enough to dissuade any facility from establishing an ETA, but there are factors to consider that may decrease the burden. Due to the typically short warning time with disaster incidents, the first ETA staffing assignments will have to be completed by staff already within the facility at the time. Team B staff have a quick response time requirement, but may be some of the first to arrive as the hospital's emergency plan is implemented and

On April 19, 1995, around 9:03 a.m., just after parents dropped their children off at daycare at the Murrah Federal Building in downtown Oklahoma City, the unthinkable happened. A massive bomb inside a rental truck exploded, blowing half of the nine-story building into oblivion. A stunned nation watched as the bodies of men, women, and children were pulled from the rubble for nearly two weeks. When the smoke cleared and the exhausted rescue workers packed up and left, 168 people were dead from the worst terrorist attack by a U.S. citizen on our soil. Rebecca Anderson, a nurse, was killed trying to rescue injured victims after the blast when a large piece of the building fell on her. She was doing what most of us would have done, but this tragic event illustrates the risks rescue work carries, as well as the additional burden placed on those trying to organize the scene and deal with the initial casualties by those well-trained and well-meaning individuals who want to help, but are not officially called to the scene. It is tremendously demoralizing to rescuers on scene to lose one of our own.

call backs initiated. Team C staff has 30–45 minutes to get to the facility. If a facility is small and these staffing requirements are beyond your reach, it is time to work with local first response agencies. The assumption with these agencies has often been "don't call us we'll be on scene" and that may be the case, but disaster epidemiology also shows us that many first responders show up on scene without being requested. This is called freelancing and is the result of well-meaning and trained personnel wanting to help. However, what it results in is a nightmare from a scene command and control perspective and in fact is very dangerous to safety.

It is reasonable to expect that agencies in whose jurisdiction the event occurs, as well as their mutual-aid partners, will be on scene, but numerous other assets from the surrounding region may be available through pre-planning, to assist with ETA operations. Recently retired first responder members or community volunteers may be interested and available to become part of your ETA team. It is worth the effort to reach out and your local emergency management agency is a great place to start. Too often we forsake responsible planning, believing it unachievable, and in doing so we begin our incubation period towards predictable poor results. Two fatal factors drive this path: first we underestimate the likelihood of an event within our capture area and second, we overestimate our own capabilities.

Demobilizing the ETA

The effective demobilization of an ETA may at first sound like a relatively straightforward operation, but it is just the opposite. Properly removing contaminated materials, equipment and decontaminating reusable equipment is tedious and requires attention to detail or you end up without critical pieces of equipment or worse yet, placing personnel at risk of exposure to contaminants.

If the collection of samples is being done to aid in diagnosis such as sending to a laboratory or for evidence purposes, proper technique must be strictly adhered to in order not to increase areas of possible contamination. Before the process of demobilization can begin, the contaminant must be clearly identified and the levels of contamination remaining on the site must be determined. This may require numerous samples from a large area, using the appropriate equipment. This is required to ensure that the proper decontamination technique, including the correct decontaminating solution, is being utilized and that there is a clear and concise knowledge of the contamination remaining and any hot spots to decontaminate are identified and then resolved.

It is often a good choice to rely on technical expertise in creating a site specific remediation program for ensuring the cleanup is thorough. The program should ensure that all contaminant has been removed and/or neutralized and that this process is documented prior to resuming normal functions in the ETA. The final step is the removal of contaminated waste to an authorized disposal site. The hospital should consult with experts in the field of waste disposal to ensure proper disposal will occur. Coordinating activities through the EOC may help identify the appropriate contractor and avoid duplicating efforts.

Any event requiring the initiation of the ETA should have an After-Action-Report (AAR) created and a Plan of Improvement written. The post-event actions need to encompass as wide a berth as possible due to the impact of the event on the hospital and its staff. Post event actions will concentrate on dismantling the ETA, providing post evaluations, and medical examinations for the HERT members and other staff members that warrant the same.

An analysis of the hospital's response to the event should be completed with recommendations incorporated as part of the review and development of a Plan of Improvement. Revisions or updating of the Emergency Response Plan is accomplished during this time and ensures a more effective plan will emerge for future events. A final step is to return the hospital to routine operations and complete any final documentation that supports the event. Final notifications and waste disposal records should be completed and documented. Hospital participation in a community-wide after-action process will greatly assist in identifying areas of possible improvement for future large events, as well as developing important relationships with support agencies.

Summary

The Emergency Treatment Area (ETA) is a designated area that provides protection to the hospital and care for patients. This area, with its designated zones and specialized equipment, is the epicenter of the emergency event as seen through the eyes of the hospital. Without it, the hospital and its staff are as much victims as anyone else and will face the disastrous effects associated with the MCI, HazMat and WMD events and contamination by default. Highly trained and equipped facilities can avert the disaster by stopping the hazard from ever reaching its doors and ensuring medical care is provided as soon as possible.

Triage Principles

- Understand the importance of triage.
- Identify the three triage stages.
- Describe a system for preventing a chaotic treatment scenario.
- Describe the color-coding triage system.

> *"If you don't know a thing, you are quite certain not to suspect it...*
> *And if you don't suspect a thing, you are certain not to look for it...*
> *And if you don't look for it, you are certain not to find it...*
> *And if you don't find it, you are certain not to treat it."*
>
> *Medical Journal, circa 1878*

Introduction

In the medical field, triage is often described as the process of doing the most good for the most victims. Some may subscribe to the theory that you are making life and death decisions while others may view triage as a seldom-used skill that we practice during mass casualty drills but rarely use in real life. It is in some ways fascinating to discuss triaging patients to see the imbalance between the allocation of medical assets in times of disasters compared to the dearth of medical care available in many developing countries. For this text, we shall consider triage to be a tool that helps us allocate resources when we perceive we have a resource shortage below normal baselines. The shortage may be caused by an increased patient load, for example, after a bus accident, or a loss of typically available resources, for example, a flood separating us from our assets. As reflected in Figs. 5.1 to 5.3, Hurricane Katrina resulted in a "worst-case" scenario in trying to ration available health care assets and/or systematically move patients towards a safe area to initiate care. Responders in Katrina could not always triage by conventional means, but were forced to adjust to the conditions before them. Once we obtain resources sufficient to return to our baseline norms, we can revert back to our typical allocation of medical assets. In times of disaster, we may find that medical assets are distributed in such a manner that communities who historically have had few medical assets are served better during a

FIGURE 5.1 New Orleans, LA, August 31, 2005—Firefighters carry an evacuee, ferried in by helicopter, to the medical triage area set up at the main staging area at I-10 and Causeway. *Photo by Win Henderson/FEMA.*

disaster than they were pre-disaster. This resource distribution can cause frustration in those communities when the assets are withdrawn following a disaster.

Triage Stages

Triage typically will occur in three stages. In the first stage, at the beginning of a disaster, bystanders will triage and transport casualties to the best of their abilities. Next, the pre-hospital field providers will triage casualties, following regional protocols, but they too are sometimes caught up in a "scoop and run" mentality. Finally, the closest hospital becomes the third triage location, along with the confluence for the two previous triage groupings. It is very easy at this point to start throwing resources at problems in front of us, adopting a philosophy that activity, any activity is somehow better than doing nothing and akin to efficiency, yet nothing could be further from the truth. The challenge your hospital staff will face is resisting the urge to do something rather than taking the short amount of time necessary to gather your wits, evaluate the event, put it into perspective, develop a plan, and then implement the plan. Your plan will succeed if you identify objectives and the resources

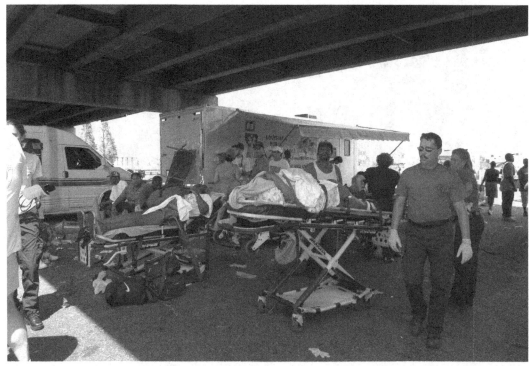

FIGURE 5.2 New Orleans, LA, August 31, 2005—Evacuees with health or medical problems are examined in the triage area set up at the main staging site. Hurricane Katrina destroyed the existing infrastructure and forced emergency workers to work in very difficult conditions. *Photo by Win Henderson/FEMA photo.*

necessary to carry out those objectives and then assign staff to do so. To immediately start throwing warm bodies at incoming patients during a disaster event will make for great news footage, but will also likely decrease operational safety and efficacy of your efforts and very possibly result in poor patient outcomes or preventable deaths. If the reader subscribes to the theory of triage being born of military conflict and necessity for returning soldiers to the battle, then adopt a military mindset to train as you plan on fighting and remember to practice, practice, practice.

Panic often ensues when hospitals are faced with the convergence of injured victims and psychological casualties, as the influx of patients can be overwhelming. Most of these victims will arrive within minutes of the incident, without having received any pre-hospital care or first aid. These hospitals will become inundated with the first wave of arriving victims who are typically the least injured, but will consume the majority of resources if you let them. It is important not to become overwhelmed early on, as it will prevent your institution from adequately caring for the most sick and injured patients, who will arrive within 30–60 minutes of the incident. The intense media coverage that follows an incident often adds to the panic and confusion.

FIGURE 5.3 Marietta, GA, September 4, 2005—The temporary Medical Triage Center at Dobbins AFB is waiting for the first Delta flight of the day. New Orleans Katrina evacuees will be health screened and needed emergency service provided. *George Armstrong/FEMA.*

Many of these problems can be anticipated and curtailed through pre-planning activities, which includes the immediate implementation of the following elements near the incident scene at safe, secured, and readily visible locations:

- Initial greeting/triage point(s)
- Access control and clear signage or direction
- Emergency medical treatment areas

It is imperative that the above stations are staffed with personnel well-trained and skilled to perform in an environment that will be unlike a "normal" emergency situation. There should be no guilt associated with performing the task of triage, as it is should be a protocol that has been practiced until it becomes second nature. Keep in mind that triage may be necessary to determine decontamination priority as well, and staff training must be robust enough to allow them to react instinctively, and not necessarily have to rationalize or engage in thought. Aside from decontamination, triage may also include immediate application of life saving interventions, e.g., tourniquets, antidotes or simply airway adjuncts. Triage purists will argue that if patients need this level of care, they should be triaged as "expected to die" and not to waste resources on them. This author feels that we must ask ourselves, "Who are you saving life-saving interventions for, if not for those in immediate distress?" It only takes ten seconds to insert an OPA airway, apply a tourniquet or administer an antidote via an auto-injector. The only possible reason for withholding such care is a facility's failure to properly pre-plan and have such simple devices available for use by trained staff.

Triage and Decontamination

In the immediate aftermath of most disasters (natural or manmade), individuals emergently seek medical care for a variety of bodily complaints. These complaints are often nonspecific and non-focal. If people are in a terrorist attack mindset, individuals may believe they have been exposed to or contaminated by a harmful agent, even though none may have been deployed. The volume of persons seeking care has the potential to quickly overwhelm healthcare resources. Hospitals impacted by the large volume of patients may not have sufficient staff available to decontaminate everyone claiming to require medical assessment and care. Triage to determine the need for decontamination is critical when it comes to allocation of limited medical facility assets. Staffing a decontamination line and decontaminating patients will consume hospital resources in a dramatic fashion and should only be employed when your assessment determines it is appropriate.

The large influx of patients associated with a disaster event should be anticipated and provisions made to direct these individuals to appropriate areas and care without overwhelming existing resources. The "walking wounded" should be directed to "casualty collection points," where they will still be under medical supervision, but will not overwhelm the acute care facilities that must attend to the more seriously injured. Members of your initial greeter/triage team should look for obvious signs, not symptoms, of toxic agent contamination in order to separate real exposures from hysteria. Following the second terrorist attack on the World Trade Center in 2001, the number of worried-well seeking medical treatment was approximately 15 times the number of people treated for smoke inhalation. In the 1995 Tokyo subway attack, the number of worried-well was five times the number of victims experiencing chemical poisoning.

If an incident involves chemicals, there may be few viable victims within the hot zone, but increasing numbers of viable victims near the outer perimeter where the agent is less concentrated. Psychological casualties will comprise the greatest number of presenting patients, and thus requires careful adherence to triage criteria to evaluate physiological status. Multiple patients displaying a toxidrome due to a suspicious or intentional event may have a chemical exposure etiology.

Timing of the onset of symptomatology is important to consider in your triage scheme as well. For instance, bomb blasts and explosions will create casualties in a very rapid fashion. Therefore, by the time victims arrive at your facility, you would anticipate these casualties to be presenting with significant complaints if they had been in proximity to the blast. Significant levels of chemical exposure will typically, but not always, result in exposure presentations fairly soon following the event and this knowledge can help guide PPE selection and your decontamination triage. Biological exposures present a secondary threat to your personnel that can normally be addressed through routine hospital PPE use. Patients rarely would present with signs or symptoms of illness without the pathogen being neutralized by the patient's actions of bathing or exposure to sunlight. Radiation can present a hazard to employees and is impossible to detect with any of our senses, which mandates routine deployment of radiation detection equipment to determine its presence or absence. Decontaminating a group of patients due to possible radiological contamination, without deploying radiation detection equipment prior to such operations, suggests your facility is inexperienced and is using personnel resources unwisely. Proper planning and training will help to limit such mistakes.

Color-Coding Triage Systems

Many agencies, communities and states have adopted triage protocols that use a color-coded system. Ideally, your country and any bordering countries should adopt identical triage protocols. Having multiple, and possibly conflicting, triage schemes results in poor allocation of resources (which once again can be attributed to poor pre-planning). This text is not advocating any one triage protocol, as they all have good points and limitations, but we will advocate the following color-coded designations:

Red color tagging means the patient has life-threatening injuries as determined by an abnormal vital sign (poor radial pulse pressure or rapid weak pulse rate, altered level of consciousness, obvious arterial hemorrhaging, or poor ventilator effort). The triage team should have the capability to immediately correct problems through application of tourniquets, insert NPA or OPA, and administer antidotes if appropriate.

Yellow color tagging means the patient may have potentially life threatening injuries but there are no outward abnormal vital signs and medical treatment will be delayed until additional assets are available.

Green color tagging means the patient ambulated to your location, can verbalize their chief complaint, can maintain their own airway, and further medical assessment will be delayed until additional assets are available.

Black color tagging means the patient visibly appears to be in extreme distress and has a lack of palpable pulse, effective respiratory effort, or consciousness, and assets are not currently available to correct the assessed problems.

Initial triage can appear to be difficult, but truly can be as simple as tagging the ambulatory who follow directions with a green tag, those with obvious mortal wounds or moribund with a black tag, and all that is left is to determine proper allocation of medical assets to the red color tagged patients. A quick way to separate the yellow from red tagged is outlined in Table 5.1.

At least for the initial triage activity, we recommend the use of colored engineer or surveyors' tape to identify the patient's triage designation. Use of this inexpensive tape allows for regular use and constant training.

HERT triage operations should be overseen by the triage team leader. This individual should be a subject matter expert in CBRNE casualty management. The triage team members will vary, depending on the size of the incident and the number of casualties expected. The triage team must train and exercise wearing their full protective equipment. The ability to triage patients is a well-entrenched skill in medical personnel around the country, indeed around the world. Triage of the CBRNE-affected or contaminated patient is a different issue and requires the members assigned to this task be thoroughly trained and become proficient through regular training and exercises. Performing triage within the Patient Reception Area or the Emergency Treatment Area (ETA) while wearing Personal Protective Equipment (PPE) will restrict certain senses that medical personnel typically use to triage. Even though medical personnel have been trained to use blood-borne pathogen protection over the years, the use of PPE designed to protect from highly toxic and dangerous substances will pose significant challenges. If protected against a chemical contamination threat, team members generally wear two or more sets of gloves with an outer work glove, bulky oversize boots or booties, restrictive outer garments,

Table 5.1 Quick Triage Category Determination Guide

Assessment	Yellow	Red
Respiratory Effort	No respiratory distress	Respiratory distress noted
Pulse/Perfusion	Strong radial/good skin color	Lack of radial or poor color
Mental Status	Oriented to situation	Not oriented to situation

and respiratory protection that confines and restricts visual, auditory and respiratory functions.

These triage members will be the front line of defense for the hospital and provide critical screening of first arrival patients. They will begin the process of bringing order to chaos by appropriate distribution of presenting patients into the correct categories. Their abilities and skills will enhance the ETA in processing patients effectively and efficiently, this alone will reduce patient apprehension and possible patient backlogging at the patient reception area. A note of importance here is the ability of the triage team to minimize a crowd disturbance, which may manifest itself should the crowd of patients feel that they are failing to receive prompt care. In many countries, quick access to medical care is considered an entitlement and has historically been available. Clear, effective communications with the arriving patients is key to maintaining calm and control, along with efficient processing.

As previously mentioned, decontamination operations are extremely labor intensive and should be deployed wisely. We can use the same triage color coded system along with a quick hazard assessment process, and our knowledge of CBRNE materials to help determine who needs to be decontaminated first and ensure operational efficiency. For Table 5.2 below:

Red Color—Indicates severe injury and/or high dose exposure to contaminant. This patient will be labor intensive from both a medical and decontamination perspective. Treatment may be required before and during decontamination for survival.

Yellow Color/Symptomatic—Indicates a serious injury and/or likely exposure to contaminant. This patient requires a priority of decontamination over medical treatment. Slightly less labor intensive and better chance of survival than red color category.

Table 5.2 Decontamination Corridor Processing Chart

Triage Color	Decontamination Corridor Processing Considerations		
	3rd Priority for HERT Decontamination	1st Priority for HERT Decontamination	2nd Priority for HERT Decontamination
Red			X
Yellow—Symptomatic		X	
Yellow—Asymptomatic			X
Green	X		

> ### TRIAGE EXERCISE
>
> You are finishing up your shift at the hospital when your windows rattle and you hear a large explosion in the distance. You look out the closest window and see billowing black smoke coming from the direction of the mall and theater complex. Almost immediately, you begin to hear sirens from every direction. You know you're in the closest hospital and the situation may soon become overwhelming. The charge nurse makes the determination to stand up the HERT and prepare for an influx of patients. You are assigned to the initial triage team and report to the reception area near the entrance to the parking lot. As you and your partner move into position, you see multiple people being carried towards you from private vehicles, police cars and even on foot. What types of medical conditions should you expect to see, and what life-saving supplies should you have with you?

> Eight members of a wedding party are transported to your emergency department with classic signs of *Clostridium botulinum* intoxication. Through the appropriate channels, you are able to obtain four doses of antitoxin for administration. Four patients went into respiratory arrest in the field after EMS arrived on scene and they have been intubated and are now on ventilators in your ED. The other four patients, while symptomatic of intoxication, still have adequate respiratory effort. Who should get your four doses of antitoxin?

Yellow Color/Asymptomatic—Indicates a serious injury with less chance/likelihood of exposure to contaminant. This patient will likely tolerate a longer wait for decontamination and benefit from medical treatment given first.

Green Color—Indicates a minimal injury or chance of exposure to contaminant. These patients can be moved through the ambulatory decontamination corridor in fairly rapid fashion. These patients should be your first choice to bus to more distant medical facilities.

Biological events come with a completely different set of triage challenges. Just as we have seen with the pandemic H1N1 virus, the question of who gets limited quantities of vaccines becomes an issue. Triage of ventilators, antibiotics and antivirals are protocols which should be developed and practiced ahead of time. This poses a challenge for a medical facility when they may have to depend upon national procurement or development and "guidance" for utilization of scarce assets. Oftentimes, the actual distribution of a limited asset is pushed to the local level, which can place unusual psychological burdens on healthcare providers. Banding together through professional organizations to develop and adopt consensus protocols may help alleviate some of the predictable contentious issues.

Proper CBRNE training and education can also help alleviate hasty emotional decisions and replace them with protocols based upon the best science, equity and inclusiveness. A good example is illustrated in the text box above.

Summary

In summary, triage may help with the initial medical assessment, but it may also be one of the most important functions when it comes to proper allocation of available resources. Regardless of the triage system you use, it requires repetitive training to the point of your staff claiming they can perform the skill in their sleep. It has been proven time and again that if you want your staff to perform a skill in an emergency, they must practice or perform the skill on a regular basis. Writing a triage protocol for deployment when a major catastrophe hits, without constant training, will result in poor performance and possibly preventable deaths. Training with your triage protocol without your employees dressed in various levels of PPE will result in poor performance as well. Be sure to mimic the actual expected event as closely as possible. This will promote confidence in your staff and in the patients they are treating.

6 ▦

Decontamination

CHAPTER OBJECTIVES

- Define decontamination.
- Describe the use of water and soap in the decontamination process.
- Describe the advantage of having a victim disrobe in the decontamination process.
- Describe the purpose of technical decontamination.
- Identify why the technical decontamination system is a separate system from the ambulatory/non-ambulatory decontamination system.
- Describe the difference between ambulatory and non-ambulatory decontamination.
- Describe the cutting and removal process for non-ambulatory patients.
- Describe the purpose of pre- and post-screening of patients/victims.
- Describe where pre- and post-screening would occur as part of the emergency treatment area.
- Describe how the term "clean" is referenced for the purpose of allowing the patient/victim to enter the healthcare facility.
- Describe what methods can be utilized to allow a patient/victim access within a healthcare facility.
- Identify who is responsible for preserving potential evidence within the Emergency Treatment Area.
- Describe the best method for preserving potential evidence while functioning in the Emergency Treatment Area.
- Describe the first task in determining the size and scope of an Emergency Treatment Area.
- Identify three sections of the sustainment program.

Introduction

The goal for any healthcare facility has always been to treat the ill and injured with the highest level of dignity and professional care. A keystone of the healthcare community is the adage "First, do no harm" when treating those who seek our aid. I believe this adage is particularly relevant to healthcare personnel who have elected to respond during a CBRN incident as part of their emergency response plan. The process of decontamination is a key factor in removing the material that has or will cause harm to an individual, and consequently may harm others. Your role will be to ensure the sufficient removal of contaminants from the victim in a way that precludes introducing any secondary contaminants into the healthcare facility, where they would pose a risk to other patients and healthcare workers.

Decontamination Principles

Many concepts come to mind when discussing decontamination, but basically we are referring to any means of removing a hazardous contaminant. Defining decontamination has produced a host of definitions, some of which I would like to share with you.

"The removal or neutralization of a contaminating substance, such as poisonous gas or a radioactive."

> Online website—The American Heritage Medical Dictionary, www.yourdictionary.com/medical/decontamination Houghton Mifflin Harcourt Publishing Company, copyright 2009.

"Decontamination is the process of cleansing to remove contamination, or the possibility (or fear) of contamination."

> Online website—Wikipedia, the free encyclopedia, http://en.wikipedia.org/wiki/human_decontamination, creative commons attribution-sharealike license, The Wikimedia Foundation Inc. Last modified on 23 July 2009.

"To remove unwanted chemical, radioactive or biological impurities or toxins from a person, object, or place."

> Online website—Encarta World English Dictionary, (North American edition) http://encarta.msn.com/dictionary_1861739276/decon.html (P) 2009 Microsoft Corporation

---

"The process of making any person, object, or area safe by absorbing, destroying, neutralizing, making harmless, or removing chemical or biological agents, or by removing radioactive material clinging to or around it."

> Online website—Dictionary of Military and Associated Terms, U.S. Department of Defense, www.dtic.mil/doctrine/jel/doddict, Joint Publication 1-02, DOD as amended through 19, August 2009.

"Decontamination means the removal of hazardous substances from employees and their equipment to the extent necessary to preclude the occurrence of foreseeable adverse health effects."

> OSHA 29 CFR 1910.120 Hazardous Waste Operations and Emergency Response, U.S. Department of Labor, Occupational Safety & Health Administration.

The goal of decontamination is to remove the hazardous contaminant as soon as possible. To do so, we use a process that has remained the same for generations. To illustrate that point, let's look at the current system. At the beginning of the process, when an individual has been exposed to hazardous material, the first step is the immediate removal of clothing from the affected areas, followed by flushing with water to remove as much contaminant as possible. Then, assuming an emergency call for assistance was placed, a HazMat Team should arrive to provide further decontamination of the individual, using water and soap. At this point, the individual would be transported to a healthcare facility where further decontamination may be performed, again using water and soap. For all of our 21st century technology and the numerous decontamination solutions we've seen brought to market, the number one recommended and most consistently used decontamination solution has been soap and water.

So what is the basis for its continued use, and why aren't we using some high-tech formulation for decontamination? There are several factors that come into play. First and foremost, if we compare decontamination to how humans have

FIGURE 6.1 Overhead view of hospital ETA decontamination setup. *Photo by Dr. Halton in memory of Tim Butcher.*

cleansed themselves for centuries, then we can appreciate the similarities between the two. For example, when we decide to bathe, we first remove all of our clothing and then use water to remove the outer grit and materials. Most of us do this by starting at the top of the head and rinsing down to our feet. We then use a soap-type product to scrub the surface of our skin, helping to remove small material and oily substances attached to our skin and hair. This is followed by another water rinse and a redressing. If I'm not mistaken, we just went through the basic decontamination process that can be found in just about any medical facility's plan.

I point this out not to claim that we should follow the same technique humans have used for ages, but rather to highlight the reasons we often choose soap and water over sophisticated formulations that may be available. So what are these reasons? First is the immediate availability of, and easy access to, water at little to no cost. Water remains the number one item we can get our hands on in an emergency, at virtually any location. We have cities and towns interlaced with pipes to supply water to virtually every building, home and street corner. Water can be stored in tanker trucks and fire trucks for immediate deployment if needed and it's always around and ready to use. Another important reason for using water is its ability to remove contaminants while doing no further harm to the individual.

CRITICAL THINKING

Water is not the appropriate solution to every decontamination situation; indeed there are numerous chemicals and substances where the application of water would cause further injury to the individual. Due caution is recommended here; the priority remains identifying the material or substance involved and following appropriate decontamination procedures for that specific material or substance. As this book is designed with the healthcare facility in mind, the focus of the decontamination section will be on healthcare facility operations as a whole. Healthcare facilities that have determined they may encounter victims exposed to hazardous materials that are reactive to water or surfactants (soap), should be prepared to properly decontaminate those individual(s) using the recommended decontamination solution for that specific material or substance.

The second factor to highlight is the use of soap (surfactants). Although soaps come in various forms, from dry to wet, mild to industrial strength, their use in the human decontamination process has remained limited. Clearly not all individuals are the same and we each have a different level of sensitivity; therefore healthcare facilities use a mild liquid type soap diluted in water for victim decontamination. The type of soap you choose will have to fit a broad range of individuals; from the elderly to the very young. The soap/water solution should be mild enough for all, yet effective enough to remove contaminants. The soap's job is to aid in removing materials that may cling to the skin surface or reside in the pores of skin or hair follicles. This brings us to an obvious yet perplexing issue: how to best decontaminate the eyes and areas near the mouth and nose. Obviously workers can't use soap in a patient's eyes, nor can they risk introducing it into airway passages, so due caution is required to effectively remove contaminants from these areas. There are special eye irrigating devices and liquids that have been designed to decontaminate the eyes, should the need arise. Many of these are routinely used in the healthcare facility setting and are readily available.

Another important step in the decontamination process is that of victim clothing removal. In fact, this step may be placed at the top of the priority list. However, although clothing removal is a sound procedural guide, there is a glitch: few victims feel comfortable removing their clothing in a public setting or in front of strangers. Certainly if the contaminant is an irritating substance, especially to the skin, then out of self-preservation the individual(s) will likely remove their clothing without being asked to do so. To what degree removal of outer clothing decreases the risk of contamination is debatable. I cannot provide a definitive percentage of contamination that is reduced by clothing removal, yet it is a reasonable procedure that maximizes contamination reduction prior to allowing an individual into a healthcare facility (see Fig. 6.2).

OSHA's Best Practices for the Protection of Hospital-Based First Receivers of Victims guidelines address the effectiveness of victim clothing removal: "For example, disrobing might remove as much as 75 to 90 percent of the contaminant arriving on a victim (Macintyre et al., 2005; Vogt, 2002; USACHMPPM, 2003a)." And again, the same guidelines state:

"The percentage of contaminant reduction depends on the type of clothing the victim was wearing when exposed. The estimates may be somewhat lower (down to 50 percent) for victims wearing short pants and higher (up to 94 percent) for victims exposed to biological warfare agents while wearing protective military uniforms (USACHPPM 2003a)."

It's obvious that the percentage of contaminant removed will vary according to the circumstances and safety should be always be considered first when deciding how effective disrobing will be. As stated earlier, reluctance to disrobe in front of strangers is human nature. Victims of contamination generally present at a healthcare facility with their clothes intact. An exception may be if the local HazMat team or emergency healthcare service has removed outer clothing prior to the victim's arrival. Victims may be willing to go through a gross water decontamination system, but likely will only remove those outer garments they are comfortable removing; any further disrobing will require the use of a privacy system.

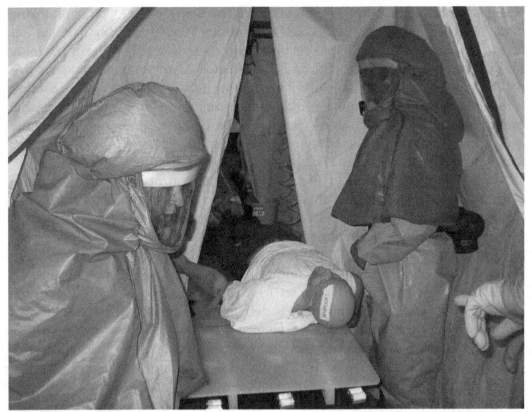

FIGURE 6.2 Patient with most clothing removed, waiting for decontamination. *Photo by Dr. Halton in memory of Tim Butcher.*

Considering the first step of decontamination, removal of victim's clothing, we can assume that between 50 and 75 percent of the contaminant will be removed. Following with water and soap will remove most, if not all of the remaining contamination on the victim. It is then reasonable to move the victim into the healthcare facility for further care and treatment. But, how do we know the decontamination process was effective? We accomplish assurance of efficacy by sampling and detection devices that confirm safe levels have been achieved. The principle of decontamination remains a basic concept, but the factors that influence the thoroughness of the process, especially human nature, remain our toughest challenge.

Technical Decontamination

Technical decontamination refers to a focused decontamination process designed to ensure the safety and well-being of the personnel assigned to decontaminate victims in the emergency treatment area (ETA). The goal is to decontaminate the outer protective garments worn by individuals in the ETA, allowing medical facility personnel to return to their normal job functions. The technical decontamination system is established exclusively for the individuals working in the ETA and is generally housed in a separate corridor from the decontamination arrangements for victims (see Fig. 6.3). You may wonder why medical facility personnel don't just use the decontamination corridor established for ambulatory and non-ambulatory patients. There are three reasons for a separate corridor. First, shift changes and relief of overworked personnel require a flow of "employee exchange" (which, incidentally, should be written in to your facility's operational safety plan). Employees need to be processed quickly and efficiently, in a separate decontamination corridor, so as not to create disruption, delay, or congestion for the patients being processed inside the victims' decontamination corridor. Second, the decontamination process for employees is focused on removing contamination from areas of their PPE and may also include exchange of batteries or cartridges or a failed component of the PPE system. The third reason is one of safety; the technical decontamination

FIGURE 6.3 Technical decontamination station in the hospital ETA decon setup area. *Photo by Dr. Halton in memory of Tim Butcher.*

corridor acts as an emergency decontamination line should any employee become ill or in need of healthcare themselves. The employee can be rapidly processed through the technical decontamination line and attended to should the need arise, all without disrupting the patient decontamination corridor.

The technical decontamination corridor may look simple in appearance; that is, the corridor may consist of a straightforward rinse, wash, then rinse again system, utilizing plastic wading pools, hoses with shower-type heads attached, and buckets with sponges, brushes, soap and water. The tools are not as important as the thoroughness with which employees accomplish the task. Your facility may well have a high tech trailer, expandable tent, or even a fixed system with numerous wash-rinse-wash stations, waste water collection systems, filtration systems for air handling, and numerous other extras to make the system work best for you, but these are not always necessary.

CRITICAL THINKING

Be sure to give serious consideration to ensuring that your system is truly functional for the atmospheric conditions you will face at any given time of the year. Extreme winter climates will obviously require warm water in the system and protection from harsh, bitter cold winds and temperatures. The exact opposite applies in extreme heat conditions, where shade, ventilation or even air conditioning systems may be necessary to provide a workable atmosphere for employees in PPE. The design features you incorporate to meet your needs will vary, but should address every reasonable eventuality.

The technical decontamination station should be one of the first corridors set up, properly staffed, and ready for operation. The safety plan should include proper preparation and readiness should a fellow team member(s) require emergency decontamination for any reason. There is nothing worse than having to wait on team members to get organized and prepared for an emergency decontamination when we know that the possibility exists and we have failed to properly prepare for the situation.

Patient Decontamination

Patient/victim decontamination is the workhorse of the decontamination system and requires the maximum effort of every team member involved. Patient decontamination is broken into two categories: ambulatory (walking wounded) and non-ambulatory (stretcher bound). The patient decontamination corridor is generally split into two distinctive lanes that are dedicated to each category of patient/victim. You may also consider allowing for male and female lanes within the ambulatory corridor. The configuration of the footprint/layout for this will vary depending on the equipment and location for setup. The layout may be a fixed setup that remains always ready for use, a portable version which will require deployment and setup of necessary shelters, equipment and tools, or a modified fixed/portable version where some of the equipment may be preset and pre-piped for use but will require others items such as roller systems, buckets and tools be deployed and staged.

We'll now focus on the differences you will face concerning ambulatory versus. non-ambulatory patients/victims, as the two corridors have vastly different requirements to ensure a complete and thorough decontamination has been accomplished.

Ambulatory Decontamination

On the ambulatory side, the obvious advantage is the ability to verbally and visually communicate with the patient/victim. Once the patient/victim has been triaged by a first receiver in the reception area of the ETA and designated to the ambulatory line for decontamination, the next task will be to communicate instructions and provide direction to the patient/victim. This may be the time you discover that the patient/victim may be hearing or sight impaired, unable to understand your native language, or mentally challenged and thus require assistance in comprehending instructions. Several alternatives are available to assist with this issue; healthcare facilities have developed and used pictorial cards that are large and clear to understand, multi-language employees may be placed at the first position in the decontamination corridor to assist with language issues, or there may be large poster boards placed in strategic locations that help guide the patient/victims through the system. The first position in the decontamination line is often the most difficult, as the individual(s) will have several tasks to perform to ensure an efficient and orderly system. The first task is to communicate clearly what you wish the patient/victim to do and ensure the instructions are understood. A brief explanation of the decontamination process the patient/victim will undergo would be helpful here as well. Next is the removal and collection of clothing and personal items. For this step ensure that you have a tracking and accountability system for personal items as part of your procedures. The system should be clear and easily understood by the patient/victim. This is critical—if the patient/victim doesn't believe in the security and accountability of your system, then precious time will be lost convincing them to give up valuable or sentimental items. Remember that among the patients/victims there may be a police officer, military member, or other emergency response individual who needs to be processed as well. Make sure you have put into place a system that allows for the securing of weapons such as side arms and other items used by these professionals. This will require advanced planning with your healthcare facility's security force, so be sure you can accomplish this task should the need arise.

Another issue that is sometimes overlooked, but one you might face, is that of a patient/victim who presents with a pet. What system do you have in place for dealing with the pet and how do you decontaminate the pet if contamination is likely? If the pet can be safely separated from the individual, then a separate decontamination line can be established that is simple and functional. A plastic wading pool or other similar type of container may be used to rinse the animal, along with a mild veterinary-approved liquid detergent solution in water for further decontamination. The animal must then be processed for confinement and control. We highly recommend contacting a veterinarian and creating an acceptable protocol for decontaminating animals if warranted. If you have addressed all those issues or have procedures in place for issues you may face when the patient/victims arrive then there is an excellent chance that the system will function smoothly and efficiently.

The next step is to have the patient/victim remove their clothing and proceed through the decontamination system. Clearly, privacy will be a concern, but this can be solved by using enclosed tents, trailers or heavy duty non-see-through curtain systems, along with male and female corridors. Once privacy concerns are addressed, then ensuring that the patient/victim follows instructions and completes the process of rinse, wash, and rinse again is the main goal. Oversight and reinforcement of instructions will be necessary to ensure the steps are completed. Patients will next go to a redress station, followed by a post-screening station that contains detection/monitoring equipment to validate the removal of the suspected contaminate.

Non-Ambulatory Decontamination

The non-ambulatory patient/victim is the most personnel-intensive section of the decontamination corridor. Processing an incapacitated individual who will arrive on a transport board, or who will have to be placed on one and then decontaminated, will require a number of decontamination team members, as well as an orchestrated system to make the process thorough and efficient (see Fig. 6.4). A patient/victim who is on a transport board is generally placed onto a roller-type conveyer system. This system allows for easy movement of the patient/victim and will position the patient/victim at about waist height for the ETA members. The process begins in the same manner as with the ambulatory patient/victims, in that they will be triaged as a non-ambulatory designation and then placed in line for screening and clothing removal. This is a multi-task operation corridor, as the

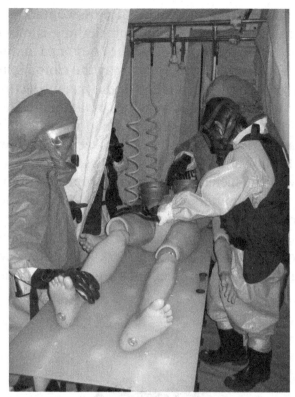

FIGURE 6.4 Mock patient on stretcher, awaiting decontamination. *Photo by Dr. Halton in memory of Tim Butcher.*

team members will have to monitor and assist in the well-being of the individual (perhaps including life support issues) while properly processing them for decontamination. This is also a physically demanding corridor, as the process of moving and manipulating patients/victims who will be wet and soapy is difficult and will require your full attention to ensure their safety as well as your own.

A systematic approach will work best for this corridor, as that way team members will be well aware of their colleagues' actions and can act as a backup system to ensure nothing has been missed or overlooked. The necessary number of team members can vary, but generally this corridor will require six personnel at a minimum to accomplish the tasks at hand. The system starts at the triage point, with removal of clothing and personnel belongings. The same tracking and accountability system used for ambulatory patients/victims will work here; part of the overall goal is to have consistency among systems and materials, so as to provide redundancy and compatibility across the entire ETA. The process of clothing removal is different here, in that the clothing is generally cut off using heavy duty safety-guarded scissors or shears, while employing a cutting removal sequence that reduces or eliminates the possibility of cross-contaminating the patient/victim. The pattern for cutting and removing clothing is based on the highest point of the patient/victim, generally using the chest area and midline as a starting point (see Fig. 6.5). The theory is to cut away the clothing, moving from high points to low points and from the midline of the patient/victim outward, which should minimize any further movement of the contaminant. The cut-away procedure starts with cutting the clothing around the torso, generally a shirt, jacket or sweater. The cut can start from the waist and travel midline towards the neck, or from the neck midline towards the waist. Regardless of where you start, you must ensure that the airway and facial area is properly protected from introducing contamination or any decontamination solutions. The next cut should be along the arms' midline, starting from the wrist towards the neck or from the neck towards the wrist (see Fig. 6.6). Then cut along the legs' midline, from the waist to the ankle, and then remove or cut the shoes (see Fig. 6.7). If the shoes are easily removed without producing any undue movement of the lower extremities or creating any

FIGURE 6.5 Midline cut to start clothing removal for decontamination. *Photo by Don Birou.*

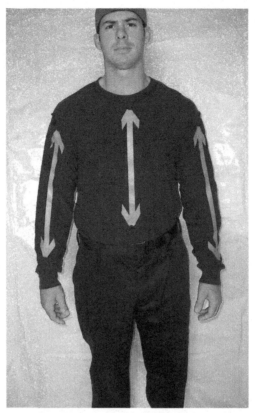

FIGURE 6.6 Cuts to torso and arms for removal of shirt or jacket. *Photo by Don Birou.*

airborne contaminant, then do so. However, if cutting the shoe is a better option, then proceed accordingly. Socks, if worn, can be removed by pulling them off if the fit is loose enough and, again, does not produce any undue movement of the lower extremities or create any airborne contaminant. If the socks need to be cut, then cut from the ankle to the toes midline, using due caution around the toes for safety. An alternative is to slightly pull the end of the sock at the toes and cut the excess off, then cut midline from the ankle to the toes. Following the cuts, the clothing will need to be removed. It is best to employ a technique of rolling the clothing from the cut edge onto itself towards the midline, with the outer clothing being rolled outside in as you go, which will reduce any movement of the contaminant. The clothing should now be below the patient/victim, but still on the transport board. At this point, the same technique you use for inspection and visualization of the back of a non-ambulatory patient/victim can be utilized to remove the clothing. The general technique is to support and maintain the neck, head and airway while rolling the patient/victim to the right or left and removing

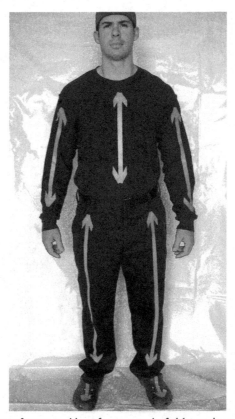

FIGURE 6.7 Cuts along midline of arms and legs for removal of shirt and pants. *Photo by Don Birou.*

the clothing as it clears the patient/victim. The clothing should be bagged, tagged, tracked and accounted for, as this will play a role in the collection of evidence and its preservation. The clothing removal station should be a three person station at a minimum, with up to five employees if necessary.

The next station is the rinse, wash, and rinse again area, where removal of any remaining contaminants on the skin is accomplished. This station will require the same number of personnel as the clothing removal station because the technique is similar. For this station the use of soft sponges is most appropriate. The technique is similar to clothing cutting, as you should start at the top midline of the patient/victim and work with downward stokes so as to use gravity to move the contaminants in the mild soapy water down and away from the patient/victim. Again, extra care is needed around the airway and facial area to ensure there is no introduction of fluids or contaminants. Generally, one to two team members will be on each side of the patient/victim and will sponge from the midline down each side towards the transport board and roller system. The patient/victim can be rolled to the right or left, allowing access to the backside for decontamination, using the same downward motion with the sponges. Take extra care when decontaminating the head and neck area, again striving to minimize any splashing of liquid onto the airway and facial area. Once the final water rinse of the patient/victim has taken place, you may wish to move them onto a clean transport board. This will accomplish two tasks; first, the clean patient/victim is now placed on a known clean transport board, and second, the contaminated transport board is now left within the confines of the ETA, thus eliminating the possibility of a contaminated transport board making its way into the healthcare facility. At this point the patient/victim is moved to the next station for drying and covering prior to moving to the post-screening station. A secondary triage and healthcare evaluation should occur at this time, before the patient/victim is absorbed into the healthcare facility setting, or transferred per protocol.

In order to effectively accomplish all the tasks assigned to this corridor, the non-ambulatory station will require the largest number of ETA personnel. Personnel change-out will also need to be addressed, as the station is physically demanding. Practice and training will hone the skills needed for this station and ensure a coordinated team effort occurs.

Decontamination Screening Process

For each decontamination corridor you establish, there should be a pre- and post- screening station. The screening process is usually part of the triage members' tasks, but may well be a separate station if personnel are available.

The screening station or process is also known as the detection/monitoring station and the goal is to determine the presence of contaminants. The screening process has two sections, a pre-screening and a post-screening. The pre-screening occurs at or near the first triage station, while the post-screening occurs following completion of the decontamination process. This screening process provides a challenge to the healthcare facility setting, as it involves the use of equipment that may be unfamiliar to healthcare facility personnel and requires

---

CRITICAL THINKING

There are a few things to keep in mind when utilizing specialized detection instruments. The first is to understand the type of instrument you are using, its design features, how it functions, and what it alerts for. Another factor to be aware of is instrument reaction time. Ideally, the instrument will quickly detect contaminants, within seconds if possible, alerting you of their presence. The last consideration is ensuring that personnel using the equipment have a knowledgeable understanding of what constitutes a risk or hazard; that is, some materials/substances may be present but do not necessarily constitute a risk to the patient/victim or the ETA team members.

the user to interpret specialized decontamination instrument readings. The goal is to determine whether or not a CBRN material/substance is present and if it constitutes a risk or hazard.

What Are You Looking For?

The answers to the above question will fall into two groups: specific and general. You may be looking for a specific, or known, material or substance that you have been made aware of prior to receiving the patient/victim. Or, you may be searching more broadly, if you have little or no information about the material/substance involved. If you know the material/substance you are looking for, then you will choose a detection instrument designed specifically to detect that material/substance. The readings you receive will allow you to determine what level of action to take. If you are looking more generally, you may very well need several different instruments to cover a broad range of hazards.

For healthcare facilities that do not have accurate or definitive information regarding the contaminant, decisions on level of risk will need to be based on the information supplied by responders, the signs and symptoms presented by patients/victims, and the readings detection instrumentation provide at the pre-screening station.

Pre-Screening

The CBRN acronym covers a broad base of materials/substances you should plan for and be prepared to detect.

The "C" relates to a very wide spectrum of chemical materials/substances, including commercial/industrial, military, and terrorist-derived substances. There are many detection instruments for this category and they are generally designed for multiple chemical gas detection and have direct readout screens. A note of caution: gas detection instruments are only capable of detecting gas, so the material/substance must be able to produce a vapor in the atmosphere you are working in. If the material/substance is a solid, or remains a solid or liquid, and is unable to vaporize due to the atmospheric temperature and pressure, then the detection instrument will be unable to alert you to its presence. The chemical family is by far the largest of the CBRN category and is the one you are most likely to encounter during an incident. This does not mean you can ignore the remaining hazards, only that you should be well prepared to detect the materials/substances that fit this category.

The "B" refers to the biological side of the family. There are a host of organisms in this category that may be used as weapons or as part of an intentional terrorist act. Although there are a limited number of biological agents available for use as a weapon, this in no way diminishes the ingenious and inventive ways an individual or group may alter or combine them to design a biological weapon. It is extremely difficult to accomplish the detection of biological materials by a handheld device that can produce identifiable results within less than a minute. You may find there is plenty of biological detection equipment on the market, but due to current limitations of instrument detection capabilities, timely results may not always be possible. For instance, it may be difficult to positively detect the presence of biological agents on the outer surfaces of the patient/victim. There are many kits designed to detect the presence of protein, but many toxic substances and materials have non-hazardous protein in them. Some biological kits can detect and alert to specific biological agents, but generally take several minutes to accomplish this task. My point here is to illustrate how time-consuming the processes of the ETA and the decontamination corridor can (and will) be. If a large number of victims are presenting and your goal is to remove the contamination as soon as possible, then holding a patient/victim for several minutes to await the results of a biological test will not be of benefit. If the biological agent has entered any of the patient/victim's internal systems, and remaining agents are still suspected to be present, then the decontamination process will remove the remaining biological hazard, if not destroy the remaining biological agents in the process.

Many companies make biological detection equipment to be used in healthcare facilities' pre-screening stations. Yet these devices cannot necessarily accomplish their tasks in a time frame that allows for quick processing and thus may delay decontamination or access to healthcare. If you find that the detection time frame is several minutes or more, I suggest you continue with a speedy decontamination process, as it will begin to remove or destroy the biological agents. Use of biological substance detection equipment as a procedural part of your facility's

---

CRITICAL THINKING

While it is best to forge ahead with the decontamination process when dealing with biological agents, the same is not necessarily true for chemical agents. By and large, chemicals have distinctive properties, either by the inherent nature of the chemical structure or by design, and based on these, the chemical may resist or repel water and soap solutions, thus making the decontamination process ineffective. It is best to know the type of chemical to which a patient/victim has been exposed, prior to starting the rinse, wash, rinse sequence. Knowing which chemical has been detected will allow you to make necessary, oftentimes critical, adjustments to the decontamination solution you are using.

decontamination process should be thoroughly discussed before determining if it will be adopted as a necessary step.

Detection for radiation or nuclear materials is the "RN" in CBRN and is a field that most healthcare facilities are already comfortable with. Many healthcare facilities have radioactive materials in use on site, on a daily basis. These facilities generally have a Radiological Safety Officer or the equivalent on staff that is available to respond to both inquiries and emergencies. Current technology and available equipment makes for easy detection of radiological materials and detection time is generally within seconds. With training, the ETA members can readily detect, and alert others to, the presence of radiological materials. The detectors or survey meters can either be handheld units or large portals that the patient/victim passes through on foot or on a transport board. Pre-screening for radiological hazards should be part of your routine process and may already exist as a current response procedure. Advanced technology equipment may reduce the need to hand sweep a patient/victim, thus saving time and effort for ETA members assigned to this task. The drawback is the cost of this advanced equipment as compared to handheld radiation survey meters. Consultation with your Radiological Safety Officer and other technical experts should provide you the best options for your facility.

Determining the level of concern (or action level) for detection of hazardous materials can be complicated and perplexing when reading the results of detection equipment. Chemicals are inherently complex and any given chemical may present no hazard below a certain level, but pose a significant hazard above a certain level. So how is one to know all the chemicals and the associated levels of concern or risk? Realistically, you can't know every chemical and its specific attributes without a chemical database readily available. The best option is to rely on the detection equipment itself; most detection devices have the capability to store preset values for determining levels of concern, action levels or alerts for levels that are immediately dangerous to life and health. These preset values are installed by the manufacturer of the detection device and are generally set at established values as indicated by government regulatory agencies or values requested by the customer. These preset values, or alert triggers, provide an audible and visual alert, freeing the user to concentrate on proper technique in obtaining a sample from the patient/victim, rather than concern over level of detection. This allows for an efficient use of detectors in the healthcare facility setting without causing undo delay or having to interpret the readings provided by the device. This does not mean that detection devices will alert for every known chemical or that they can provide a definitive answer as to the presence of a hazardous material or substance. However, if properly used by well-trained, knowledgeable, and skilled individuals, detection devices will greatly enhance your team's ability to detect the presence of a hazard and ensure effective decontamination has occurred.

Detection Devices: It would be of little value to list detection devices by manufacturer, brand or model, as these devices are routinely updated, modified or discontinued. Instead, I will provide a broad overview of the type of devices commonly found in use and their relevance for use in the pre- and post-screening station of an ETA.

CRITICAL THINKING

Serious discussion concerning the use of detection devices in the ETA setting has occurred among experts in the field and debate still lingers on the merits of their usefulness and the type of device that best suits the healthcare facility mission. Before acquiring any detection or monitoring equipment, be sure to solicit, review, and discuss information from experts in the field of CBRN response detection, regarding their recommendations for the most applicable devices for your facility.

A brief history of how these devices have evolved for use in the field of hazardous materials response may provide some insight into the appropriateness of their use in the healthcare facility ETA. Early handheld field-functional detection devices were basic instruments derived from industry and government use for specialized needs. The devices were basic in design and features and were primarily used to detect radiation, corrosive liquids, and flammable or explosive atmospheres. Detection devices typically were non-specific and could only detect general hazards. For example, a device could detect the presence of a flammable or explosive atmosphere, but could not indicate which specific material was producing it. Today's devices are highly sophisticated and not only provide detection of specific chemicals, but also have simultaneous multiple hazard detection and alerting capabilities. Some handheld instruments can simultaneously detect up to four specific atmospheric gases as well as the presence of a wide range of volatile organic compounds (VOCs). Table 6.1 details some of the available devices and the compounds they are able to detect. The demand for field-functional identification of specific materials and substances has produced several advanced instruments that are used by emergency response teams around the world on a daily basis. These instruments sample solids, liquids, and gases and are now capable of identifying compounds. Due to terrorist acts and the related use of weapons of mass destruction (WMD) materials, we have seen the development and deployment of highly advanced instruments for the detection of chemical warfare agents, industrial/commercial chemicals, explosives, and biological agents. Some of these instruments are designed for simultaneously detecting

Table 6.1   General Detection Device Matrix

Detects	Device Type
Radiation, Alpha & Beta	Radiation Survey Meter, Pancake Probe
Radiation, Gamma & Neutron	Radiation Survey Meter, Any Probe
	Radiation Pagers
	Radiation Isotope Identifier
Chemical—Commercial/Industrial	Multi-Gas Detection Devices
	Photo-Ionization Devices
	Flame-Ionization Devices
	Fourier—Transform Infrared
	Ion Mobility Spectrometry (laser)
	Raman Spectroscopy (laser)
Chemical—Warfare, Nerve, Vesicant	Multi-Gas Detection Devices
	Photo-Ionization Devices
	Flame-Ionization Devices
	Fourier—Transform Infrared
	Ion Mobility Spectrometry (laser)
	Raman Spectrometry (laser)
Biological Agents	Immunoassay
	Disposable Matrix Devices
	Hand-Held Immunochromatographic Assays
	Hand-Held Advanced Nucleic Acid Analyzer
	Lateral Flow Immunochromatography
	Nucleic Acid Amplification
	Polymerase Chain Reaction
Multi-Capability Single Device	Ion Mobility Spectrometry/Radiation Survey
Gamma Radiation	
Chemical Warfare Agents	
Pepper Spray and Mace	

radiation and chemical nerve and blister agents and irritants, while others may group certain types of materials and have a more broad response (see Fig. 6.8 for examples of detection devices).

In the end, we expect the device(s) to detect and then alert us to the presence of hazardous materials, substances or agents. Advanced technology does provide us

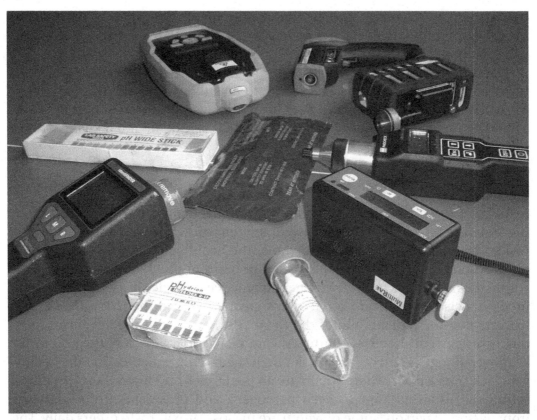

FIGURE 6.8 Detection devices. *Photo by Don Birou.*

with the capability to detect multiple types of hazards with instrument response times that are generally less than a minute. Having this capability is a huge advantage as it provides us with information regarding the level of risk to the patient/victim, the personnel in the ETA, and the healthcare facility and its occupants. When ETA team members are proper trained and utilize CBRN field detection devices, the value of the information it provides cannot be underscored enough. The pre-screening and post-screening detection information, when immediately communicated to the decision making members of the healthcare facility incident team, will allow for a more fully informed response to occur. When better informed, better decisions are made to improve response, safety and patient care.

Post-Screening

The purpose of the post-screening station is to validate that the decontamination process was thorough and that no additional decontamination is necessary. The instruments of choice for this station are the same as the detection devices used in the pre-screening station. The post-screening process provides personnel the opportunity to check the patient/victim thoroughly, especially in places where contaminates may be concealed or may be difficult to decontaminate. The post-screening station should also provide an overview of the effectiveness of the decontamination process as it relates to how thoroughly the team members are working. This can be helpful in determining when team members are over-extending themselves, or alert you that fatigue is setting in and a change-out of personnel is necessary.

Determining How Clean Is Clean

Some relative perspective is warranted when placing a value on, or establishing a marker for, the term "clean" when referenced to allowing a patient/victim inside the healthcare facility. As a whole, the healthcare community and hospitals work diligently to limit the spread of harmful pathogens and organisms within the healthcare facility setting. The practice of hygienic aseptic technique in all aspects of healthcare services has greatly reduced the risk to healthcare workers and the patients under their care. But, even with the advanced techniques in current practice, the healthcare facility remains a battleground for keeping pathogens and organisms at bay. It seems contradictory that the healthcare facility as a place where you invite all the ill, sick and injured to one central setting and then attempt to keep pathogens and organisms from migrating from person to person, some of whom are in close proximity to others daily. The healthcare facility accepts that the patient checking in or coming through the emergency room may very well have a disease, pathogen or organism that is now within the walls of that facility, and that eradicating that disease, pathogen or organism will take time and effort and place others at risk. The crux of the matter is that the healthcare facility allows a reasonable amount of disease-bearing pathogens and organisms to reside within the structure and on its equipment, as it would be impractical if not impossible to eliminate every last organism that posed a risk.

The same philosophy can be applied to determining the level of contamination reduction, degradation or neutralization that will have to occur before acceptable levels are achieved, thus allowing the patient/victim entry to the healthcare facility. There is complexity in determining acceptable levels for such a broad range of materials or substances, including unknowns.

If you take the OSHA Best Practices for Hospital-Based First Receivers of Victims document and reference the percent of removal for contaminant by only disrobing, it indicates between 75% to 90% removal (Macintyre et al., 2000; Vogt,

2002; USACHPPM, 2003a). If you assume the minimum (75%) and then factor in the next step of the decontamination process—using water and soap for between three and six minutes (OSHA Best Practices for Hospital-Based First Receivers of Victims, USACHPPM 2003a, SBCCOM 2000b, MCDRT, ATSDR 2003), then you can assume that perhaps over 80% of the contaminant has been removed. The remaining contaminant now has to be classified for type (solid, liquid or gas), persistence, toxicity, and molecular size, which then will assist in determining the hazard risk remaining. If you factor in that some materials and substances are resistant to water and soap and may continue to reside on the patient/victim, then the risk of hazard and cross-contamination of others is higher. The answer to "What is clean enough to allow entry into a healthcare facility?" remains unclear and the dynamic complexities of chemical substances, biological agents and radiological materials make it difficult to assess in an emergency decontamination setting using the detection devices that are currently available. In truth, there is no definitive answer to the question and so the answer is found in the process itself. The removal of clothing, the rinse, wash, rinse process with soap and water, and the pre- and post-screening for detectable contaminants, remains the solution whereby the maximum amount of hazard reduction has been achieved in the least amount of time.

Achieving absolute removal of the contaminant, and verification of such, should not necessarily be the ultimate goal. The goal of getting the patient/victim in to the healthcare facility for additional medical attention has to be weighed against the potential of remaining contaminants and the contaminant's ability to cause further harm.

Evidence Preservation

Incidents and events may unfold in any part of the world and any healthcare facility may be called upon to deal with the aftermath of an accidental, intentional and/or possible terrorist act. The preservation of items, materials and substances that may prove beneficial in the investigation, arrest, and final prosecution of, the individual(s) responsible for these crimes starts with the professionals who first make contact with the victims. The responsibility for preserving potential evidence within the ETA will fall on the team members operating in the first receiver area, which generally includes the triage, pre-screening and clothing removal stations. Proper accountability for tagging and tracking will provide the best opportunity to preserve evidence from patient(s)/victim(s) and allows the team members to note unusual or suspicious items or indications of something suspicious (see Fig. 6.9).

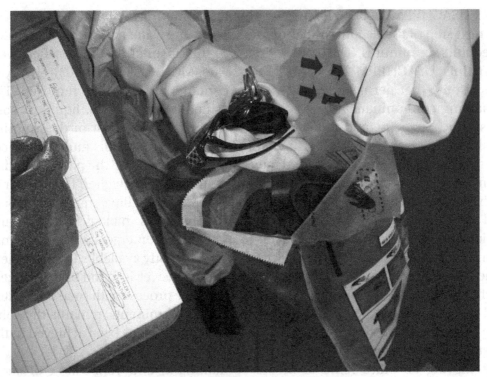

FIGURE 6.9 Personal items being bagged and tagged. *Photo by Don Birou.*

CRITICAL THINKING

It is important to mention the possibility of a patient/victim arriving and then being designated as deceased during triage. At this point, the deceased and all items with the body are considered evidence and should be preserved until law enforcement authorities take control of the body.

The possibility also exists that during the terrorist or intentional act the perpetrators were seriously injured and are now part of the patient/victims arriving or being transported to your healthcare facility. Preservation of any and all items on that individual(s) would of course be paramount in the investigation. If your healthcare facility has an evidence collection protocol or guideline in place, then you may very well adjust or modify it to accommodate its use in the ETA. If no protocol or guideline currently exists for your facility, then contacting your local or government law enforcement agency for assistance in creating one would be an excellent start.

What needs to be clear is that evidence preservation is a low priority, considering that the purpose of the ETA is to preserve life and health for those in need. But, every attempt should be made to recognize, capture, collect, and preserve items that may well turn out to be key evidence in an act of terrorism or intentional act to harm individuals. Creating clear guidance on, and procedures for, the collection of evidence, including preservation of bodies as potential evidence during a large mass casualty event, would be prudent, especially if your current morgue capacity is limited.

Decontamination Team

Recruitment & Development

The creation of an ETA team can be a daunting task, as your key resource "personnel" will have primary jobs within the healthcare facility. You will need to identify personnel who are willing to take on the additional responsibility of functioning on the team, as well as identify personnel with specialized skill sets unique to this operation.

The first task of determining the size and scope of the ETA team will depend a great deal on the size and scope of the healthcare facility. The number of personnel you may be able to allocate for the team may be small, perhaps three to five people, or your facility may be able to accommodate a twelve to sixteen person team (see Fig. 6.10). Regardless of size, each facility will face the same challenge of identifying individuals who match the skill sets for the ETA

FIGURE 6.10 HERT decontamination sub-group. *Photo by Dr. Halton in memory of Tim Butcher.*

positions and accommodating for the loss of that individual from their primary job position.

The ETA positions and functions are varied and will likely include personnel from numerous departments, such as emergency, security, engineering/maintenance, nursing, administration, and finance, as well as physicians. Besides looking at personnel in your departments and their obvious skills, you can query employees on their past experiences and untapped skills. There may be employees who have knowledge and skills relating to military service, active or reserve status, National Guard service, fire department service, fire or police rescue and hazardous materials response, emergency healthcare services, or private environmental hazardous materials response. These skill sets could prove beneficial in creating a team and serve as a source for technical assistance. Within the decontamination station several positions must be filled and may include:

- Triage—Pre-decontamination/pre-screening/patient tracking and accountability
- Clothing Removal Position(s)
- Wash/Rinse Position(s)
- Post decontamination/post-screening
- Team Leader—Decontamination corridor
- Safety Officer—Decontamination corridor
- Recovery/Remediation—Equipment decontamination and recovery, waste material and water disposal

Practical Training Tips

Training for personnel involved with, or in support of, the decontamination corridor should be considered robust and may require meeting standards or regulations from agencies such as OSHA, EPA, Joint Commission, NFPA and other governmental agencies. Some basic training requirements and highlights are presented here to provide an overview. Be sure to research and the training requirements, regulations or standards for your area, as to cover every training requirement for every location is beyond the scope of this book.

From the "OSHA Best practices for Hospital-Based First Receivers of Victims from Mass Casualty Incidents Involving the Release of Hazardous Substances" document, the following are excerpts on training personnel:

First Responder Operations Level training is required for employees (including security staff) who have a role in the Hospital Decontamination Zone, as well as the hospital's contamination cleanup crew. (OSHA HAZWOPER 29 CFR 1910.120q Standard)

First Responder Awareness Level Training is required for ED clerks and ED triage staff who might identify unannounced contaminated victims (then notify the proper authority) and security staff working outside the hospital Decontamination Zone.

A briefing at the time of the incident is required for employees whose roles in the Hospital Decontamination Zone could not be anticipated before the incident ("skilled support personnel"—e.g., healthcare specialist or a trade person, such as an electrician).

Information similar to hazard communication training is recommended for ED staff and other employees who work in the ED (Hospital Post-decontamination Zone), provided contaminated victims would not have access to them.

Examples of HAZWOPER First Responder Operations Level training curricula are available for hospitals preparing employees to conduct decontamination activities (HAZMT for Healthcare, 2003; CA EMSA, 2003a; VA, 2003; Sutter health, 2002). However, these curricula are not necessarily designed as 8-hour presentations (some are longer; others are shorter and intended for use when employees are able to demonstrate specific areas of competency).

Staff who might identify contaminated victims that arrive unannounced require specific instructions for handling the situation. Once ED clerks or staff suspects a patient is contaminated, they should be well trained in the following procedure:

- Avoid physical contact with the patient.
- Immediately notify supervisor and safety officer of possible hospital contamination.
- Allow other properly trained and equipped staff to isolate and decontaminate the victim according to EMP (Emergency Management Plan).

Personnel (employees) whose participation in the Hospital Decontamination Zone was not previously anticipated shall be given an initial briefing at the site prior to their participation in any emergency response. OSHA also recommends some form of basic training for employees who work in the Hospital Post-decontamination Zone and who would not be expected to come in contact with unannounced victims, their belongings, equipment or waste.

Obviously training must meet certain regulations or standards, but the application of those standards should provide a sound basis for the practical aspects of each position as it relates to their tasks, equipment and skills.

Training options vary and may include an internal training program that allows for minimizing down time of employees, with no travel or incidental compensation. This frugal approach works well in accomplishing the task, but may not provide the advantages of external training programs that may be available, including free government support courses. Joint training programs or exercises with other healthcare facilities in your region may be an opportunity to provide a collaborative training environment along with reduced financial costs.

Wherever possible, training should be broken down into segments where individual team members can focus on details of the tasks they may have to perform during decontamination. As each segment is completed, cross-training of individuals can then occur, allowing for adaptive task cross-over of personnel when the need arises.

Practical training segments and practical exercises provide the best scenario for employees to gain skills and knowledge concerning the tasks they must perform. Although classroom presentation of the subject matter is a must to ensure team members are informed and knowledgeable, practical exercise and training provide the greatest opportunity to instill and refine skills and knowledge under realistic conditions.

Sustainment of Decontamination Capabilities

When you have accomplished the task of establishing, training, and equipping your healthcare facility decontamination response team, you will then be faced with maintaining a viable response team and its associated equipment. The decontamination team is by far the largest segment of the ETA for a healthcare facility to sustain and manage. Your healthcare facility has spent time and money establishing a decontamination team; its inability to respond efficiently and function effectively during an incident could result in unfavorable consequences for the patient/victim, healthcare facility, and its staff.

The sustainment program should include three sections:

- Personnel
- Equipment
- Knowledge and Skills

Personnel sustainment may pose the most difficulty if staff retention is a recurring issue for your healthcare facility. Once trained as part of the decontamination team, the individual is a valuable asset and the loss of that individual would require recruitment and training of a replacement, as well as replacing job-related personal equipment. All of this comes with a price, monetarily as well as in time and effort. Personnel assigned to your decontamination team should, if possible, show a dedication to fulfilling the position with the intention of a long-term commitment. While it is not possible to obtain a binding commitment from each team member, every effort should be made to highlight the necessary dedication and commitment to the team that is required of each member.

Personnel will require annual refresher training and routine practical training or exercises to remain up-to-speed on current techniques and equipment. Standards and regulations call for required refresher training, which will vary depending on the level of training they currently meet and the standards or regulations for your location. Most regulations indicate a minimum number of hours that team members must meet for refresher training and/or the competencies involved in their position. It is often less-than-desirable to just minimally meet the standards or regulations you are attempting to follow. You will want team members to have as much information and training as possible in order to feel fully competent in all aspects of the anticipated tasks following an incident.

Equipment sustainment and maintenance will be similar to any current equipment program the healthcare facility has. Particular attention is warranted concerning equipment with a shelf life as indicated by the manufacturer. Manufacturers generally void all liabilities and warranties associated with their equipment once the date on the shelf life has expired. Check with the manufacturers for storage and cleaning requirements for the equipment you wish to utilize. Most decontamination equipment is fairly rugged and should hold up fairly well if properly maintained. Issues with deterioration of decontamination equipment are generally associated with residual moisture that remains after use. Proper drying and storage locations with adequate ventilation can minimize deterioration or damage due to water and moisture, but routine inspection with replacement or repair of items will be necessary to ensure a fully functional decontamination system.

We touched on maintaining knowledge and skills in the personnel section above, with a focus on standards and regulation requirements. The remaining knowledge and skills will be gained through a direct program, often provided by the healthcare facility itself as it relates to internal emergency response information. Personnel on the decontamination team will need routine updates regarding changes or alterations to the emergency response plan itself or changes that affect the deployment of the decontamination system. These may include physical changes, such as building construction that would affect the footprint and/or location of the decontamination system site, access to equipment or response access points the team members may have to negotiate, connection points for water and electrical equipment, waste water collection, the reception location for first receivers of patients/victims, vehicle access points, and security perimeter control points.

The healthcare facility should provide routine skills and knowledge checks on internal issues or particular items unique to their facility. Most healthcare facilities have many common procedures or protocols that are the same from facility to facility, but many others have unique, design or functional attributes that must be addressed to fulfill the emergency response plan. These could run the gamut from the very small rural facility with limited or no outside support system available, to the teaching facility with numerous research programs and affiliations with multiple universities and government-based healthcare facilities.

Healthcare facilities have many available options for maintaining the knowledge and skills of personnel assigned to the decontamination team, from web-based programs to the classroom setting and practical exercises. These options allow for the distribution of information and skill check validation necessary to ensure personnel are ready when they are needed most during a CBRN incident.

Case Study—Hospitals Face Chemical Exposure Nightmare

August 30, 2008   St. Louis, Missouri   3 pm, Saturday

SSM DePaul Medical Center	454 bed facility
St. Anthony's University Hospital	576 bed facility
St. Louis University Hospital	356 bed facility
Barnes Jewish Hospital	1,332 bed facility

Sometime before 3 p.m. on Saturday, August 30, 2008, workers at the Ro-Corp Plant in East St. Louis, Illinois, dropped a container filled with nitroaniline, a dry powder chemical.

Nitroaniline is:

- An organic chemical compound: water soluble powder, yellow to brown in color
- Used as a chemical intermediate in manufacturing dyes, pesticides, gasoline, certain pharmaceuticals and poultry medications
- Highly toxic; it is readily absorbed through the skin and toxic if inhaled
- Exposure can result in methemoglobinemia which impairs blood cells and reduces the capacity to transport oxygen
- Symptoms of toxicity may occur as late as 12 hours after exposure and include cyanosis, nausea, vomiting, convulsions, tachycardia, and dyspnea

The workers did not report the release and instead cleaned up the spilled powder and placed it into a waste dumpster. The workers showered onsite and then traveled home.

At around 3 p.m. an SUV with three plant workers from the Ro-Corp Plant arrived at the emergency room of SSM DePaul Medical Center. The SSM DePaul Medical Center is approximately 30 miles from the Ro-Corp Plant, across the state line, in Missouri. On arrival at DePaul Hospital the driver rushed into the lobby of the waiting room and stated, "I've got two people really, really sick in my car." Two security officers and one medic assisted the plant workers out of the SUV and into a fixed decontamination unit at the emergency room ambulance entrance. Both security guards and the medic were exposed to the chemical and deemed contaminated and in need of decontamination themselves. Unfortunately, one of the security officers was the hospital decontamination team leader. A hospital representative indicated that due to recent renovations the personal protective equipment for response team members was still in its old location, awaiting movement to the new location just outside the decontamination room.

As information trickled in from outside sources, it was discovered that three more contaminated patients were at a hospital some 40 miles away and that two contaminated patients were at hospitals in the metropolitan St. Louis area. Within the first hour, the magnitude of the situation had progressed to the point where 15 employees of DePaul Healthcare Center needed decontamination and the entire facility was in a lock-down mode (also known as "Black Diversion").

From that point, DePaul Medical Center began the process of incident management with further information from the SUV driver, who identified the chemical involved as nitroaniline. Additional assistance arrived from regional response agencies who then established a decontamination area in the parking lot outside the emergency room. An environmental company was brought in to assist the St. Louis County HazMat Team in determining remediation of the contaminated sites inside the hospital. The Center for Toxicology and Environmental Health in Little Rock, Arkansas, provided technical expertise through a six person team that determined the extent of contamination within the hospital. The process required air sampling for up to 12 hours and a visual check of hard surfaces using an ultraviolet light. The team then searched the homes of the patients to determine the extent of contamination and gain a better picture of the situation. The DePaul Medical Center emergency room reopened at 2 p.m., Sunday August 31.

A review and debrief by representatives of DePaul Medical Center, responding fire and police agencies, and the remediation companies, has provided insight to several areas they wish to improve. The first action sited was to move the personal protective equipment to the emergency room entrance for immediate access. Communications were a second issue, as limited information was initially available, creating an "unknown chemical" response incident. In addition, there was miscommunication among the hospital staff during the lock-down and inaccurate information was received concerning the number of individuals exposed (with numbers reaching over 50 at one point). During the lock-down phase of the incident, people within DePaul Medical Center had received erroneous reports of "people dead all over the place" stated John Mueller, Director of Safety, Security, and Emergency Preparedness for DePaul Medical Center. Mr. Mueller also stated, "Nurses and clinical people immediately think, okay, we've got to save the patients, actually, that should be the number three priority. That always freaks them out, My God, why is patient care number three? Because care of the caregiver is number one. You've got to protect yourself first and then you've got to protect your building"(Riecher, 2008).

Beyond the contaminated locations at the hospital, there was also the issue of decontaminating equipment in the hospital itself. Wheelchairs, chairs, stretchers, trays, and numerous others items all needed to be decontaminated along with the SUV the three initial victims had arrived in.

In all, this case highlights the speed at which a no-notice incident can destroy a perfectly good CBRN response plan. DePaul Medial Center had established a disaster plan and had practiced it utilizing the National Incident Management System (NIMS) and the regional Incident Management System (IMS). The hospital had personal protective equipment available, just not where they needed it to be when the staff was ready to respond.

This incident illuminates significant issues of concern (though many were out of the hospital's control):

- The incident occurred at a commercial/industrial plant a fair distance away from the hospital. Distance and time were on the hospital's side, but the employees at the plant failed to report the incident, which in turn provided no activation of the emergency response plan and reporting system at the plant site.
- Plant employees traveled home and waited until signs and symptoms were significant enough to warrant seeking medical care at hospitals in various locations throughout the St. Louis area.
- Plant employees failed to immediately inform the hospital staff of a chemical exposure and release.
- Hospital staff initially reacted to what they thought was a medically ill victim, thus cross-contaminating the facility.
- Timely and accurate information was not communicated, resulting in erroneous information being spread and causing panic.
- Pre-staged hospital personal protective equipment was stored in an unsuitable location following renovations.

- Identification of eight chemically contaminated patients seeking medical assistance across the metro hospital system was ineffectively communicated, resulting in the loss of advanced warning for other hospitals.

The end result for all the affected hospitals was one of confusion, cross-contamination and exposure of hospital staff (with the quarantining of sections of the hospital structure and grounds). This of course caused loss of services to the community as a whole and loss of business to the hospital, not to mention cleanup and remediation costs.

Some have been critical of the ineffective response by the hospitals in protecting their staff and building, others have pointed to the failure of the system as a whole in providing a safe response. The incident does hinge on a single key component, that of deception on the part of the plant employees in failing to report or communicate the chemical exposure. Had the employees properly reported this incident, or immediately informed hospital personnel as to the nature of the injuries, the decontamination team could have readied themselves and responded appropriately. The earlier hospital staff are informed of a hazardous materials situation, the quicker they can mobilize and protect themselves, the hospital, and others.

Reference

Riecher, 2008. "St. Louis ER's Face HazMat Crisis" *Industrial Fire World, Hazardous Exposure, Volume* 23, No. 6, pg 8.

(For additional information sources, see references for Chapter 3.)

Appendix A

Checklist for Developing HERT

Activity	Responsible Party	Progress Notes
Development team made up of representatives from all participating departments determines a mission statement for your HERT		
Develop a hazard/vulnerability assessment for your hospital capture area		
Conduct a gap analysis based upon the hazard vulnerability analysis and current hospital capabilities		
Develop concept of operations for your HERT		
Obtain administrative buy-in for your HERT program		
Develop list of implementation issues, regulatory requirements, and timelines in establishing your HERT program		
Consider need to re-approach administration to proceed		
Determine if outside assistance is required at this point to help develop HERT program		
Develop budget including equipment, supplies, communications, logistics, safety, education, training, exercise and sustainment costs		
Adopt training curriculum, develop policies, procedures and protocols from HERT notification to deactivation		
Develop HERT staffing requirements, recruitment and participation guidelines		
Determine if PPE and respiratory protection program is robust enough to support HERT and augment as appropriate		
Implement training program for staff passing PPE health screening assessment		
Revise as necessary policies, procedures and protocols based upon discoveries during training		
Conduct joint training with community partners		

Appendix B

HERT Level C PPE Donning and Doffing Guide

Level C Personal Protective Equipment

Prior to donning PPE, personnel should undergo pre-entry medical monitoring as soon as possible. Only personnel meeting inclusion criteria and having met the required training standards will be allowed to dress in PPE.

Don PPE Level C

NOTE: Team members should follow local protocol regarding taping.

- Each team member should obtain a chemical protective suit, PAPR with hood, gloves, and a pair of boots.
- Conduct a safety check of the PAPR as covered in class, including flow rate to be sure it meets rate specified by the manufacturer.
- Remove jewelry & clothing.
- Put on inner nitrile gloves.
- In COLD WEATHER: Put on inner suit. Tape gloves at wrist & zipper at neck.
- In WARM WEATHER: Put on scrubs and ice vests.
- Put on outer chemical protective suit to waist. Put on boots & outer chemical protective gloves.
- Connect PAPR to hood with hose; turn airflow on. Put on butyl hood (position the inside shroud between suits). Pull chemical protective suit up and on.
- Ensure zipper is covered & secured, put tape on top.
- Belt PAPR to waist.
- Put outer butyl hood shroud over suit.
- Stretch arms, pull suit sleeves OVER gloves, tape in place.
- Pull suit cuff over boot top if present and tape in place.
- Place a piece of chemical resistant tape on the hood exterior and label with the employee's name & time that employee is entering Hospital Decontamination Zone.

Self-Doff PPE Level C

- Wash hands thoroughly.
- Still wearing PPE, wash self, starting at the top of the head and working down to the bottom of the boots. Have a partner wash your back.

- Untape boots and gloves, but do not remove them.
- Unlock PAPR and place it on chair/gurney/floor, etc.
- Remove the outer suit—roll the suit away from you, inside out (with help from a partner). Remove outer gloves along with the outer suit.
- Remove PAPR hood, place in large garbage can.
- Step out of boots and suit into final rinse area (keep inner gloves and clothing on). Wash and rinse thoroughly (with partner's help).
- In COLD WEATHER: Remove (inner) suit, place in waste.
- Remove nitrile gloves: first pinch one glove and roll it down partially, then place thumb in other glove & remove both gloves simultaneously.
- Wash again, removing inner clothing, then step out of decontamination shower and into towels/blankets.

Technical Decontamination-Doff PPE Level C Adjustments

- Remove tape (if used), securing gloves and boots to suit.
- Remove outer gloves, turning them inside out as they are removed.
- Remove suit, turning it inside out and folding downward (first loosen and secure PAPR belt). Avoid shaking.
- Remove boot/shoe cover from one foot and step over the clean line. Remove other boot/shoe cover and put that foot over the clean line.
- Remove respirator. The last person removing his/her respirator may first wash all other respirator hoods or facepieces with soapy water and thoroughly wipe PAPR fan housing, then clean his/her own equipment before removing his/her suit and gloves. Place the masks in plastic bag and hand the bag over the clean line for placement in second bag held by another staff member. Send bag for decontamination. Discard items that cannot be effectively cleaned (e.g., it may not be possible to completely remove persistent contaminants from PAPR belts).
- Remove inner gloves and discard them in a drum inside the dirty area.
- Secure the dirty area until the level of contamination is established and the area is properly cleaned.
- Personnel should then move to a shower area, remove undergarments and place them in a plastic bag. Double-bag all clothing and label bags appropriately.
- Personnel should shower and redress in normal working attire and then report for medical surveillance.

Appendix C
HERT Ambulatory/Non-Ambulatory/ Technical Decontamination: Decontamination Lane Setup

Ambulatory Patients

Decontamination Procedures for Ambulatory Patients

There are several different methods by which the ambulatory patient may be directed to the appropriate location for receiving. Signs providing instructions on where to go and what to do may be posted, provided the hospital has been notified of possible victims. If no notice occurs, then verbal instructions or amplified voice (megaphone, bullhorn) may be utilized to provide instructions. Patients should be directed to an area with an enclosure such as a tent or trailer that provides modesty (as best available) and protection from the elements.

Clothing Removal Station
- Ambulatory patients will be directed to go to the decontamination trailer or field decontamination lane.
- The victims/patients will be directed to remove contaminated clothing, place them in labeled clear plastic bags for disposal or evidence in case of a CBRNE event. Personal items (watches, rings wallets, etc.) should be placed in clear plastic bags, tagged and set aside (pre-incident planning should address jewelry, watches and other expensive personal items).

Wash/Rinse Station
- Patients shall shower and wash and rinse their entire bodies with soap and warm water (for at least two to three minutes).
- Water temperature should be suitable for patient comfort without inducing hypothermia and yet not too hot as to open pores more than necessary.

Survey Station
- Medically survey patient and provide basic life support care as necessary. A medically qualified individual should be assigned to this position.

- Survey patient utilizing available detection equipment, such as M8, M9, pH sticks or other equipment to determine if decontamination has been successful.

Clothing/Redress Station
- Patients shall be redressed with appropriate and suitable garments so as to provide modesty and comfort. The garment(s) selected should include footwear suitable for walking on rough surfaces found outside the hospital and protection from the outside elements.

Triage Station
- Following clothing/redress, the victims/patients should be walked to the Triage Station.
- Triage team member can do a further survey of the patient's medical condition.
- They should pay special attention to wounds, cuts or lacerations, and rinse these areas with clean water or a saline solution to ensure they are clean of any contaminants.
- Bandaging and dressings should be applied to cover these areas to protect them from further contamination and possible infection.

Advanced Life Support in ETA
- Patients exhibiting signs and symptoms of exposure, who require advanced life support care, should be provided that care at this station before they are sent to the hospital's emergency department, if such care is possible.
- If not, then a further survey of the patient's condition should be done here and that information forwarded to the hospital's emergency department staff and the patient taken there immediately. The ETA should be stocked with equipment and medical supplies necessary for providing advanced emergency patient care. An experienced doctor and nurse should attend and oversee this station.

Hospital Emergency Department
- Once patients are provided the required care, they should be moved to the hospital's emergency department where additional care, hospital admission, or transfer can be provided or arranged.

Equipment List for Ambulatory Patients
- One lane of the three lane deployable decontamination shelter
- Flexible and extendable hand water sprayer nozzle system

- Orange safety cones, 10 each
- Triage tag system, 100 each
- Barrier tape, red, "Hot Zone"
- Barrier tape, yellow, "Do Not Enter"
- Garbage bags, heavy duty, large 35 gallon, one box
- Garbage bags, heavy duty, small 5 gallon, one box
- Liquid soap
- Sponges
- Water resistant overhead light system inside shelter
- Patient personal item collection and tracking system kit
- Towels for drying off
- Redress garment and footwear
- Megaphone/bullhorn, battery operated, hand-held

Non-Ambulatory Patients

Decontamination Procedures for Non-Ambulatory Patients

The non-ambulatory patient may arrive with notice by ambulance or as a no-notice arrival by privately owned vehicle. Once discovered and presented, the victim(s) should be directed to the Emergency Treatment Area (ETA) for decontamination. Once placed on a stretcher or backboard the patient should begin the non-ambulatory decontamination process as soon as possible.

Clothing Removal Station
- Move stretcher with patient on backboard to the non-ambulatory roller system in the decontamination corridor and position stretcher for transfer to the roller system.
- Transfer patient on backboard to the roller system.
- Contaminated clothing should be removed or cut away utilizing the CDP Cut-Out procedure; see cut-out document.
- Contaminated clothing shall be placed in labeled clear plastic bags for disposal or as evidence in case of a CBRNE event.
- Personal items (watches, rings wallets, etc.) should be placed in plastic bags, tagged and set aside (pre-incident planning should address jewelry, watches and other expensive personal items).

Wash/Rinse Station
- Under a portable or fixed shower system, the patient should be carefully washed and rinsed with soap and warm water.

- The victim/patient's entire body should be washed with soap and warm water and rinsed (for at least two to three minutes). Water temperature should be suitable for patient without inducing hypothermia and yet not too hot as to open pores more than necessary.

A specific process will be used to wash and rinse the victim/patient:

- From head to foot
- From front to rear
- Midline down both sides
- Giving special attention to head and hair, underarms, groin, etc.
- The victim/patient should then be transferred to a clean stretcher/ backboard.

Survey Station

- Medically survey patient and provide basic life support care as necessary. A medically qualified individual should be assigned to this position.
- Survey patient utilizing available detection equipment, such as M8, M9, pH sticks or other equipment to determine if decontamination has been successful.

Clothing/Redress Station

- Provide suitable patient cover for modesty and as protection from the elements.

Triage Station

- A triage team member can do a further survey of the victim's/patient's medical condition.
- They should pay special attention to wounds, cuts or lacerations.
- Bandaging and dressings should be applied to cover these areas to protect them from further contamination and possible infection.

Advanced Life Support in ETA

- Patients exhibiting signs and symptoms of exposure who require advanced life support care should be provided that care at this station before they are sent to the hospital's emergency department, if such care is possible.
- If not, then a further survey of the patient's condition should be done here and that information forwarded to the hospital's emergency department staff, and the patient taken there immediately. The ETA should be stocked with equipment and medical supplies necessary for providing advanced

emergency patient care. An experienced doctor and nurse should attend and oversee this station.

Hospital Emergency Department
- Once patients are provided the required care, they should be moved to the hospital's emergency department where additional care, hospital admission, or transfer can be provided or arranged.

Equipment List for Non-Ambulatory Patients
- One lane of the three lane deployable decontamination shelter
- Flexible and extendable hand water sprayer nozzle system
- 1 & 5 gallon size buckets, plastic
- Orange safety cones, 10 each
- Triage tag system, 100 each
- Barrier tape, red, "Hot Zone"
- Barrier tape, yellow, "Do Not Enter"
- Liquid soap
- Garbage bags, heavy duty, large 35 gallon, one box
- Garbage bags, heavy duty, small 5 gallon, one box
- Bleach, 1 gallon
- Soft bristle brushes
- Sponges, small
- Sponges, large
- Clothes cutting shears
- Patient roller system
- Backboards, plastic with straps
- Patient personal item collection and tracking system kit
- Water resistant overhead light system inside shelter
- Detection devices—M8, M9, pH paper, radiation survey meter, multi-gas monitor

Technical Decontamination

Personnel working in PPE will be required to undergo proper decontamination before exiting the decontamination corridor. The number of decontamination steps and the decontamination solution required are hazardous substance specific and the suggested procedure for the specific substance should always be followed. Generally a good surfactant and water may provide the best decontamination process, but obtaining the specific product identification and utilizing

200 HOSPITAL EMERGENCY RESPONSE TEAMS

the specific decontamination solution is always best. Product identification and/ or specific decontamination procedures may be obtained from several different sources such as the CDC, ATSDR, CHEMTEC, EPA, TOXNET or from product manufacturers.

It is assumed that due to limited personnel on the HERT that the HERT members shall themselves become the Technical Decontamination Team and prioritize the sequence of personnel from the most highly contaminated to the least likely contaminated during the technical decontamination process. HERT members with the most contamination will enter the technical decontamination station first, while members who encountered less contaminant will be cycled last. The last two members will then self-decontaminate.

Equipment Drop

The HERT personnel will proceed to the technical decontamination station and drop any tools and/or survey equipment that they may use again or will be used by other personnel. Arrange for a designated equipment drop site.

Wash/Rinse Station

Step 1—Direct Member into Shuffle Box
The shuffle box is the first step in the process and consists of a simple container on the ground with a short brim or lip. The container should be large enough to safely stand in and may be filled with an absorbent material or liquid solution that is designed to reduce the contamination or hazard on the boots.

Step 2—Direct Member into 1st Wash/Rinse Pool
Step into the first wash/rinse station utilizing a side-step motion with a face-to-face orientation, while stepping into and out of decontamination pool. Be sure the member uses a support device such as a four point walker or other device to ensure stability during ingress and egress from decontamination pools.

If a loose-fitting hooded PAPR is worn, then an additional team member may be needed for assistance. The additional member shall remove the rear filtration system and battery with belt and hold the assembly up and away from the member being decontaminated. This ensures that the filter cartridges and battery are not saturated with decontamination water or solution and that the battery continues to power the pack supplying filter air to the member. Shorting out the electrical system or introducing large quantities of water or decontamination liquid into the cartridges will either stop or significantly reduce the airflow through the system, thus creating an emergency situation for the wearer. A free-standing support item may be used in place of the additional member to support the PAPR assembly, but if this is the case, ensure it will remain stable during decontamination process and that the item is disposable or can be decontaminated.

Wash and rinse team member starting from the top of the head, moving toward the toe. Use brushes with all strokes, starting at the highest point and traveling downward only. During this process, special attention should be directed to the hands, front of garment from neck to the waist, and bottom of boots, as these will be the most likely places of increased contamination. The hands should be washed so as to minimize the possibility of getting decontamination water or solution inside the garment at the point where the garment sleeve mates with the glove (the garment sleeve is on the outside of the glove and taped). To lessen the possibility of inducing decontamination water or solution at this point, have the member hold their hands in a slightly downward position so as to allow the decontamination water or solution run with gravity from the arm down the hand and off the fingertips. Ensure thorough washing of areas indicated by the member that require special attention such as the front of the garment, which may have made repeated contact with areas of the patient or roller system. Wash thoroughly the bottom of the soles of the boots by having the member rotate the boot to an "on toe" position with one foot at a time (ensure member utilizes the support device during this phase). Rinse member from head to toe while minimizing the splash from the wash sprayer.

Step 3—Direct Member into 2ⁿᵈ Wash/Rinse Pool
Repeat above steps

Change-Out Station

If the need is to replace filters on the loose fitting PAPR system or APR and return to active operations in the decontamination corridor, then this can be accomplished at this time. If no change-out is needed then skip this station.

Step 4—Direct Member to a Seat with No Sides or
Back or Stool for PPE Removal
With member seated, start the process of removing the Chemtape from the wrists, ankles and front zipper area (if an APR is being used remove the tape around the mask).

Have member stand up and remove the outer work/chemical glove by placing their hands together open palm and placing them in between their knees. Using a slight amount of pressure pull the outer work/chemical gloves off; gloves then go into a receptacle.

Unzip the suit at the midline and starting at the neck roll the garment inside out clearing the shoulders and progressing to the waist and knees.

Have member sit back down and remove the garment a leg at a time, as each foot comes out of the garment have the member rotate the foot to the clean side of the station till member has rotated both feet and torso to the clean location.

Place garment and boots in receptacle.

Remove inner Chemtape on the glove that covers the Silver Shield glove if taped.

Remove Silver Shield glove, place gloves in receptacle.

Remove loose fitting hooded PAPR or APR.

Have member remove inner glove by the inside out method and place into receptacle.

Step 5—HERT Team Member Receives Medical Evaluation with Emphasis on the Specific Chemical Toxicological Hazards
The member's medical records and documentation shall be complied and forwarded to the appropriate hospital department for record keeping.

Equipment List for Technical Decontamination Station

- Garden hoses × 2 at 50 feet each
- Hand sprayer wand with control valve and variable water spray pattern, 1 gallon
- Hand sprayer wand with control valve and variable water spray pattern, 5 gallon
- A one to four garden hose manifold with shut off valve for each hose connection
- Four 1 gallon buckets
- Four 5 gallon buckets
- 6 soft bristle brushes with long handles
- Liquid soap
- Two decontamination pools, 4' × 4' each and 6 inches deep, plastic
- Orange safety cones, 10 each
- Garbage bags, heavy duty, large 35 gallon, one box
- Garbage bags, heavy duty, small 5 gallon, one box
- Two - Four point support walkers
- Sponges, large, 6 each
- Sponges, large, 6 each
- Bleach, 1 gallon size, 1 each
- Barrier tape, red, "Hot Zone"
- Heavy duty plastic stool or seat, 2 each
- IV pole, extendable, wide base, four wheel, 2 each
- Detection devices—M8, M9, pH paper, radiation survey meter, multi gas monitor

Appendix D
HERT Decontamination Techniques

Decontamination is the process of reducing and preventing the spread of contamination by people and equipment present at a CBRNE or hazardous materials incident by physical and/or chemical processes. The techniques used to accomplish decontamination will vary. Decontamination of ambulatory and nonambulatory patients varies in that the latter cannot aid in their decontamination.

Patient Decontamination Procedures

Ambulatory Patients

- Each patient should be triaged to determine need for life-saving care, ability to survive long enough to make it through decon, and priority for decontamination. Assignment of a triage tag will also aid in tracking of clothing and personal items.
- Treatment should be limited only to those interventions deemed life-saving by the HERT Medical Officer.
- Direct patient to ambulatory Decon Sector using signs and barriers, if possible.
- Children should be kept with their parents if at all possible; if no parent or older sibling is available then a Decon Team member should provide needed assistance to a child. Notations should be made with a grease pencil on the triage tags of family members to help keep families intact.
- Patient should be given a personal decon kit as soon as it is available and be given concise instructions on its use—two strategies are to have laminated posters (in multiple languages if appropriate to locale) or to have a taped message on self-decon procedures. If not, someone will have to provide instruction.
- The kit stays with patient as they proceed through the process.
- Patient should quickly remove all clothing, putting valuables into the clear plastic bag and clothing into the large bag, then put both bags into a final bag and cinch tight with triage tag number in pack. Patient should keep triage tag around their neck and wear it through decon and treatment.
- The clothing bag should be set aside in a secure area.

- If staff is available, patient's name and triage tag number should be recorded on the patient decon record.
- Patient should continue forward into the Decon Sector with remaining part of personal decon kit.
- Patient should quickly rinse themselves from head to toe with water, using either the hand-held sprayer, garden hose, or shower head.
- Patient should next wash with soap and washcloth or brush from the kit in a systematic fashion, cleaning open wounds first and then in a head-to-toe fashion for 5 minutes when the agent is non-persistent and 8 minutes when a persistent or unknown agent is involved. Discourage the patient from rubbing too vigorously while washing. Eye irritation may require the use of a topical anesthetic before irrigating.
- A member of the Decon Team should closely observe each victim to ensure they are thorough in washing themselves. Particular attention should be made to ensure they wash the axilla, creases, folds, and hair. Help should be offered as necessary.
- Once the washing is complete, each patient should thoroughly rinse themselves (this should require about a minute to complete).
- Decon soap, washcloths, brushes, and sponges should be put into a nearby trash can and NOT carried into the Cold Zone.
- After the rinse/wash/rinse cycle is complete the patient should next proceed to the towel-off area to complete drying off. Patient should leave the towel in the trash can.
- Following drying off, the patient should put on the patient gown and proceed to the Triage Officer for reassessment and assignment to a treatment or transport sector for disposition.
- Decon Team members should be alert to the possibility that an ambulatory patient may clinically deteriorate and require immediate removal to the Non-Ambulatory Sector via backboard, stretcher, or wheelchair.

Non-Ambulatory Patients

- Each patient should be triaged to determine need for life-saving care, ability to survive long enough to make it through decon, and priority for decontamination.
- Treatment should be limited only to those interventions deemed life-saving by the HERT Medical Officer.
- Patient should be brought to the Decon Sector and tended to by a minimum of 6 decon personnel.

- Each patient should be put onto a backboard or EMS stretcher with the pad removed.
- All patient clothing should be removed, valuables put into the clear plastic bag, and clothing into the large bag then put both bags into a final bag and cinch tight with triage tag number in pack.
- Attention should be paid to minimizing the aerosolization spread of particulate matter (radiation contamination) by folding clothing inside out as removal is being done and dabbing the skin with sticky tape and/or vacuuming.
- Patient should have their triage tag around their neck and wear it through decon and treatment.
- The clothing bag should be set aside in a secure area. If staff is available, the patient's name and triage tag number should be recorded on the Patient Decon Record.
- While resting the backboard on sawhorses or other device, or with the patient on a stretcher, quickly rinse the patient from head to toe with water using either the hand-held sprayer, garden hose, or shower head; protection from aspiration of the rinse water should be ensured.
- Next, the patient should be washed with soap and either a brush or washcloth in a systematic fashion, cleaning airway first followed by open wounds then in a head-to-toe fashion for 5 minutes when the agent is non-persistent and 8 minutes when a persistent or unknown agent is involved. Avoid rubbing too vigorously.
- The patient should be rolled on their side for washing of the posterior head, neck, back, buttocks and lower extremities by 2–4 personnel; attention to a possible neck injury should be given.
- Careful attention should be given to washing the voids and creases such as the ears, eyes, axilla, and groin.
- Topical eye anesthetic may be required before effective eye irrigation is done.
- The patient should then be rinsed for about one minute in a head-to-toe fashion that minimizes contamination spread. Overspray or holding the rinsing device too close, so as to irritate the skin, should be avoided.
- Decon Team members should be alert to the probability that the non-ambulatory patient may require ABC support (airway positioning, suctioning, O_2 administration, spinal stabilization, etc.) and administration of life-saving antidote administration by IM injection. If IV therapy is needed, the extremity site for the IV should be deconned quickly before the IV is started. If IV therapy is needed the patient should be pulled out of line in the

Decon Corridor but remain in the Decon Sector. This will require dedicated medical personnel in addition to decontamination line staff.

- The patient should be dried off, put into a hospital gown, and transferred to a clean backboard (or clean off and dry the board they are already on if additional boards are not available). Patients on a stretcher should be transferred to a clean backboard. Any medical materials applied in the decontamination corridor may need to be removed and replaced with clean items prior to movement to the post-decon area.
- Decon soap, brushes and sponges should be put into a trash can and not carried into the Cold Zone. O_2 material should remain in the Decon Sector.
- The patient should be taken to the Triage Officer for reassessment and assignment to either the treatment or transport sector.

FACILITATOR NOTE

Remind team members to wash the victim from head to toe, keeping modesty issues in mind.

The decontamination team should make sure that the cutting device and gloves are rinsed with a decontamination solution before coming into contact with the victim. The cutting tool should be dipped in the solution before each cut.

Discuss the flowchart available for cutout procedures:

- Begin removing clothing by cutting with shears from the waist up to the neck of the shirt or blouse.
- Cut the sleeves up to the neck.
- Peel back the clothing from the victim, using the inside of the shirt as a barrier (this action removes decontamination from the victim's airway).
- Cut from the cuffs of the pants up to the waist, and then peel back the pants from the victim. Undergarments must also be removed.
- Use local protocol in removing shoes, boots, etc.
- Remove footwear (if a sock does not pull off, use the shears to cut a small hole in the toe of the sock, and cut up the sock).
- Team members will dip both gloved hands into decontamination solution before touching or lifting the victim.
- Ensure team members dip both gloved hands and shears into the decontamination solution after each cut.
- Survey the victim.

Cutout and Decontamination Procedures

NOTE: Team members should exercise appropriate safety precautions when lifting and transporting patients.

- Place the patient between the buckets containing diluted bleach. WARNING: The bleach is for cutout tools, including gloves and scissors only. Bleach should not touch human skin, as it may cause severe burning and/or damage.
- One, or ideally, two, team members will cut the clothing, while another person maintains the patient's airway and controls the operation. Another person will communicate any change in the condition of the patient and provide support as needed.
- Team members should not straddle patients and should not kneel on the ground (to avoid cross-contamination or damaging their protective garment).
- Decontaminate scissors and gloves after each cut and before touching skin.
- Since most serious injuries and death from hazardous materials result from airway and breathing problems, remove clothing nearest the airway first.
- Remove the shirt by first cutting up the front to the neck area then cut the sleeves to the neck area. Peel the shirt back from the patient and use the inside of the shirt as a barrier for the patient. If present, remove the bra at this time.
- Remove pants starting at the cuff. A cut is made upward from the bottom of both legs to the waist. Peel the pants away from the patient and use the inside of the pants as a barrier for the patient; remove underwear.
- Cut shoestrings and remove the shoes. Use the inside of the shoe as a barrier for the patient's foot.
- Remove the socks by gently pulling up on the sock (if a sock does not pull off, use the shears to cut a small hole in the toe of the sock, and cut up the sock).

Patients with Special Needs

Glasses/Contact Lenses

- Patients with glasses should keep them if they cannot see without them. They must be washed and rinsed thoroughly during the decon process before being worn. Otherwise, the glasses should be placed in the valuables portion of the clothing bag.

- Contact lenses should be removed and placed in the valuables portion of the clothing bag.

Canes/Walkers

- Patients who use walking assist devices may retain them, but the device must be washed with soap and water during the decon process before being allowed into the transport or treatment sector.
- Patients who are unsteady standing and/or walking should be given a walker upon entry into the Decon Corridor. The walker should be used to assist with ambulation until they get to the end of the line, when it should be retrieved, deconned, and returned to the front of the Decon Corridor for the next patient who needs it.

Percutaneous Lines/Saline Locks

- Unless contaminated, percutaneous lines and saline locks should be covered with Tegoderm or Saran wrap before the area is decontaminated.
- Contaminated percutaneous lines or saline locks should be removed before being decontaminated. After the area is cleaned, a temporary dressing should be applied until the patient is in the Treatment Sector, where antibiotic ointment and a new bandage should be applied.

Hearing Aids

- Hearing aids CANNOT be immersed or otherwise be soaked with water. Thus, they should either be removed and placed in the valuables portion of the patient's clothing bag or, if they must be used by the patient because there is no hearing without them, they should be carefully wiped off with a slightly saline moistened 4 × 4 gauze, dried off, put into a clear plastic bag, and handed to the patient. The cleaned hearing aid is NOT to be worn until the patient has completed the decon process (including washing the ears) and is in the transport or treatment sector.

Dentures

- Unless the oral cavity is contaminated, dentures should remain in place and no decontamination is necessary.
- If the oral cavity is contaminated, then the dentures should be removed, placed in a clear plastic bag with the patient's name or triage tag number placed on it. The dentures should later be decontaminated in accordance with instructions received from the Poison Center and/or a dentist. The patient's mouth should

be decontaminated with mouthwash or saline that is gargled and safely spit out into a bio-hazard bag. Note that, depending on the contaminant, it may not be possible to decontaminate plastic items, such as dentures.

Law Enforcement Officers with Weapons

- In most cases, law enforcement personnel who have been injured on the scene will have had their gun(s) removed before arrival and given to a fellow officer. However, if that is not the case, the weapon should be left in the holster and the gun belt removed by a Decon Team member and placed in a clear plastic bag labeled with the patient's name and/or triage tag number. The bag should then be passed to the Treatment Sector where it should be given to a fellow officer or hospital Security Officer for safekeeping until it can be given to a representative of the injured officer's department. **THE GUN SHOULD BE LEFT IN THE HOLSTER IF AT ALL POSSIBLE.** If the gun must be removed, it should be handled by a Decon Team member familiar with firearms, rendered safe, placed in a clear plastic bag marked with the patient's name and/or triage tag number, and given to a fellow officer or hospital Security Officer in the Treatment Sector.
- Decon Team personnel should be aware that oftentimes an officer may have a backup weapon usually found in a holster near the ankle, in their pocket, in a ballistic vest, or near an armpit. The holster with the weapon in place should be removed and secured as described above.
- An officer's gun belt may also contain items that could prove dangerous if allowed to get in the wrong hands. Thus, the belt should be collected and separately bagged ASAP and passed to a fellow officer or hospital Security Officer in the Treatment Sector. **DECONNING OF AN OFFICER'S WEAPON AND/OR GUN BELT WILL BE THE RESPONSIBILITY OF THE POLICE DEPARTMENT.**
- If the officer is wearing a ballistic vest it must be removed prior to undergoing decon. The vest is usually easily removed by loosening the Velcro straps and then pulling the vest apart and off the patient. It should then be placed in a large plastic bag identified with the patient's name and/or clothing number on it and passed to a fellow officer or Hospital Security Officer in the Treatment Sector.

Appendix E
HERT Emergency Treatment Area Exercise (7-hour exercise)

This exercise will provide an opportunity for the team members to establish an Emergency Treatment Area (ETA) and all its associated activities. It is not designed as a no-notice event but it will be a complex and longer-running event which will place some stress on the team members. Safety or gross errors will be corrected immediately by the facilitators, but other issues will be addressed at the hot wash wrap-up.

Team members will be given a scenario briefing (using current date and weather conditions) about a planned community event which may require activation of the Hospital Emergency Response Team (HERT). Team members will be given about 90 minutes to pre-plan for the event by setting up their command structure, including the decision on who will be dressing out for decon and staffing all areas of the ETA. The exercise will commence in real time, and the facilitators will feed information to the group as time goes on. The exercise will be hands-on with patients (live and manikin), plans written, and communications implemented as needed with outside entities which will have to be role-played by facilitators. Facilitators should record on paper any input they provide, to allow for consistency among facilitators, to assist in after-exercise review, and for consideration of incorporating into future exercises.

> **Facilitator Note:** Allow up to 7 hours for this exercise. Facilitators should refer to specific task guidelines if they are not familiar with them at this time.

The estimated timeline for this exercise is as follows:

1015–1025	Scenario read for team members
1025–1200	Team members prepare IAP for community event
1200–1300	Lunch
1300–1530	Operate ETA
1530–1545	Deactivate ETA
1545–1600	Medical screening
1600–1630	Debrief exercise

After team members have been read the scenario they will be expected to establish an IMS structure that enables them to work together as a HERT to perform as many realistic tasks as possible within the confines of time, resources, equipment, and the enviornment. Objectives we are looking for include:

Command Function

Conduct a situational anaysis
Create an IAP
Work within community command structure
Determine appropriate PPE level
Establish rehab area
Establish and maintain communications throughout
Ensure safety and security of hospital and HERT members

Operations Function

Determine site for decontamination coridoor
Establish ETA, including equipment necessary for all operations
Don PPE
Staff pre-decon triage area
Staff cutout and decontamination area
Staff post-decon medical assessment and treatment area
Establish and maintain communication with command
Recognize need for security
Recognize need for detection and monitoring equipment and deploy properly

Checklists to help team members and facilitator in the command area are attached for use as appropriate.

Facilitator Note: Prior to lunch, team members will be responsible for conducting a discussion and carrying out such activities so that by lunch time they have:

1. Conducted a hazard vulnerability assessment appropriate for the specific event/threat intelligence they have received.
2. Evaluated their current status/census.
3. Discussed and obtained information from local EMS, Public Health, Fire, and Law Enforcement on their projected status for the community event and/or other pertinent considerations.

---

4. Developed guidance for employees on reporting of suspicious behaviors, events, or items.
5. Determined and established recommendations on the need to restrict or direct employee and visitor ingress and egress from the facility and/or grounds.
6. Establish a PIO and prepare to monitor media and local news reporting.
7. Review callback notification procedures.
8. Establish triggers and stages as appropriate for implementing emergency plan.
9. Discuss methods to declare an emergency staffing crisis and handling credentialing issues and use of volunteers.
10. Review hazard specific responses for threats to your facility.

Team members will be responsible for strategic thinking and development of a pre-incident plan prior to lunch and after lunch should be able to go tactical and implement their plans. This may include establishing an Emergency Treatment Area, including a command function, decontamination corridor, post-decon assessment and treatment, and a rehab station. Proper pre-decon triage will reveal that not all patients require decontamination. Ambulatory, technical and nonambulatory decontamination may be covered as time permits. Prior to beginning the exercise, manikins with signs/symptoms appropriate for initial triage need to be readied, manikins allowing IV and intubation interventions should be used if available, and all equipment required for ETA operations obtained. Not all team members will be dressing out for this exercise but they will need to be prepared to operate the decontamination corridor for a length of time determined by their commands situational analysis.

During the team members' planning time, facilitators are encouraged to listen to discussions but allow the team members to move at their own pace with direction. Adequate documents and IMS forms must be available for the team members as well as several facilitators to role play community agencies if the team members seek input.

It is anticipated that the team members will be "leaning forward" on the establishment of the ETA and will find that due to pre-planning they can be up and running more quickly. This emphasizes the value of pre-planning as well as building confidence in their ability to perform this operation at their hospital.

Facilitator Note: Two facilitators are needed to prepare and staff the command and rehab areas. They may elect to be dedicated to one activity or float as appropriate based upon activity and flow. Prior to the exercise the primary facilitator will ensure all items necessary to operate the areas are available and in working order. Facilitators should also be well versed in any community interaction roles/information they may need to provide.

One facilitator should prepare and staff the pre-decon triage area and be prepared to ensure manikins and/or role players are in position and properly identified with triage and other pertinent medical findings. A minimum of 8 victims per hour will be needed for this exercise. The patient arrival does not need to be in specific order but should be spaced to give teams a variety of issues to deal with. At some point during the scenario, information regarding a possible suspect or vehicle will be injected by the lead facilitator.

One facilitator will be present anytime team members are donning PPE and will move with them to the decon operational area, announcing on the facilitator radio net when the team members are "on air." The same facilitator will be responsible for moving the team members back to rehab at the end of their PPE cycle. In between, they will remain in the decontamination area and act as the primary safety officer.

Three facilitators will be present in the decontamination corridor (1 in cutout area, 1 near decon line, 1 near hot/warm line). Facilitating the team members through proper operational issues is one task, but just as important is maintaining close observation for signs of heat stress, watching for trip hazards, and ensuring the safety of team members dressed out in PPE. Facilitators should emphasize the need to balance personnel workload of evidence collection against the need to move critical patients rapidly through the corridor. Team members should be presented with the need to apply some type of critical medical intervention pre-decon and then determine the need to replace any intervention material before exiting the post-decon area. Facilitators will apply common sense and review the situation rather than use theoretical cross-contamination as the rule.

One facilitator will be present in the post-decon area to observe reassessment of patients and appropriateness of medical interventions and/or transport decisions. Patients will have the option of being admitted into the hospital or moved off for transport to other areas or facilities.

If adequate attention is not being paid to collection of evidence, facilitators may interject verbal inquiries regarding triage tag numbers and clothing descriptions.

Rehabilitation

Part of operating the HERT is conducting the medical monitoring of staff to ensure their ability to function.

Typical tasks are conducted as follows:

- Hydrate and provide nourishment for staff.
- Provide a safe haven where staff can take a time out from incident response.
- Provide ongoing monitoring to identify potential heat- or stress-related illnesses or injuries and any other health-related issues.

- Immediately identify, treat, and report any potentially serious medical conditions detected during evaluation.
- Treat and report any traumatic injuries.
- Classify personnel into three categories:
  - Return to duty.
  - Remove from duty (evidence of illness or injury).
  - Transport to a medical facility for further evaluation.

Scenario

The annual Petunia festival draws thousands of spectators and participants from around the region. This year, record numbers of people are expected to gather to participate in the various activities, which include horse racing, live entertainment, exhibits, and a carnival atmosphere.

The organizers of the event have received a credible threat of an organized disturbance. Law enforcement agencies believe this is designed to draw attention away from the prison, where a high profile execution is scheduled to take place.

A multi-agency Unified Command System has been set in place to handle the scheduled festival, as well as prepare for the potential new threat. Your hospital has had a liaison representative active in the planning process.

Instructor Note: Team members should be allowed 90 minutes to pre-plan and prepare and write an IAP based on the potential activity from the festival and for the "credible threat." The planning should also include discussion on:

- Conduct a hazard vulnerability assessment appropriate for the specific event/ threat intelligence they have received.
- Evaluate their current status/census.
- Discuss and obtain information from local EMS, Public Health, Fire, and Law Enforcement on their projected status for the community event and/or other pertinent considerations.
- Develop increased awareness guidance for employees relative to the threat intelligence on reporting of suspicious behaviors, events, or items.
- Determine and establish guidance recommendations on the need to restrict or direct employee and visitor ingress and egress from the facility and/or grounds.
- Establish a PIO and prepare to monitor media and local news reporting.
- Review callback notification procedures.
- Establish triggers and stages as appropriate for implementing emergency plan.
- Discuss methods to declare an emergency staffing crisis and handling credentialing issues and use of volunteers.
- Review hazard specific responses for threats to your facility.
- Discuss staffing strategies to ensure continuous decontamination operations.

At 1300 hours an explosion occurs in the grandstand near the concession area of the horserace at the Petunia festival. The hospital is advised of the situation, told to anticipate multiple casualties, and that a triage & treatment area is being set up on scene.

The first patients arrive POV within 15 minutes with an assortment of non-life threatening traumatic injuries including burns. Radiation burns typically present differently than thermal burns—immediate pain is rare (itching, tingling, erythema, and edema are more common signs and symptoms).

Facilitator Note: Command area facilitator should allow the team members to: 1) Analyze the situation's potential, 2) Establish their command structure, 3) Begin assignment delegation (which should include preparation for decontamination), and implement their IAP. Do not prompt team members to establish communications network; if they fail to do so, it will be self-discovered.

Having had close pre-planning communication with the event Unified Command team, the hospital should advise Unified Command that the hospital is receiving patients. If they do this early, the Command will advise the hospital that they have gotten some "hits" on their radiation detection equipment and are conducting a more detailed scene assessment.

If the hospital does not communicate early, this information will not be provided until the first POV patients have been processed. The lead facilitator may choose to allow some minimal, non-threatening spot hits for radiation in the POV that brought the first patients.

The hospital receives an update from EMS Transport advising that two ambulances are enroute to your hospital with a total of four patients, two of which are critical. Unified Command then contacts your hospital and advises they believe now that the event was likely a "dirty bomb." According to witness statements and area damage it appears a significant explosion occurred. They also have definite radiation readings on scene. They advise the hospital to screen all persons coming to area hospitals.

Facilitator Note: This announcement should occur approximately 10 minutes after the initial patients arrive at the hospital. The lead facilitator may delay or speed this up depending upon team members' performance up to this point.

The first ambulances arrive with assorted significant traumatic injuries. However, these patients are also complaining of nausea, vomiting and diarrhea.

> **Facilitator Note:** These patients should have "detectable" radiation on their bodies.
>
> Nausea and vomiting that occurs in less than two hours is classic for the Acute Radiation Syndrome Prodome and represents a severe degree of exposure.
>
> CDC standards of care indicate that treatment of the traumatic injuries should take precedence over decontamination as long as the caregivers are protected. Simple removal of clothing eliminates a majority of the contamination. Facilitators should also become familiar with REACTS and any suggestions they might give for treatment.
>
> If contacted, the other hospital is reporting that they are also receiving multiple patients.
>
> If the liaison has contact with command/operations/EOC they should be advised that all available medical air transport is being used to transport patients to the Level 1 centers.

Victims continue to arrive via ambulance and POV with an assortment of injuries ranging from minor to critical.

> **Facilitator Note:** The exact number of victims will depend on the players and manikins available. It may be possible to "recycle" victims back through to increase the complexity of the exercise.
>
> At intervals (approximately 45 minutes), a lull in patients will occur. This will give team members the opportunity to change roles (as well as actual rehab). It is also an opportunity to communicate among staff and update the IAP. Considerations include:
>
> - Surge capacity
> - Transport to tertiary care (resources are still limited)
>   - The military base may be a resource if proper channels are followed
>   - Activation of National Strategic Stockpiles if available
>   - Communication with On-Scene command
>   - Duration/Magnitude

Most of the patients should have traumatic injuries ranging from minor to critical. A small percentage of patients should have "detectable" radiation which will be placed by the facilitator. Several patient complaints should be "psychological" in nature (fear, anxiety)—with and without actual injury.

Anticipated Results
Situational Analysis

- The potential for multiple patients should be anticipated based on the type of event and the area of the event.

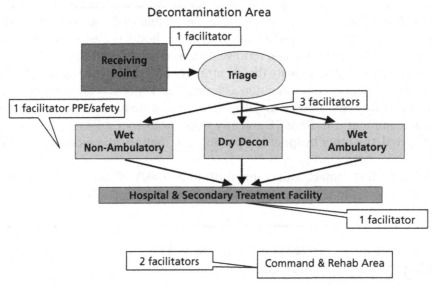

FIGURE E-1 Decontamination area.

- While the distracter is the trauma patients, the likely potential for contaminated patients should be prepared for.
- References should be pulled for radiation when this information is available.

Create an IAP

- Hospital Incident Management Structure
- Decon team including relief rotation and rehab
- Triage & Treatment areas in the appropriate zones
- Contingencies for immediate and long-term surge capacity and capability
- Integration concerns:
  - While the number of patients is not overwhelming for most facilities, the type of event and the potential for a continued flow of patients make this a significant event.
  - Many area resources will be involved in the response to and mitigation of the event.
  - Integration may include communication with on-scene command, local EOC, poison control/chemtrec, law enforcement (security), and other healthcare facilities.

Performance Objectives

- Set up Triage, Decon, Treatment & Rehab areas
- Establish internal & external communications

- Differential diagnosis
- Agent caused vs. medical respiratory/cardiac event
- Decision on which patients to decon

Facilitator Note: The following script should be utilized when introducing and advancing the exercise.

The annual Petunia festival draws thousands of spectators and participants from around the region. This year record numbers of people are expected to gather to participate in the various activities, which include horse racing, live entertainment, exhibits, and a carnival atmosphere.

The organizers of the event have received a credible threat of an organized disturbance. Law enforcement agencies believe this is designed to draw attention away from the prison, where a high profile execution is scheduled to take place.

A multi-agency Unified Incident Command System has been set in place to handle the scheduled festival, as well as prepare for the potential new threat. Your hospital has had a liaison representative active in the planning process.

You have until lunch to:

- Conduct a hazard vulnerability assessment appropriate for the specific event/threat intelligence they have received.
- Evaluate your current status/census.
- Discuss and obtain information from local EMS, Public Health, Fire, and Law Enforcement on their projected status for the community event and/or other pertinent considerations.
- Develop increased awareness guidance for employees relative to the threat intelligence on reporting of suspicious behaviors, events, or items.
- Determine and establish guidance recommendations on the need to restrict or direct employee and visitor ingress and egress from the facility and/or grounds.
- Establish a PIO and prepare to monitor media and local news reporting.
- Review callback notification procedures.
- Establish triggers and stages as appropriate for implementing an emergency plan.
- Discuss methods to declare an emergency staffing crisis and handle credentialing issues and use of volunteers.
- Review hazard-specific responses for threats to your facility.

Facilitator Note: Script Continued-

1130—Advise team members they have 30 minutes to wrap-up and document their pre-planning efforts.

1200—Advise team members they should go to lunch and be back, ready to work at promptly 1300.

1300—"An explosion has just occurred in the grandstand near the concession area of the horse race at the Petunia festival. Expect multiple casualties. EMS is establishing a triage and treatment area on scene."

1315—First patients arrive via POV.

1320—"Hospital Security to HERT Command, be advised we have significant traffic trying to gain access to the ED entrance, we're doing our best to direct them wherever you want them." HERT Command should consider making request for additional security and give clear guidance to security on where vehicle traffic should go. They may need to make arrangements for triage elsewhere.

1325—"EMS Transport advises two ambulances en route with 4 patients, 2 critical."

1325–1335—These patients will arrive when the lead facilitator deems team members are prepared.

1335–1415—Patients will continue to be staggered in as the lead facilitator deems appropriate.

1355—"Scene Command to hospital be advised we have a lot of press down here. Our PIO is going to try and put together a statement, suggest you consider the same and coordinate with our PIO."

1415—"Scene Command advises an additional device has been located in a vehicle near the scene and all on-scene personnel are evacuating; no additional patients will be transported until the device is rendered safe."

1415–1430—This downtime will allow for rotation and rehab of staff. The lead facilitator will determine if the time should be extended.

1430—"Scene Command advises that car was not a threat; scene operations resuming."

1435—"EMS transport advises 3 ambulances en route to your hospital."

1440–1525—Continuous flow of patients from both ambulance and POV.

Facilitator Note: Script Continued-

*1500—"Scene Command to all community agencies, police are asking agencies to help them locate subject of interest (insert age and description of role player to be injected at 1510).

*1510—Individual arrives on scene, says they are reporting for work. They have a backpack with them. Role player should be recognized as person of interest and directed to location with security. If they do not challenge, see how far into command area they can get.

1530—Advise team members no more patients and they should begin deactivating ETA.

1545–1600—Move to medical screening.

1600–1630—Lead facilitator conducts debriefing.

Command Disscusion Guide

Team members identify who will fill roles within IMS structure

Team members staff IMS as defined

Have team members draw out IMS structure

Team members list initial response objectives

Team members define initial response priorities

Team members identify resources required: beds, staff, ventilators, etc.

Determine current hospital surge capacity

List protection/isolation notification measures

Define triggers and phases of emergency plan implementation

Identify role of public health, LRN, reporting, case definition, prophylaxis of vaccination recommendations

Have PIO prepare at least one statement for the press: provide the public information on what the hospital is doing to protect their staff, patients and the community. Advise the public on what they should do if they think they have been exposed to any harmful substances.

Team members should assess gaps in ability for hospital to be self-sufficient

Prepare all appropriate IMS forms

Ensure communication is maintained throughout team

Questions to Generate Discussion

What are some problems that affected the success of the operation?

Was the HERT operated in a safe manner to staff and patients?

What are major concerns that must be taken care of first?

What steps could your hospital back home take today to become better prepared?

When a suspicious person is located, does IMS structure change, does the plan or objectives change, should other agencies be notified, and do they need to take additional security measures?

Instructor may choose to have team members capture key decisions, strategies, challenges and successes on paper.

Appendix F
HERT Emergency Treatment Area (ETA) Drill (short, intense 2.0-hour drill)

This is designed to be a "no notice" exercise. This exercise should not be attempted until the HERT team has had other opportunities to establish an Emergency Treatment Area (ETA), including a decontamination corridor; practice triage; perform cut out and retention of clothing and personal effects; conduct decontamination activities; and medically evaluate and treat casualties suffering a variety of problems. This exercise is conducted as a no-notice event to place some stress on the team members and it is expected some mistakes will be made. Safety or gross errors will be corrected immediately by facilitators, but other issues will be addressed at the hot wash wrap-up.

The on-duty HERT Team leader will be given a brief scenario which should spark activation of the Hospital Emergency Response Team (HERT). Team members will be given 20–25 minutes to "prepare" for the event by setting up their command structure, including the decision on who will be dressing out for decon and staffing all areas of the ETA. The exercise will then commence and run in real time, and the facilitators will feed information to the group as time goes on. The exercise should be hands-on with patients (live and manikin), plans written, and communication implemented as needed with outside entities which will have to be role-played by facilitators.

> **Instructor Note:** Allow up to 2.0 hours for this drill. Instructors should refer to specific task guidelines if they are not familiar with them at this time.

The estimated timeline for this exercise is as follows:

Ten minutes:	Scenario read for HERT team
Twenty minutes:	Team prepares ETA to receive patient
One hour:	Team operates ETA
Fifteen minutes:	Doff PPE & deactivate ETA
Fifteen minutes:	Post-drill medical screening

223

After Team members have been read the scenario they will be expected to establish an Incident Management System structure that enables them to:

Command Function

Conduct a situational anaysis
Create an Incident Action Plan
Determine appropriate PPE level
Establish rehab area
Establish and maintain communications throughout

Operations Function

Determine site for decontamination corridor
Establish ETA, including equipment necessary for all operations
Don PPE
Staff pre-decon triage area
Staff cutout and decontamination area
Staff post-decon medical assessment and treatment area
Establish and maintain communication with command

Facilitator Note: HERT Team members will be responsible for establishing an Emergency Treatment Area, including a command function, decontamination corridor, post-decon assessment and treatment, and a rehab station. Proper pre-decon triage will reveal that not all patients require decontamination. Ambulatory, technical, and nonambulatory decontamination may be covered as time permits. Prior to beginning the drill, manikins with signs/symptoms appropriate for initial rapid triage need to be readied. If possible, manikins which allow IV and intubation should be utilized along with all equipment typically required for ETA operations. HERT Command will need to be prepared to operate the decontamination corridor for a length of time determined by their situational analysis.

Facilitators will need to prepare and staff the command, rehab, decontamination and ETA areas. They may elect to be dedicated to one activity or float as appropriate based upon activity and flow. Prior to the drill, all facilitators will ensure all items necessary to operate their areas are available and in working order. Facilitators should also be well versed in any community interaction roles/information they may need to provide.

The facilitator staffing the pre-decon triage area should be prepared to ensure manikins and/or role players are in position, properly identified with triage and other pertinent medical findings. A minimum of 8 victims will be needed for this exercise. The patients should arrive in the following order:

POV—2 patients (require decontamination)
Ambulance—2 patients (critical trauma, do not require decontamination)
Ambulance—2 patients plus 2 crew members (require decontamination)
POV—2 patients (decontamination not required but prudent to do so)

One facilitator will be present anytime team members are donning PPE and will move with them to the decon operational area, announcing on the facilitator radio net when the team members are "on air." The same facilitator will be responsible for moving the students back to rehab at the end of their PPE cycle. In between, they will remain in the decontamination area and act as the primary safety officer.

Facilitator Note: Three facilitators should be present in the decontamination corridor (1 in cutout area, 1 near decon line, 1 near hot/warm line). Facilitating the students through proper operational issues is one task, but just as important is maintaining close observation for signs of heat stress, watching for trip hazards, and ensuring the safety of team members dressed out in PPE. Facilitators should emphasize need to balance personnel workload of evidence collection against need to rapidly move critical patients through the corridor. Team members should be presented with the need to apply some type of critical medical intervention pre-decon and determine the need to replace items before exiting the post-decon area. Facilitators will apply common sense to the entire picture rather than use theoretical cross-contamination as the rule.

One facilitator will be present in the post-decon area to observe reassessment of patients and appropriateness of medical interventions and/or transport decisions. Patients will have the option of being admitted into the hospital or moved off for transport to other areas or facilities.

If adequate attention is not being paid to collection of evidence, facilitators may interject verbal inquiries regarding triage tag numbers and clothing descriptions.

Rehabilitation

Part of operating the HERT is conducting the medical monitoring of staff to ensure their ability to function.

Typical tasks conducted are as follows:

- Hydrate and provide nourishment for staff.
- Provide a safe haven where staff can take a time out from incident response.
- Provide ongoing monitoring to identify potential heat- or stress-related illnesses or injuries and any other health-related issues.

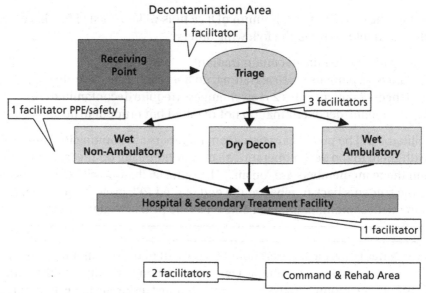

FIGURE F.1 Decontamination area.

- Immediately identify, treat, and report any potentially serious medical conditions detected during evaluation.
- Treat and report any traumatic injuries.
- Classify personnel into three categories:
  - Return to duty.
  - Remove from duty (evidence of illness or injury).
  - Transport for further evaluation to a medical facility.

Scenario

Car vs. Freight Train MVA

At 1500 hours, a car collides with a freight train, causing the train to derail. The two local hospitals, which routinely monitor the EMS channels, hear the initial dispatch information.

Facilitator Note: This scenario and knowledge of hazardous materials transported by rail should spark a heightened index of suspicion to the point of activation of the HERT—or at the very least some discussion and planning.

As the scenario builds, it may become important to emphasize that the other local hospital is also involved with patients from the event. However, planning to transfer patients to the tertiary care centers is appropriate.

When the first units arrive on scene, they report (on the EMS channel) that in addition to two critical patients trapped in the vehicle, one of the rail cars has spilled its contents of a powdered substance which has created a large cloud blowing into a populated area.

> **Facilitator Note:** Command area facilitator should allow the team to: 1) Analyze the situation potential, 2) Establish their command structure, 3) Begin assignment delegation (which should include preparation for decontamination), and 4) develop an IAP. Do not prompt the team to establish a communications network, if they fail to do so, it will be self-discovered.

The hospital receives an update from the field advising that they have visualized a placard on the derailed car with the ID number 2783 (Parathion—Guide No. 152). Field Command also advises to anticipate multiple patients.

> **Facilitator Note:** This announcement should occur approximately 10 minutes into the initial planning phase.
>   Parathion is a potent organophosphate insecticide. Signs and symptoms are varied and can be delayed, depending on the route and extent of exposure. Team members in the command area will be expected to research the product and pass along pertinent information.

The first patients arrive by POV complaining of bloody nose, cough/shortness of breath, and chest pain. These patients were in close proximity when the accident happened and had direct inhalation exposure to the initial "cloud of dust." Although the symptoms are respiratory in nature, THESE PATIENTS NEED DECON.

> **Facilitator Note:** These first patients can be "live" or "manikin" and the scenario simply adjusted to the availability (they could easily be "unconscious"). Two or three patients are sufficient to begin the decon process. Non-ambulatory decontamination is appropriate.

The next patients to arrive by ALS ambulance are the critical trauma victims from the MVA. They have had no direct exposure to the substance and the accident was upwind of the spill. However, the EMS/Fire Personnel have maintained SCBA protection as a precaution. **These patients should be triaged while in PPE, but could bypass decon.**

Facilitator Note: Bypassing decon is a risky decision and should only be made after appropriate evaluation and questioning. However, in the situation described, bypassing decon because of the lack of exposure and the critical nature of the patients may be appropriate.

　　These patients should be unconscious with assorted critical injuries, and the use of manikins is most appropriate to allow aggressive patient care. They should arrive at the hospital as they normally would—full immobilization, IVs, oxygen.

　　If the team members choose to decontaminate, the facilitator should verbalize the patient's condition deteriorating to the point of cardiac arrest prior to exiting the decontamination corridor.

The next patients arrive via ambulance, complaining of perfuse sweating and involuntary muscle contractions. These patients were good Samaritans who walked through the spill to get to the trauma patients and had direct contact with the powdered substance. Signs and symptoms will progress to include nausea/vomiting, diarrhea, abdominal cramps, dizziness/headache, and miosis and they will hemodynamically deteriorate. The ambulance crew is complaining of similar symptoms. THESE PATIENTS NEED DECON.

Facilitator Note: The ambulance crew should be live patients; however, the transported victims can be manikin if necessary. Because some "role playing" would be appropriate, use of live patients is desired. If role players are used, the ambulance crew can utilize an ambulatory decontamination process.

The last group of patients to arrive by POV is complaining of general respiratory distress. They have had only indirect exposure (or no exposure). **These patients should be triaged while in PPE, but could bypass decon.**

Facilitator Note: These patients can have chronic respiratory problems or simply anxiety related to the event. Either manikins or live victims can be used. The goal is differential diagnosis, and the realization that patients unrelated to the event will continue to arrive at the hospital.

Facilitator Note: The scenario will run approximately 1.5 hours. The lead facilitator will be responsible for determining, in consultation with other facilitators, when to call the drill. It is appropriate for command to decide rotation times for staff in PPE; let them determine if they rotate during the drill. If they have not considered the need to rotate, the facilitator should question the command team since they do not know how long they may need to perform the operation.

Anticipated Results
Situational Analysis

- The potential for multiple patients should be anticipated based on the type of event and the area of the event.
- While the distracter is the trauma patients, the likely potential for contaminated patients should be prepared for.
- References should be pulled for Parathion when this information is available. The effects of Parathion can be delayed depending on the exposure, so the possibility of an extended event should be realized and planned for.

Create an IAP

- Hospital Incident Management Structure
- Decon team including relief rotation and rehab
- Triage & Treatment areas in the appropriate zones
- Contingencies for immediate and long-term surge capacity and capability
- Integration concerns
  - While the number of patients is not overwhelming for most facilities, the type of event and the potential for a continued flow of patients make this a significant event.
  - Many area resources will be involved in the response and mitigation of the event.
  - Integration may include communication with on-scene command, local EOC, poison control/chemtrec, law enforcement (security), and other healthcare facilities.

Performance Objectives

- Set up Triage, Decon, Treatment & Rehab areas
- Establish internal & external communications
- Differential diagnosis
- Agent caused vs. medical respiratory/cardiac event
- Decision on which patients to decon

Facilitator Note: The following script should be utilized when introducing and advancing the exercise.

Begin Drill—"At 1500 hours today, a car has collided with a freight train, apparently causing a derailment. Our hospital should be prepared to receive patients in the next 20–30 minutes."

1510—"EMS unit on scene reports 2 patients trapped in vehicle, one railcar container has been breached and a large dust cloud is moving towards a neighborhood. Unknown what the product might be at this time."

1512—"Police unit on scene advises they see placard # 2783 visible on the railcar responsible for the dust cloud."

This is the last scripted communication the team members should receive. The facilitators in the command area should be prepared to provide replies to request for information from the command area to specialists such as poison control, chemtrec, law enforcement, other health care facilities, etc. If in doubt about what information to provide, consult with the lead facilitator or fellow facilitators to make the best decision. Facilitators may provide other hospital status and HERT team members may elect to transfer patients directly from post-decon.

Command Disscusion Guide

Team identifies what roles within IMS structure are required
Team staffs IMS as defined
Have team draw out IMS structure
Team lists initial response objectives
Team defines initial response priorities
Team identifies resources required: beds, staff, ventilators, etc.
Determine current hospital surge capacity
List protection/isolation notification measures
Define triggers and phases of emergency plan implementation
Identify role of public health, LRN, reporting, case definition, prophylaxis, or vaccination recommendations
Have PIO prepare at least one statement for the press. Provide the public with information on what the hospital is doing to protect their staff, patients, and the community. Advise the public on what they should do if they think they have been exposed to any harmful substances.
Team should assess gaps in ability for hospital to be self-sufficient
Prepare all appropriate IMS forms
Ensure communication is maintained throughout team
Questions to Generate Discussion
What are some problems that affected the success of the operation?
Was the HERT operated in a safe manner to staff and patients?

What are major concerns that must be taken care of first?

What steps could your hospital take today to become better prepared?

When a suspicious person is located, does IMS structure change, does your plan or objectives change, and should other agencies be notified, and do they need to take additional security measures?

Facilitators may choose to have team capture key decisions, strategies, challenges and successes on paper.

Index

233

Printed in the United States
By Bookmasters